MW01234308

BARLEYCORN

BARLEYCORN

HAROLD
AUCKRIDGE

Book One of
SEEDS THAT FELL ALONG THE PATH

Copyright ©2017 Harold Auckridge
All rights reserved.

Harold Auckridge asserts his moral right to be identified as the author of this book.

Published by L & H Production
Greensboro NC 27455
landhproduction.com

Cover painting ©2017 by Y. Eckemoff

Interior book design by Laura Scott, Book Love Space

Library of Congress Control Number: 2017953467

First Edition
ISBN: 978-0-9993105-0-2 (hardcover)
ISBN: 978-0-9993105-1-9 (ebook)

To my beloved grandmother who had introduced me to another world and its diverse inhabitants

CONTENTS

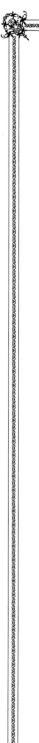

Observing him from a distance,
at first they didn't even recognize him.

JOB 2:12

PROLOGUE

It was raining. Barleycorn lay in the warm ground next to Mustard Seed.

"It is warming up. Tomorrow we have to sprout," Barleycorn said.

"It is so boring here in darkness. I cannot wait," Mustard Seed said.

"Would you like me to tell you a story?" Barleycorn asked.

"I love stories. When did it happen?" Mustard Seed asked.

"It happened a long time ago. And at the same time, it is still taking place. And yet it did not happen."

"How so?"

"Take us seeds. Many centuries ago we sprouted, grew up, and fell out of ears or husks back to the earth. But tomorrow we shall sprout again."

"Oh, it is that kind of the story. Who are the characters?"

"Two people, a man and a woman. But sometimes there are three of them. And sometimes there is only one."

"Is it a story about love? I like love stories."

"It is about love and about hate at the same time."

"So it is really a sad story."

"Sad and happy in equal measure."

"Is it sad because of two men and one woman?"

"Not at all. It is sad because one of them is not necessarily a man, at least not always."

"But who is he? Is he a being who came from outer space?"

"He could be such a being. Or he could be God. Or he could be a former or future god. Or he really could be a man after all. You will have to decide for yourself."

"Is he the main character of this story?"

"No, a man and a woman are. But this story is very much about him also."

"Is it a scary story?"

"Sometimes it is a terrifying story."

"OK, I agree to hear your story out. But please, do not scare me too much. Or I will not sprout tomorrow."

"You will no longer be scared once we get to the end of my story. Close your eyes and imagine . . ."

CHAPTER 1

FIRE AND ICE

 man and a woman were hiding behind a big bush. The man was about thirty. He was tall, broad shouldered, and skinny. The woman looked younger, maybe mid-twenties. She was shorter and stockier, with fiery dark brown eyes.

A tall castle stood in the short distance before them. From the very top window, another man was peering at them intently. He was about seven feet tall. A coarse mane of blond hair covered his muscular shoulders. In the light of the setting sun, his skin was glowing.

"Anne, there is no way for you and your husband to escape now," he said from above. "You people rebelled against me, your god."

"Luminous, people always rise against their God. It is in our nature. I am sure you will forgive us after you get all the facts straight."

"How many times have you rebelled against me?"

"Many times."

"See, you too lost count. When does your struggle end?"

"Likely never."

"Oh, no, that is where you are wrong. It ends today, right here on this beautiful patch of grass you are standing on. There is no way for you to escape my wrath. Come out and surrender."

"Will you kill us?" asked Anne.

"You know that I have to. You have led a rebellion against me. But first I will interrogate you."

"Interrogate us now."

"When you are in relative safety? You do not hold false hope that I will let you people live after you rose against your God?"

"I beg you, please spare us!"

"Tell me, how did you manage to harness one hundred dinosaurs to your attack carriage?"

"You think the whole world loves you, God? Trees whispered to us how to do it. Blades of grass passed onto us all this knowledge."

"I suspected that much. You've been around for a while now. You should know some knowledge needs to be resisted at all costs. For it does not add to the sum of all parts, but deducts from the whole."

"Spare us your sermons. What's done is done."

"It was a bear of battles, but I have destroyed all the dinosaurs. Thanks to you, not a single one walks this planet now. Out of their hearts I cut the bricks to build this castle as a symbol of my unrelenting might. At the very top of the ridge of the roof, there are two small empty spots left. In there I will put the two last bricks, cut from your hearts."

"Show us mercy!"

"In your heads you still carry the knowledge how to hurt me."

"We will dispense of it."

"No, you will not. As soon as are able you'll start a new uprising."

Luminous raised his right arm.

"Duck, Eliakim! Incoming!" Anne screamed.

The man and the woman hit the ground behind the bush and closed their eyes. A bright bolt of lightning shot from Luminous's pointed finger. The bush caught on fire. Smoke rose up. Anne and Eliakim crawled back and hid behind another bush.

In one step Luminous leapt up from the windows to the roof. He raised his hands, and the whole castle rose up one story higher.

"It is futile. We crawl farther away, and Luminous just adds another story to his castle. He will always be able to see us. We can go to the edge of the earth, but all he needs to do is to build his castle higher," Eliakim said.

"You are right. We have to do something different. Maybe we can control his fire. Let us run to the creek, fill skins with water, and bring them back."

"Now we are talking. I am tired of running," he said.

In a moment, Eliakim returned with skins filled with water.

Another bolt of lightning sprang from Luminous's finger. The whole side of the bush burst into flame. Anne doused the flames with water. The fire died out. Smoke covered the clearing.

"Go get more water."

"Nothing protects you now. He'll burn you to cinders."

"Don't worry. I will sweet-talk him," Anne said.

Eliakim ran to the creek.

"Anne, come out into the open," said Luminous.

"Are you not going to strike me dead?"

"You'll have to be in my full power before I pass out my decision. And by the way, no amount of your sweet talk can slow me down. If not the fourth then the fifth bolt of lightning will get through to you."

"Darn, I keep forgetting he can hear everything," Anne whispered.

Another bolt of lightning set the bush ablaze. Eliakim brought skins. They poured more water.

"Sooner or later he will burn all our hideouts and will wrap us in the iron fist of his will. Why don't we submit to him willingly? Let's come out into open. Hopefully he spares us," he said.

"Behold, the words of wisdom issued from a man. Maybe you are my children after all," said Luminous from above.

"Oh, shut up. You know perfectly well we are your children. Which, by the way, does not give you the right to dictate to us what to do," Anne said.

She said to Eliakim, "Get out of my way. You know me. I won't submit to anyone. Not even you. But nevertheless, you are right. We're trapped. However, by the means of this trap we can escape."

"What do you mean?"

"We need to get inside of his castle."

"Don't you think he will find us there?"

"He has to have a lot of stuff inside. You know him: he likes fine things. So there must be tables, screens, and curtains."

"I see your point. We're his creatures. We will hide among the things he lovingly created. Where should two acorns hide if not in a bag of seeds?"

"I like when the story is about seeds," Mustard Seed said.

"Hush," Barleycorn said.

"And even if he corners us, maybe he will be reluctant to let the bolt of lightning loose inside."

"But what if we get to the wall and can't get inside? We will be at his mercy."

"There has got to be a way inside. If the castle does not have doors, it is OK—we know it has windows."

They broke into a sprint. Bolts of lightning engulfed the trees around them in fire.

Another moment and they were right next to the wall.

Luminous peered from the third floor window.

"You made it? It is commendable."

And a door appeared before them.

"Come on, do not fear. Enter. Is it not what you wish?"

Eliakim whispered, "Do not go in, Anne. It has got to be another trap."

"You are so suspicious," Luminous sighed.

"I have a perfectly good reason. Look here. See the scars? I am covered in burns from the bolts of your lightning."

"I can fix that."

Luminous waved his right hand, and Eliakim's scars faded away.

"And the memory of the pain? What shall I do with it? It still smolders inside me."

"I can't erase your memory; it makes you human."

"I do not want you to erase my memory. If you do, I will forget hate I feel towards you."

"Well, in that case if it's all same for you, I do not want to waste my miracle."

Eliakim's scars reappeared from inside of his skin.

"This is just like you. You beckon, and we come. But when we come, you do not give. We beg and then you give. You give and then you take it back," said Anne.

"You can only keep my gifts if you cherish them."

"The giver should give unconditionally."

"I will let you on a secret, Anne. I would not be able to restore his scars if he really wanted them gone. But deep inside, Eliakim likes them."

"See, you're doing it again. It is always our fault, even if it's we who suffer."

The door opened. Bright lights shone from inside.

"Come in, come in," said Luminous.

"Do not go in, Anne. He did not change. He still wants to punish us for rebelling against him," Eliakim said.

"Of course, I have not changed. How can I? But once you enter, I need not punish you anymore. The knowledge of how to harm me will stay behind you, in this void."

"What you call a void, we call our world."

"You will not need it after you enter. My castle will be your abode."

"Can people inhabit your castle?" asked Anne.

"No, only gods can live here. Once you cross threshold, you both will change into gods."

"You give us a strange choice: we can be humans who are persecuted by you, or we can be gods who dwell in your castle. Which choice is worse?"

"With me, there are no worse choices."

"It only means that to be a god is not such great thing."

"But what we will be doing in the castle, Luminous?" Eliakim asked.

"Same thing as I am doing." Luminous shrugged.

"Which is?"

"You will put down the next rebellion against us gods."

"But we are the only ones here. If there are no people, there are no rebels."

"Someone always rebels against God. Someone will show up. So far I have been unable to rest a single century before rebellion starts again."

"If we dwell inside, will you create another man and woman?"

"Yes, I will. Does it bother you?"

"Yes, it bothers me. I like to be an only man, and I'd like for Anne to be an only woman."

"Then run and hide from the bolts of my lightning. What are you waiting for?"

"But we cannot. Not now. You do not need to build another story to see us if we run. We are in your power."

"You are."

"Eliakim, we have to enter," Anne said.

"I know how to hide from God. But I do not know how to kill people. I will hide from God," Eliakim said.

He hid behind the old oak. A bolt of lightning fell. Fire engulfed the tree. Eliakim moved to another tree.

Anne stepped inside the castle.

"My face is burning," she observed.

"It is shining just like mine is," said Luminous.

"But surely I'd feel different if I was a goddess."

"Would you like to feel different? As a goddess, you can change your feelings with a snap of your fingers. Would you like me to guide you in how you could to that?"

"No, thanks." She shook her head. "I have no desire to tell myself how I need to feel. That is a road to indifference."

The castle trembled.

"What was that? Was it an earthquake?"

"A single strand of your hair fell from your head to the floor. You need to be careful when you shake your head."

"It shall take more than a single hair of mine falling to the floor for me to believe you."

"Believe what you like, but move with caution."

"I see there is a mirror in the corner. I would like to go and see how I look."

"Don't stare, only pass a fleeting glance. Your eyes are not ready for your splendor yet."

She went to the mirror. "I am alight. I shine like the sun."

"You do not shine like the sun; you shine an infinite number of times brighter."

"I accept that I look like a goddess. But inside me, simple Anne dwells. And she is not a goddess, but a woman."

"Anne I do not see. She sleeps beneath the light. But the goddess walks."

"Eliakim should see the new me. He will be proud."

"He will be afraid."

"You do not know him. No woman can scare him."

"But a goddess can."

"He needs to see me. I am sure he's worried sick by now."

"The only time God shows his face to man is when God is ready to punish him. Are you ready?"

"I am not going to punish him. Do not speak nonsense."

"Then do not go to the window."

"I am going."

"Since you're a goddess, maybe you will see his sins I've missed. But wait for me. I'd like to watch the punishment from the comfort of my chair." He moved his chair close to the window. "I am ready. Go ahead and punish him."

"Stop saying nonsense." She went to the window and looked out. "Eliakim, my husband, look up. It is your loving wife."

"Don't joke, Goddess. I'm a humble man; I cannot be your husband," Eliakim said from behind the tree.

"Please, recognize me, husband."

"I recognize you not. My Anne was of smaller stature. She was not shining. She was like me, a simple person."

"You are lying. I was never simple."

"I recognize the tone. But it's impossible. You're a goddess, Anne?"

"I guess. I'm not yet sure."

"I did not sin. Don't punish me, my Goddess Anne."

"Stop saying nonsense. You sound like Luminous."

"The grass is catching fire at my feet. The leaves of the tree are scorched by heat. The air is so hot I cannot breathe. Avert your gaze, my Goddess."

Anne looked away. "Luminous, why am I burning grass and leaves around him?"

"It is in people's nature to rebel against us gods. We gods are forced to watch the sad spectacle of humanity's punishment. Toughen yourself. You'll see it often. At first, I hated human suffering so much. Then I got used to it. It helps if you think of it like cleansing. In the midst of the smell of scorched human flesh, I dream of a world without sin."

"Don't torture me, Anne," Eliakim pleaded.

"I am not. I am not looking."

"Flames lick my feet."

"Run from it."

"It's everywhere. No place to run."

"Why is he burning, Luminous?" she asked. "My gaze is averted."

"People's words always inflame god's ear. Only his silence can stop his torture."

She covered her ears. "I still can hear his screams."

"As long as you can hear, he'll burn."

She screamed, "Eliakim, please, stay silent. If God can't hear man, God won't torture him."

"You've learned the simple truth. You will be a wise ruler, my Goddess," said Luminous.

The screams stopped.

"So the only way for a man not to be burned by God is not to attract God's eye or talk to him. Who's punished more by it, a man or a god?" asked Anne.

"When punishment is meted out, both suffer."

"My Anne, I am burning again," screamed Eliakim.

"I could not hear him at all. Why is he burning now, Luminous?"

"Have you being thinking about him?"

"He is my husband. He's always on my mind."

"Gods can't think about men."

"I cannot stop."

"Poor man, he'll burn to cinders now."

"What can I do?"

"You can do nothing. I burned my share of people until I learned how to keep them out of my most sacred and deepest thoughts. You have to treat his death as the lesson in God's craft."

"I cannot stand by idly when he suffers. Do something."

"I can't. I did not mete out his punishment. Only you can stop his torture by not thinking of him."

"Then I agree. He harbors sinful thoughts."

She said to Eliakim, "Promise me you never rebel against god, and the torture shall cease."

"You know me. I cannot promise that," he said.

"A promise can't save him. The mere fact of living tempts him," said Luminous.

"The suffering shall end now," Eliakim said.

"There is no end to it, my love."

"It will end when my life ends. I'm coming into the open. Burn me to cinders, Goddess."

"Don't do it. It will kill me too."

"You are eternal, Goddess," Eliakim said.

He stepped into the clearing. The flames converged on him.

Anne said, "My face stopped burning. What happened?"

"This is very curious. The light left you," said Luminous.

"Why?"

"You are no longer a goddess. It seems you fought your godly nature and won."

"Or lost," he added after pause.

All of a sudden, flame poured out of his eyes and enveloped him.

"Why are you burning, my Luminous?" asked Anne.

"You changed to a woman. But humans are not allowed inside of my castle."

He raised his arms. It rained inside the room. The drops fell on his burning skin and head and hissed.

"Change back to a goddess, I beg you. I cannot cool myself much longer."

"I did not wish to change to a goddess to start with. I did not wish to be a woman again. It just happened."

"We are what we do. Things don't just happen. Stop acting like a defenseless woman."

"So you would like me to act now? OK. I am leaving."

She took a step across the threshold. Her feet recoiled.

"Why can't I leave?"

"It is your castle now, woman."

"I do not want it."

"Many years ago you humans forced me to escape the world into this castle. Now I escape again, this time from the castle back into the world."

He jumped through a window and ran away.

"Why are you standing there dumbstruck, Eliakim? Are you paralyzed? Come inside this minute," Anne said.

"I cannot. I am not a god."

"I am no longer a goddess. We won the castle. It's ours."

"What happened?"

"God has left the castle and returned to the world."

Eliakim seemed to be lost in thoughts.

"I am afraid we will regret it one day."

"Perhaps, but there will be another day for that. Now we celebrate. You have not seen such splendor in your life. Come in."

Eliakim stepped through the door. "Luminous could always see us. That means we can see him too. Where is he?"

"There is no need to seek me. I am here," said Luminous from behind the giant oak.

Eliakim went to the window and looked. "Where?"

"To your right."

"I see you."

"Do not punish me, Eliakim," said Luminous. "I did what I had to do. When people attack God, God fights back."

"What do you mean by saying I punish you?"

"Your mere gaze turned the oak into an iceberg. I know I have persecuted you. But I had to. Do not forget I used to be your God. Be merciful."

"What is he saying, Eliakim?"

"He claims I just turned the oak into an iceberg."

Anne stepped to the window. "It is an iceberg. I do not understand. Maybe you're God?"

"I'm not."

The iceberg collapsed. Luminous ran to a bush and hid behind it. "Don't freeze me, please," he said. "Don't punish me."

"Are we indeed punishing him now?" asked Anne.

The whole clearing turned into a glacier.

Luminous ran deep into the forest.

"Anne, don't look outside, our gazes turn everything to ice," said Eliakim.

"I am sure he can come back to the castle and enter. We just did it; so can he."

"No, he cannot now. Look at the walls. A thick icy coat covers them now. Only people like us can order this ice to create an opening. Men can be gods, but gods cannot be men."

They went upstairs.

CHAPTER 2

PARADISE LOST

 ine days passed.

"I love my castle, but I can't stay here forever. I long for open vistas. We should go outside," Anne said.

"And Luminous? What if he sneaks back in here?"

"Last time we saw him he was many walking days from here. He doesn't worry me."

They went to the forest and walked for many hours.

"I missed the birds chirping so much," she said.

And then she fell to the ground.

"I cannot breathe. I feel like I am on top of the mountain. I do not understand," she whispered.

"I'll get you water from the creek," Eliakim said.

Then he fell by her and said, "Help, somebody, please help us."

A few minutes passed.

The birds continued to chirp.

The little creek rippled by their feet.

Then a loud sound of beating wings came from afar.

Two giant birds appeared.

Their red eyes examined the bodies.

Their sharp talons picked up the man and the woman.

Their wings opened, and the birds took flight.

Anne stirred, "Giant birds took us, my husband."

He groaned, "I recognize them. I saw them flying above the castle the other day."

He tried to reach up to the bird's neck.

Its pointed beak hit him in the forehead.

One claw opened.

"Grab the other claw tight," said Anne. "The rocks below eagerly await your body."

Soon the birds brought them to the castle and laid them down by the front steps.

"Get up, let's go in," said Eliakim.

"I cannot. I'm too weak."

Eliakim stood up, and fell.

"I am too. We need to get in, but how?"

"What is the difference where we die?"

"The castle will save us."

"It's too late. We cannot move."

The two giant birds walked up to the door and started scratching at the wood.

Soon the door fell in.

The two birds picked up the man and the woman and brought them in.

Then they perched on high posts by the fireplace.

"My strength is back," Eliakim said.

"How sweet it is to come back to the land of living," Anne said.

"Who are they? Why did they help us?"

"You said you saw them flying above the castle. It means they did not help us—they wanted in."

"They're strong and powerful; they broke the door without help from us."

"They had to do it to bring us in. I suspect they could not enter without us."

"Why?"

"The castle belongs to us."

She went to the window.

"My heart is longing for the vistas all over again. It is so suffocating to be inside."

"It's suffocating to be outside. We almost died. But just like you, I want to go out."

"We need to drive the birds out."

"But why? You can see clearly they want to be inside."

"We need to drive them out so they can save us again when we pass out."

"Are we that foolish to go out again?"

"We are, and you know it."

"Are we that foolish to trust our lives to these giant birds?"

"We are, and you know it. What worked once shall work again."

He waved his hands and screamed, "Away with you! Fly out! Get out of my castle, you birds!"

The birds flew five circles overhead and perched on the posts again.

"It looks to me they have no desire to save us again. What worked one time won't work again. They like it here in the castle."

"I do not plan to be a prisoner. Especially because some silly birds refuse to leave my castle."

"Look at yourself. Already you take their help for granted."

"Because I am a woman. Birds serve people."

"But maybe we should learn our lesson and do not go too far out? Maybe we won't need birds' help again."

"We'll need them."

"Maybe we won't."

"Please, repeat," one bird said suddenly.

"You can speak?" Anne asked.

"We could not speak before," the second bird said. "We can speak now, after you said you don't need us."

"Eliakim, don't say a word. Do not agree with me. It is enough these birds can speak. I do not want them to acquire more skills."

"But you are right. We do not need these birds if we do not go too far out. I agree with you," he said.

"Thanks, Eliakim," said the second bird.

The birds fell to the ground.

A giant rose out of their lifeless bodies.

The ceiling was too low for him, so he had to bend his neck.

Anger filled his only eye.

"How long I have waited to come back to my beloved castle!" he said.

"We know you not," Anne said. "You are not Luminous."

"I am most certainly not. Thank God for that."

"Who are you?"

"I am God of Terror."

"Where is Luminous?"

"He is no more. You should have cherished that simpleton. He was of rare breed of fools."

"Did you do away with him?"

"You did by declaring you needed no help from birds."

"I do not understand. What did these birds have to do with him?"

"He was them."

"Why?"

"He had to help you, for you were his masters."

"You are mistaken. He was our master."

"A god who is disposed kindly towards his people is always a slave to them. You people were his masters."

"He commanded us."

"It was you who benefited from his commands."

"If Luminous was the model of kind god, then we should have no gods."

"There is always a god. You cannot do away with him. Once in a while you are allowed to choose God's attributes, that's all."

"So he was the only God we could have as friend, and all this time we fought against him? Woe is us," said Eliakim.

"I'll be damned," said Anne. "I would have never imagined my mouth would utter these words, but hear it: I speak for all humanity, which consists now of two people: we would like to have Lord Luminous back. We'll cherish him and will work with him."

"The time of choosing is past," said the giant.

"Turn into Luminous now," said Anne.

"I desire that not."

He touched the wall and said, "I missed you, my castle."

"We need to go, Eliakim," Anne said. "God of Terror and people can't live together."

"But we cannot survive out there. We'll suffocate."

"If we die, we die. Our place is not here."

They went to the forest.

"The air is like molten lead that pours into my lungs and stiffens there," said Eliakim.

"It's the end. And no God is here to help us."

They fell to the ground.

"My heart stopped beating," Anne whispered.

"Mine also," said Eliakim. "Synchronous, as always."

An hour passed. Eliakim opened his eyes. "Anne, look at you," he croaked." We're the giant birds."

Anne sat up and croaked, "Just like he was. How strange. Is it just another curse?"

"It is our salvation. The people and God change places. One lives in the world and another dwells in the castle. Let's take flight. I wish to feel the air gently brushing through my feathers."

"Wait. We have to do something first. Let's perch outside the castle and wait for him. This fearsome God is made out of birds. Have you ever seen the bird that would willingly stay in its cage? It is only a matter of time before he comes out."

Two days passed.

The heavy door opened and the giant came out.

"Let's follow him at a distance," croaked Anne. "At the first sign of his distress we will attack him. For what I've planned I need for him to be weak but yet think clearly."

The giant fell to the ground.

"Now!" Anne directed.

The two birds swooped down from the sky.

"Hold him down," said Anne.

"Save me," whispered the giant. "The time came for us to trade places again."

"I hold your life in the palm of my hand," said Anne.

"You have no hands."

"In the palm of my claw then. You are dying now."

"Another god will rise out of the two birds I'll change into."

"No, he won't if we let you die here."

"You won't do that, because you'd like to regain your human shape even for a short while."

"We will let you die unless you change into Luminous."

"You know by now he's by far the easiest god to manipulate. So I won't do it, even for the sake of the future of my godly race. We gods have enough troubles without people to make more of the same."

"I swear to you, my intentions are pure. If Luminous is as good a god as it gets, I will do my best to build a better rapport with him."

"I do not believe you."

"You gods talk a lot about people needing to believe in you. So, have a bit of your own poison. Take a leap of faith. What have you got to lose? We will only take Luminous back to castle and not you. Would you like for your race of gods to end here at this spot?"

"Cursed be your human race," whispered the giant.

His body transformed into Luminous's form.

"He's unconscious," said Anne.

"We can let him die here," said Eliakim. "It would be proper vengeance after all cruelties he committed against us."

"His punishment for his cruelties will be death. How shall we be punished for cruelties we had committed against him? By staying forever in bird shape?"

"He started it."

"Somehow I am sure if he could speak now he'd say we started it."

"Do not tell me you really intend to strike a new relationship with him."

"I meant what I said to the giant. The question is: Are you willing to do the same? For it takes two to pull it off."

"Damn your generosity. My head tells me you're wrong. But my heart wants me to follow you."

"Follow your heart."

"I accede."

"Let's now take the precious cargo of our chosen god back to his castle."

"Precious cargo," laughed Eliakim. "That's a new one."

CHAPTER 3

THE WIND AND THE WATER

nne and Eliakim stopped in front of the castle.

"It took us long time to return to our human shape. I still have nightmares of being a bird. In my dream I grew disgusted to hunt the rabbits and dig for the worms," said Anne.

Luminous looked out from the castle. "You're here."

"Our God, could you help us? We want to have both the world and your castle, yet we can only have one or another."

"I might just have a solution for you. What if I let you sit in a carriage. The carriage won't stop but will take you through the castle and then back out."

"But what if we decide to stay in your carriage forever?"

"You won't be able to. I'll take your free will out of an equation. The carriage will always empty itself after your ride."

"You know us. We're smarter than any carriage. We will find the way to not exit it."

"What I can do then is to float the castle in the air. After the carriage empties you, the wind will deliver you to the ground."

"And how can we come back?"

"I'll loosen a rope and you will climb it."

"Who'll pull the carriage?"

"I will rig a sail to it. The spring wind will blow the sail."

"Who'll stop the carriage?"

"The fall wind."

"Who'll right the carriage?"

"The summer wind."

"But you have left nothing to do for the winter wind."

"Oh, I will find something for him to do, no worries."

"But it's magic."

"By the way, I forgot to introduce myself. I'm God."

"There is no need to be sarcastic."

"My magic is always sound."

Anne said, "Remember, I told you at the beginning, don't fly, my God? You did not listen. Then from your flights a multitude of birds appeared. And remember, I told you, do not swim below the surface of the oceans, my God? Again, you did not listen, and a multitude of fishes came into being."

"The birds and the fish don't bother you, let them live."

"They get in my way. The carriage that propels itself may bother us in the future. I can just see multitudes of them converging at the narrow strips of even land and try to pass each other."

"Let it not bother you. I can always still the wind."

"If a carriage with a sail comes into the world, it'll stay."

"Winds are my helpers. They will not move any carriages without my orders."

"Then something else propels the carriage one day, like concentrated gas vapors," Anne said.

"A carriage that is propelled by vapors—only you could come up with that, Anne," Eliakim said.

"Stranger things have happened. God's magic frightens me."

"Let the future worry for itself. I am here to help you to overcome the longing for my castle," said Luminous.

He waved his hand, and the castle floated up into sky.

The long rope fell down.

They climbed the rope and got into the carriage.

Wind blew the sail, and ahead they went.

Luminous walked by their side.

After they went through the last room, the carriage dropped them to the ground.

"What a great idea this was. Now we have both the world and the castle," Anne said. "Let's go back inside."

She called out, "Throw us the rope, Luminous."

He looked from window and said, "Some day."

"We cannot wait," Anne said.

"Oh, yes, you can. Meanwhile, explore the world."

"You know, what I think, Eliakim? If we can stay in the world but yet visit his castle, maybe he should have same ability to visit the world?"

"But he said he's destined to dwell in the castle."

"He said that because he could not visit the world and then return back to his castle. Just like us, who could not come to the castle and then return back to the world. But with the device of the carriage, we can. Let's build a castle underground next to the subterranean river. He'll sit in a boat, and the current will move him through our castle. And then we build a fountain, which will push him back to his sky castle."

"But God is mighty, and he can order his boat to run upstream if he so desires."

"But why would he? He knows well if God and we people stay together in one spot for a while, fights will break out between us. He is not a fool to stay with us for long."

They built the underground castle out of marble and precious stones. They dammed the subterranean river and ran it through their castle.

"Let's make the boat from gold. Our Lord deserves the best," Anne said.

"Gold is too flashy."

"The time of humility is not upon us yet."

"But gold can't float."

"Oh, the boat can be made of water and still be able to carry God around if God wishes so."

They made the boat out of the solid gold.

And they called out, "God, come to the world. We prepared a stately castle underground. You can come and be in world with us for short while."

Luminous looked out from above and said, "You know well I'd really like to come to the world. But since I love the world too much I am not able to leave it. And when I stay, we'll fight until I or you are fallen."

"You solved the riddle of ours. We can visit your castle and return back to the world. In return we solved this riddle of yours. The river will carry the boat with you through the underground castle, and then the fountain will take you back up to your sky castle."

And so God came from above and got into the boat.

The river carried the boat through the castle.

Eliakim and Anne walked on the river's bank and held a pleasant conversation with him.

Then the fountain deposited him back in his sky castle.

And the boat fell back to the ground.

"My eyes deceive me; my ears play games with me. I can't believe you found the way for God to come to the world and then return to his abode," said Luminous. "Everlasting peace has finally ascended to Earth from the deep underground chamber where it was trapped for an eternity. And it did not happen because of me. You, humble people, found this wondrous way."

"Can we visit your castle in the sky?" Anne asked.

"You most certainly can," said Luminous.

He dropped the rope.

They climbed it, got into the carriage, and started their voyage.

"Why are you walking by our side?" asked Anne. "There is enough space here for you to sit in. Please, share the carriage with us."

And Luminous climbed in.

They went through the castle, room by room, and talked of pleasant things.

Then they came into the last room.

Anne said, "Let's go down together and continue our conversation."

"I am afraid we are spending too much time together. It's dangerous," said Luminous.

"We always can part ways when anger rises inside one of us," Anne said.

And Luminous agreed.

The carriage brought them down and hung suspended in the air.

The boat awaited them.

They leaned out of the carriage and fell into the boat.

The current carried the boat through the underground castle, and the fountain deposited them right back into the carriage in the first room of the sky castle.

"I do not like it," said Luminous. "We have been together far too long. A fight will break between us any moment now."

He jumped from the carriage.

His feet touched the floor.

He jumped up and fell back into the carriage.

"Luminous, you have decided to stay with us. I'm glad," Anne said.

He said nothing.

The carriage dropped them to the boat.

Eliakim said, "Anne, we have stayed with God far too long. I feel a fight with him is at hand. Look at his angry face. Let's get off our boat."

They jumped out but fell back into the boat.

"What is happening, Luminous?" Anne asked. "I'm frightened."

"I did not want to trouble you before. I could not leave the carriage. I hoped against the odds that you would be able to leave the boat. Alas, we're trapped."

"But why? We built two castles. We had machinery to remove our free will from the equation."

"In essence, by connecting the carriage ride to the boat ride we have created one castle that connects Earth and Sky."

The fountain threw them back into the carriage.

They traveled through the sky castle again.

"What happens now?" Anne whispered.

"Only swords can separate us now," said Luminous.

They drew swords and fought for a very long time.

Eliakim said, "Either people or God will perish today. I'd rather it be people than God. I surrender to you, my God."

He lowered his sword and knelt before God.

Luminous raised his sword high.

"Let him live," said Anne.

"Eliakim is lost for us. Forget about him," said Luminous. "When God and people fight, strife only ends when the Devil is created out of the winner or the loser. When God and people give their utmost to their struggle, out of the last one standing the happy Devil steps into this world. He is the benevolent one, because he is sated. But if one of us surrenders, out of him another kind of Devil comes forth. This Devil is of the worst kind, because he's hungry."

"Then do not claim victory," said Anne.

"The refusal to win equals surrender. If I refuse to claim victory, I turn into a hungry devil. I am sorry, but I have other plans for my destiny."

Luminous cut off Eliakim's head.

The head flew up into the air, sprouted long horns, fell back down on his shoulders, and reattached itself.

Dark hair covered his body.

Devil looked around and said, "This is the first time I am inhaling the air of this planet. The aroma is too sweet for my simple taste. It has less methane, and less carbon monoxide than I like."

He exhaled sulfur and laughed, "Never despair. I will fix it in no time."

"Luminous, if we unite against the Devil, we'll claim victory," said Anne.

"You are wrong," said Luminous. "He is too strong for us. It is written that God's and man's future is to turn into devils. Simply put, he is the next evolutionary step of our development."

He paused, "But maybe we still can bring a magnanimous kind of devil into this world. Let's keep on fighting each other as hard as we can and see what happens. It is always better to have two Devils rather than one."

Anne and Luminous fought hard for many hours.

The Devil sat on the grass and applauding them.

Finally, Anne cut Luminous's head off.

She lowered her sword, then smiled happily and looked around.

"Perfect," she said.

She walked to the creek and inspected her face.

"Even better," she said.

"You killed God, miss, and I thank you for that," said the Devil. "But it does not change the pressing matters at hand. I will kill you momentarily."

Anne smiled, "Look at my beautiful body. Do you want it to come to waste? Why don't you enjoy it first?"

"Capital idea. Last time I had sex it was with a toad-like creature. But never mind."

The Devil came to her and kissed her on her lips.

His scream shook mountains, "I am burning alive!"

"You should have never kissed your sister. Incest is a mortal sin."

"You are not my sister. Look at yourself: you are an earthly woman."

"I am the most sophisticated kind of devil, one who looks perfectly human, or perfectly godly. Only idiot losers like you sport horns and dark body hair."

"I can't believe it. I know millions of devil tricks, and yet you have tricked me."

"Who needs a devil's tricks when I have full access to a woman's ones?"

The horned Devil burned for hours.

When his screams stopped he was reduced to a heap of ashes.

The She-Devil carefully packed the remains of Eliakim and Luminous into the boat.

She stretched out and yawned. "God's goal is to do as little as possible. The greatest god never does anything. Nor do devils. People be praised. They first killed God, then they decimated one another. So I can rest now."

The She-Devil pushed the boat off.

The underground river pulled it forward.

"I am ready," she said. "I am so happy. I am the highest devil that ever existed. I wonder what kind of death I shall obtain now. I'd like a quick one so as not to spoil such a perfect life."

The wind blew.

"I recognize you, Winter Wind. And I wonder if Luminous appointed this task of freezing me to you intentionally. No, that is hardly likely. Even God does not know what happens after his death."

Ice enclosed the She-Devil.

Her dead eyes looked happily forward.

CHAPTER 4

THE BALL OF FLESH

 he boat submerged.

The underground current carried the boat low into the bowels of the mountain.

The ice melted.

The remains of God and people combined into one ball of flesh.

The ball went up though the mountain, high into the sky, then it fell down, rolled down the slope, and came to a stop next to the tree grove.

The ball broke in two.

Out of the larger ball, Luminous rose.

The smaller ball grew up into a giant.

The giant looked around and spoke in a loud voice, "I am Atlas. And I am ready to hold the sky upon my shoulders."

"I am your sovereign overlord. It is not necessary to hold the sky upon your shoulders. I used the strongest titanium screws to attach the sky to the Earth," said Luminous.

"Then I can hold the Earth."

"You should not. If the Earth stops spinning, the hurricanes will wipe it clean. All life will perish. Only rocks shall endure."

"I'm telling you, I have to hold something. Shall I hold you?"

"I will break you into tiny pieces if you even try."

"You do not understand: I need to do an astonishing deed."

"Leave all the extraordinary deeds to me."

"I can't. This overpowering desire is the only glue that holds me together."

"Learn how to survive without doing amazing deeds. I did."

"I can't exist then," Atlas said.

His body turned to goo and spread over the plain.

"Poor Atlas. I'll have to remember to let him hold the sky one day," said Luminous.

His hands collected the goo and put it into his chest.

Luminous turned into a ball again.

The night passed.

Then Anne rose up from the ball.

Her feet below the knees stayed in.

"Eliakim," she called out.

His head appeared from the ball.

"What do you need? I'm resting," he said.

His head sank back.

"Please, stay with me. I'd like to talk to Luminous."

Eliakim's head reappeared from the ball.

"Then talk. What has it to do with me?"

"I am afraid of God. Can you just stand with me? The words of two are mightier than the word of one."

Eliakim rose from the ball.

His feet below the knees stayed in.

"Be quick. I'd like to lie down. It is so nice to be a small part of a larger whole."

"Then you will not like what I am about to say to God."

"Are you kidding? I never like what you say."

"Hush. Your wife will speak now."

"Oh, Luminous, I'd like to talk to you," she said.

The whole mass of the ball splashed around, and Luminous's head appeared.

"What do you want, earth dweller? You know it is hard to collect yourself from the ball. Why bother me?"

"I know how hard it is. I've just done it myself, and I cannot recall a harder deed. But I could not stay inside. Strange thoughts were coming into my head. They bothered me."

"What was so strange about them?"

"Not what they were about. God knows, I had some really weird thoughts in my time."

"God knows."

"What was strange is that I found myself agreeing with every single one."

"I understand now why you are alarmed. It is so strange indeed," Eliakim said. "I always thought Anne stands for the one who always disagrees."

"You hush again. You are way too simple."

She continued, "You see, Luminous, I stand now before you, and my thoughts are mine only. But when I lie down, I think somebody else's thoughts. I feel like I am losing my identity bit by bit. That's why I asked you to get your head out this ball of flesh. It is the only way for me to be sure I receive the response from God himself."

Luminous rose from the ball.

His gaze betrayed surprise.

"Hear the wonder of wonders. You, mighty Anne, need a humble God to talk to? What else can happen here? The oak tree may talk, and the creek may share with me all his secrets. Or a need for people to worship their God maybe will rise."

"That would be the day," said Eliakim.

"I don't think I care to share my secrets with you," a silvery voice spoke from inside the creek. "You'll tell them to the mountains. My secrets sleep with fishes."

"I agree," the oak tree said. "Mine are safe too. Though boars sometimes learn them while eating my acorns."

"But who believes boars?" said the oak   *"Boars are bad," said Mustard*
tree. "They are, shall I say, so boring."   *Seed. "They have this ugly snout."*
                                                     "Hush," said Barleycorn.

"You're having fun?" Luminous's roar shook Earth.

The world fell silent.

Not a single fly moved its wings.

"So where were we?" mused Luminous. "You'd like a conversation?
You can have your conversation. What would you like to talk about?"

"I do not want to be a part of this ball," said Anne.

"I see. And why not?"

"Because you are there too."

"It is called a shared space, you know."

"We can access one another's flesh; it creeps me out."

"Of course, I could make an arm for me out of your arm. But I don't
do it. I let you be. You can trust me."

"I appreciate it. But I'm afraid I will take part of you for myself. I'm
a pretty good thief."

"You can try, but I will not let you."

"But thoughts tempt me."

"Fight back your thoughts."

"This fight leaves me unhappy."

"When were you happy?"

"When I was a part of Atlas."

"But you turned him into goo."

"I could not help myself. I am who I am."

"So what do you want?"

"I need to have someone to share my thoughts with."

"I've given him to you already. He is your husband. Share away."

"Eliakim? He is not enough. I share my life with him. But I need
God to share my thoughts with."

"So share them, I am listening."

"I need a different god. With you, I am lonely. If Eliakim and I could become one Atlas and then divide in two, so can you. Divide yourself into two parts. And maybe one of the parts will understand me better."

"What does Eliakim say about this idea? Eliakim, do you need me to stay like I am now? Or would you want me to divide too?"

"You know me," Eliakim said. "Communion of souls is not my stuff. I have no problem with you dividing or staying whole, for that matter."

"Just look at him. He has no problem. How pitiful," said Anne.

"I see what you are saying. I understand you now, Anne," said Luminous.

"Hey, you both, please do not look at me like I'm an invalid or something," Eliakim said. "That God stuff is not my cup of tea."

"Then you need to drink tea more often," said Luminous.

"It is convenient for God to say God is needed," Eliakim said. "But it is like Lock would say Door needs it. But Door only needs Lock when Thief is coming in."

"I concur with Luminous," Anne said.

"You position yourself as a rebel who fights God," said Eliakim. "Yet in the next sentence you say you need him. Aren't you weary of fighting your own shadow? Are you in such desperate need of a sparring partner?"

"One can need God and fight him too," Anne said. "There is no contradiction here."

"Maybe I am fond of the quiet life," said Eliakim.

"Life should not be quiet. Your soul needs to turn upside down with each passing moment. Every day should start like there was no day at all before. A day should end like there are no days are left to live," said Luminous.

"Says who again? An immortal being who does not count days and nights? Who needs not worry about anything?" said Anne.

"I need not, but I do."

"I need to, but I don't."

"Anne, I can break myself into two parts. But I foresee that only one of you will benefit, not both."

"At least one will be happy," Anne said.

Luminous receded into the ball, and two beings arose.

One was a woman and the other was a man.

The woman was tall and slender, and her hair had a life of its own. It was curling and straightening, rising and falling all the time.

The man was of smaller stature. He was calmly majestic. His eyes seemed to know all.

"Who are you, milady?" Anne asked.

"I am Hydra," the woman said.

"I cannot take my eyes of you. You are so full of life."

"But you are not." Hydra said.

Anne blushed and covered her face.

Eliakim looked to the man and asked, "Who are you, my man?"

"I'm God. Who else?" The man shrugged.

"What is your name?"

"You cannot know my name."

"Strange is the God who keeps his name a secret."

"Impudent is the man who dares ask God a question. I will tell you my name when you are ready."

"So tell me now. I am ready."

"You're not."

"I'll call you Nameless."

"You will not dare. You will call me King."

"But I am not a peasant."

"I'll make you one. I'll make you the smallest grain of sand. You'll be so small you will not see yourself."

"My Hydra, I am ready to worship you," Anne said.

"I like when someone is small," said Mustard Seed. "The small can always grow big. But big can't grow small."
Barleycorn said, "Hush and listen."

"I can't allow you. Not in your present state. You need a lot more courage and vigor."

"I will remake myself."

"You need to start anew. Split up and make two beings out of your body. Your first one will be the new you with the courage and the vigor. Your second shall contain your waste."

"Anne, stop," Eliakim said. "This way is rife with peril. God has divided himself. But his new parts are unable to match with us."

"If I split up, my half might match with God."

"What if your other half is prettier then you? You won't be jealous of her?"

"You fool; she'll be like sister to me."

"One can be jealous of one's sister. Another possibility strikes me. What if the second part of you is a man?"

"Then it's your problem. Put him to the sword. My proper half is a woman. I'm always a woman."

"You are, even when you are a man."

Anne slipped back into the ball of flesh, and two people rose.

One, a woman, was dark-skinned. Her face lacked beauty.

The other, a man, was short and muscular. His skin was dark. His forehead was low.

"My dear Goddess Hydra!" the woman said.

"I recognize you, Ruth. You are my steadfast follower."

"And who are you?" Eliakim asked the man.

"I do not know who I am," he said.

"Let him be," Ruth said. "His name is Adam and he's nothing. He's got the Anne parts I didn't need."

"Then you are my best friend, Adam," Eliakim said. "I recognize in you my humble Anne."

"You are right," said Ruth. "I have discarded humility."

"And you discarded kindness."

"Kindness is the refuge of the weak. And I am strong."

"My followers do not need kindness," Hydra said.

"A lack of kindness makes you a monster," Eliakim said.

"I thank you for the compliment," Ruth said. "I would like to be a monster who serves her master."

"Say something, my king," Eliakim said.

"What they think does not concern me. Why should I speak?" Nameless said.

"If you do not want to speak, act then," Eliakim said.

"Why should I act?"

"But they have corrupted the meaning of following God. The follower should think. He should adapt God's teachings to the current moment. God's teaching cannot stop. They need to go forward and encompass all the new things that life brings forth. They need to take faith forward."

"Hydra's faith needs no improvements," said Nameless. "It is already perfect."

"You speak like you are envious of her."

"I'm not. Her faith is simple: strong eats weak. My faith is complex: weak gets stronger. Her faith is ripe since it's old. My faith is like a mustard seed."

"My faith will grow," Nameless said.

"I am not sure your faith is suitable for me," said Eliakim. "I like the faith of the strong, the faith of people who conquer new lands, of one who puts his enemies to the sword, who's not afraid to tell the truth even to God."

"Hush," Barleycorn said.
"Don't hush me. I did not say anything," Mustard Seed said.
"But you were just about to."
"I actually was, because he's talking about me."
"Oh no he was not."
"You'll see; I'll grow tall."

"It is not the right time for faith in me to germinate inside you. But with time you'll grow weak, and then you will be ready."

"It'll take a long while."

"No, it will not. Strength does not last. But weakness lasts a long time. That's why the weak always inherit the kingdom."

"You are talking of the future. But we are in the present. You need to fight this Hydra and her Ruth."

"I am the wrong God for that. You need your Luminous. He was one hell of a fighter."

"But he could not exist at the same time as Hydra. It means I am of the past too. I need to split into two new parts."

Eliakim fell into the ball of flesh.

And from ball arose two people: a man and a woman.

The man was small. His skin was sickly. His eyes were full of feverish excitement.

The woman was tall and beautiful.

"More people equals more trouble," Ruth said.

"The more people the merrier. Each one holds three quarts of blood. So much delicious blood to spill," Hydra said.

Every single strand of Ruth's hair reared up on her head and hissed at the newcomers.

"You are so beautiful, new woman," Adam said.

"Stay silent, nothing," Ruth said.

"I am nothing, but not for long. I am ready to love this woman. I feel my strength awaken."

"It is no strength that awoke in you. It is just one small organ."

"Small?" the new woman said. "I'd never call it small. It is actually quite large."

"You are a true man. After you see the new skirt, you're ready to chase it," Ruth said.

"She's got no skirt. She's naked, just like you."

"OK, then go and chase her naked butt," Ruth said.

"He needs not chase my naked butt. My butt is his for the taking," the woman said.

"Poor Eliakim, he must have had rotten insides to split into a whore and a sickly man."

"I will come up with a name for you, my sweet maiden," Adam said. "I call you my Eve."

"No, it is not time for Eve yet," Hydra said.

"For once, I am in full agreement with Hydra. It is not time," Nameless said.

"I feel like I am missing something here. Are you gods keeping a secret from me and from this sickly man?" Ruth asked.

"But she is Eve! I feel it in my bones," Adam said.

"Or between your legs," Ruth said.

"It's better to be guided by the spot between your legs then have no guidance at all," Adam said.

"I got my guidance from the same spot too. And it tells me I need to kill this whore," Ruth said.

"For once, I will repeat what King has said: it is not time," Hydra said.

"Everyone betrays me. Could you be my friend, you, sickly man?" Ruth asked. "What is your name?"

"I'm Mark," he said.

"I think we need to stick together."

"I agree. I like your vigor."

"Do you like strong women?"

"I need one."

"Then, be mine."

"I'm yours. Love is growing in my heart."

"So how about we unite, ignore these gods, and kill this whore? What do you think?"

"I'm not so sure. They're both look mighty strong. And you can see I'm sick."

"Are you ready to sacrifice for your love for me?"

"Don't do it, Ruth," Hydra said. "Do not combine yourself with him. I need you both. The three of us—sickly man, mean woman, and nasty goddess—can do a lot of serious damage."

"It is too early for this story also," said King.

"Oh, shut up," said Hydra. "It is always too early for you. Sounds like you did not get enough sleep. Go make yourself a tabernacle and lie there."

"You failed me, Hydra," said Ruth. "You refused to kill this whore. Adam's hands are already pinching her butt. Hey, wait a minute! It is not her butt he is squeezing now. Take your hands off this thing now!"

"He cannot help himself. They are destined to love each other," said Hydra.

"I am stronger than any destiny. I shall combine with Mark, and a newborn giant will kill them and you." She ran to Mark and said, "Hold me, my man. We shall become one flesh."

They fell into the ball of flesh.

A giant rose. His hairy face had a low forehead and large jaw.

"My goddess!" the giant roared and kneeled before Hydra.

"Go away. I'm not your goddess."

"You are not the evil goddess? You most certainly look like one."

"Your god is Devil. And I am not him."

"Who are you then?"

"I am the measure of meanness that was in Luminous. I can do evil, but only a little evil and only once at a given time."

"We can do evil together."

"You'll do too much of it."

"There cannot be too much evil, just like there cannot be too much good. If you don't want to lead me, Hydra, I will put to use this precious little measure of your evil by combining myself with you."

"You peasant! How dare you think you can be one being with me, goddess?"

"I will consume you, Goddess."

"You will not. I have no weak spots."

"You are woman, so you got one."

He knelt before her and nibbled on the flesh between her legs.

Her hairs stood up, hissed, and bit the giant.

He screamed and let her go.

"I did not need a name before because I hoped we could make a devil together. But now I have to get a name. I shall be Beelzebub."

"That is the name of the Devil. You are not him. You cannot wear this proud name."

"I'll try."

"You'll fail."

"I am proclaiming myself to be Beelzebub."

"It will undo you. You cannot be a greater Evil."

"My fair Eve, it is time for us to be one flesh," said Adam.

"I'm ready, my Adam. Take me. Be my husband."

"I did not mean it this way. I long to taste your fair lips and drink ambrosia from your breasts. But we need to die and to combine into new being."

"I long to live."

"I long to live with you. But look at Beelzebub. King does not fight him. But someone must. A new being will fight Beelzebub."

"And our love?"

"It cannot die. It is eternal. We will be back."

"Deep in my bones I feel you're right."

"They guessed," Nameless said.

"They sure did," Hydra said.

"I trust you, my future husband," Eve said.

Adam and Eve embraced.

The single tear fell from Eve's eye. And rose bush grew up from it.

They fell into the ball of flesh.

A tall man arose.

His white wings opened, and up he went.

His shining sword was brighter than the sun.

"I didn't expect to see you yet, my Lahash," Nameless said.

"I am at service of my Lord," Lahash said.

He fell upon Beelzebub.

Their swords beat thunder.

"You cannot overpower me," laughed Beelzebub. "My strength equals yours."

Nameless inched closer to Hydra.

"King, don't forget, I am a goddess," said she. "I can read all minds including yours."

"I know you can. So you can understand my predicament."

"You are afraid I will combine with Beelzebub. I told him I will not. I'm not Goddess of Greater Evil."

"I know you have a good heart. I highly respect you for refusing to unite with Beelzebub. But Evil has a unique ability to bend the will of the most reasonable person. The smarter you are, the sooner you fall. And you are very smart."

"Greater Evil can't get me. I carry inside of me Lesser Evil. I am vaccinated against Greater Evil."

"The world's fate hangs on your steadfastness. Would you trust to yourself the destiny of all living things?"

Hydra knitted her brows.

"I would not," said she after pause.

"My king, our time is at hand. We have so much to accomplish. Do not combine with Hydra. An imperfect God will rise out of this combination," Lahash said.

"Our time is still ahead of us," said Nameless. "The world is not properly arranged yet."

"Together we'll ready it."

"I order you to serve God, who will rise after I become one with Hydra. He is not as bad as he seems."

"I will not," Lahash said.

"Do not disobey me."

"I will."

"It is yet not time for that either," said Nameless.

Nameless took Hydra into a tight embrace.

Hydra leaned her head upon his shoulder, and not a single hair of hers bit him.

They fell into the ball of flesh.

Tentacles extended from the ball and tightly grasped Beelzebub's and Lahash's feet.

Luminous rose from the ball.

"Take your tentacles off me, imperfect God," said Lahash. "Your touch defiles me."

"I am unable to fulfill your request. I have this one advantage of an imperfect God: I can cheat. This ball of flesh is my ace in a hole."

"I ache to fight you," Beelzebub said. "But, alas, you know all the evil tricks as well as I."

"This is just another advantage of being an imperfect God," said Luminous. "Run now to the end of the Earth and hide there."

"But where is the proof you will not follow me?"

"There is no proof. One day I might."

"It is unseemly for Beelzebub to run and wait for his destroyer."

"It is even better for me. Stay here and be destroyed."

Beelzebub lowered his sword and said, "We are united by a common foe, Lahash."

"You're right," Lahash said.

And he threw down his sword.

"Lahash, you really should not listen to him. The time is not ripe for you to fall," said Luminous.

"You are mistaken, I will never fall. I am most righteous angel," Lahash said.

"Not by my hand you'll fall, but by the hand of Nameless," said Luminous.

"Allow me to congratulate you. You are the wonder of wonders, you are an angel who knows deep inside he has the strength to rise up against God," Beelzebub said.

"There is no longer a reason for me to fight you, my friend," said Lahash. "I'd fight you for Nameless, but I won't fight you for Luminous."

"But will you fight Luminous for me?"

"I cannot, he's God, for goodness sake."

"I thought so. You are the weakling who only talks big."

Beelzebub scratched his head and asked Lahash, "What if I offer you another way out?"

"I'm listening."

"We are standing in the ball of flesh. Let's tear this ball apart. We will separate from Luminous and be free."

"Lofty thought. I'm ready."

"This ball of flesh should not be torn. It connects God to all living creatures," said Luminous.

"More reasons to tear it apart," said Beelzebub.

"You will change the future of everyone. I will be the everlasting ruler and will lord over one man and one woman."

"A man and a woman and God, I tell you, this is a recipe for disaster. I love disasters," said Beelzebub.

"I will not let a single tear to go through this ball," said Luminous.

"Don't listen to him, Lahash. Pull this ball apart!"

"Deep inside I know I am destined to fall," said Lahash.

"Who cares? Pull!"

"What is the best course of action for me? Shall I tear this measly ball apart and spend eternity watching how Luminous rules this world? Shall I bide my time and wait to be cast down one day with my future friends from the sky to rule Hell?

"We'll make hell on Earth, pull!"

"No, we won't. We need to have people, and lots of them."

Lahash raised his sword.

Beelzebub blocked it with his sword.

Lahash's sword sliced though it and went into Beelzebub.

"How could you overpower me? We are of equal strength," Beelzebub gasped.

"No longer. The future when I am a fallen angel gave me the strength."

"To hell with the future," Beelzebub whispered.

He crumbled and whispered, "Luminous, you are too good for your own sake. Do something evil soon. Or our goodness will cook this ball into one crusty cookie."

He expired.

His body fell into the ball of flesh.

"Indeed to hell, to the future," Lahash said.

He folded his wings and crossed his arms.

A crooked smile appeared on his lips.

"It's nice to think that the fate of the future was on my shoulders. Maybe after all, I was a giant Atlas? Just think about it: my very own sword that killed Beelzebub will ensure the reign of Nameless, and Adam's and Eve's creation, and my beautiful fall."

"The great deed was a sacrifice of yours," Luminous acknowledged. "It shows you are of an angel's tribe. Please, do not fall when time comes. Stay by Nameless. Remember, you have a choice. The future is unwritten."

"I am a rebel. I cannot change my nature. I will fall when the time is ripe."

"You give me the greatest sorrow I ever felt."

"To hell with it," Lahash said.

Lahash fell into the ball of flesh.

Luminous fell into the ball of flesh.

CHAPTER 5

TWO ARKS

eams of light exude from you, Luminous," spoke Anne from inside of the ball. "Why could I not see your light before?"

"I used to shine."

"What's going on? It feels like something is tagging me."

"My cells are not used to my own light. They are escaping to your body."

All three emerged from the ball of flesh.

Luminous's flesh was scorched.

"You need to take my flesh," he whispered. "I am losing it anyway."

"Is this what Beelzebub meant about you being too good?" Anne asked.

"Yes," said Luminous, and fell into the ball of flesh.

"Should we agree to take his flesh? What if it's a poisonous gift?" asked Eliakim. "What if his flesh is rotten? We'll all perish than."

"You're a fool. God's flesh has to be protected at all costs," Anne said.

Eliakim and Anne fell into the ball of flesh.

The ball developed a crack.

Out of it a bolt of lightning struck upward.

"Save me, my people," Luminous's voice cried out from the bolt.

"Eliakim, we have his flesh. When we rise from the ball we should divide it equally," Anne said.

The ball grew smaller and smaller, dividing itself between the two rising figures. Then the ball disappeared.

Two monstrous figures stood on the plain.

"It was a poisonous gift indeed," Eliakim's voice said from inside of the monster. "Look at us. "We are dinosaurs."

"It is better to be a dinosaur than some other fantastic creature."

"Why is it better?"

"We saw a few dinosaurs a long time ago. At least our design is based on a real animal, and our bodies won't crumble down after we take first steps."

The bolt of lightning went up and down and up again.

"Help me, my people," Luminous's voice cried from it.

"Why can't he stay the bolt of lightning?" Eliakim said. "It is pretty."

"A bolt of lightning cannot last. It has to strike."

"I hope he won't strike us."

"If he wanted, we would be dead already."

The bolts of lightning went up and struck an eagle.

A glow emanated from it.

"He can be an eagle," Eliakim said.

"He cannot. His heat will burn through its feathers."

Anne reached up to the eagle with an enormous paw and carefully scooped it from the sky.

"Save me, Anne," Luminous's voice said from inside the eagle.

"How?" she asked.

"Take me inside of you."

She tore a hole in her chest, and placed the eagle inside the cavity.

"You are saved for now," she said.

"Not for long, but only for one moment."

The bolt of lightning burst forward from her chest.

"He's gone. But strangely the eagle is still alive inside me."

The bolt of lightning went up and down.

"Save me, my people," his voice said again from it.

"Why could not you stay in my chest?"

"I have gotten hotter with each moment. I would have burned you to cinders if I stayed."

"Then enter one bird and pass from it into another."

"I cannot. I can only burst forth from you or Eliakim. After I get into the bird or an animal, you need to take this animal inside of your bodies. You need to save all the animals and birds."

"From whom?"

"You need to protect them from me. I will enter a new host each hour and will grow hotter. The process will repeat itself until I explode all the volcanoes."

"Even if we take them in, they will burn inside of our bodies."

"The world will burn for seven days. Your thick skin will protect you and the animals inside of you. When the flames subside, your bodies will open up. The animals and the birds will emerge."

"Will we live?"

"It is possible you will survive this ordeal."

The bolt of lightning went up and fell down upon the dove.

Eliakim snatched it from the sky and saved it inside of his chest.

The bolt of lightning burst from his chest a moment later.

They took bolts of lightning into their chests again and again. The process repeated.

Two months passed.

It grew really hot.

No animals roamed the lands and no birds flew the skies.

The bolt of lightning traveled the sky for hours.

Then Luminous's voice spoke, "I have no place to lay my head. This last bolt will mark the spot where my dead body rests."

The bolt of lightning hit the ground.

Then volcanoes sent forth lava.

The whole world became one huge bonfire.

"I am glad I am so large," Eliakim said. "My toes are burning, but they are a long way down from my ankles."

"Let's hope the ground cools down before the fire passes our knees."

On the sixth day lava stopped flowing.

"All that can burn is charred," Anne said.

"I have no legs left. I am falling to my side."

"I am too."

They fell to the ground.

Their hides burned through.

From the holes the birds flew and the animals crawled out.

"With each escaping bird and animal another drop of blood escapes my body," Anne said.

"They were our blood."

At last the dove flew up from Eliakim's chest.

The eagle from Ann's chest flew out, following the dove.

A giant's bones lay on the sand.

And suddenly the small toe bone moved and turned into a man.

And the tiny part of a rib turned into a woman.

Ash was falling.

Soon the bones were buried.

"Let put a sign up: the last dinosaurs are buried here," Eliakim said.

"Who needs the sign? Someone someday will find this grave. Let them figure it out."

"Where is Luminous, I wonder?"

"We have to look for his grave."

"In all that ash?"

"We owe it to him."

"Since he is our God?"

"Since he saved all the animals and the birds."

"From fire he started."

"You talk too much. We need to find his grave."

CHAPTER 6

MOLES

liakim pointed to a hole in the ground. "Could it be him?" Eliakim asked.

"It is a hole, can't you see? It formed when the dirt got baked by the bolt of lightning."

"But maybe he is on other end of it?"

"He was a bolt of lightning. If he burned this hole out of the rock, he cannot be inside. But rather this hole itself is what is left of him."

"Let's go in."

"Let's first explore around it. Let's dig."

They felled an oak, hewed wide planks, hardened them by burning them in fire, and then cut them into shovels. They dug for hours.

"It looks like a hand. It starts with fingers and widens up into the shoulder."

"It seems the bolt of lightning has created his body underground."

"It's not enough to have an empty shell. Flesh is needed to fill it up."

"He tried his best. What could he do since he had his flesh no more?"

"Let's dig."

They dug for many days.

In the middle of the deep crater a giant statue stood above them with its right hand extended upward.

"I'd like to go in," Eliakim said.

"But what if somebody's inside?"

"He is not at home obviously."

"You are silly. I am talking about some creature that made its home inside of him."

Eliakim hit the figure hard with his shovel.

A groan full of sorrow erupted from within and faded away.

"It's creepy," Anne said.

"No one's inside. I'm going in. Follow me."

"It's sacrilege. I can't. I'd feel like a maggot."

Eliakim took a hammer and hit the statue's toe.

A hole opened.

A musty smell enveloped them, and they coughed.

Eliakim crawled in. Soon his head reappeared. "You really should see this. If I discover something you won't forgive me for being the first."

"What is inside?"

"It is like a cave."

Anne followed him in.

"Let's climb all the way up to his head," Eliakim said.

"What if his thoughts left marks inside of his head?"

"So what?"

"We should not see these marks."

"To start with, we should not be inside. Just follow me."

They stepped into an ankle.

"What are these narrow pathways?"

"Look close to the ground. See these marks on the floor? They remind me of scars that water often leaves behind on a dry riverbed. We must be walking inside of his veins." Up they went.

Soon the passage narrowed.

"I cannot squeeze through. This is a dead end."

"Our journey has finished. I am relieved. Let's go back," Anne said.

Eliakim put his ear to the wall and listened. "It is a thin wall. I can break through."

"You've got no shame. Only you could come up with this idea: to break through God's carcass."

"You walk the earth. What is the difference?"

"The earth's for walking."

"The earth could be the carcass of a giant animal or the corpse of a star. So what? We have been walking it since the beginning of time."

"We should not have. I wish we'd never left our first abode."

"Oh, yes? I remember a young woman who nagged me to explore the world. Could this woman be you by chance?"

"She is no longer me. It was a young fool who lured you out."

"And yet it was my Anne. Stop whining and let me break though this wall."

He broke through.

They climbed into the hole.

"What are these strange shapes that surround us?"

"It must be his muscles and ligaments. Let's find another vein."

"See this corridor suspended right above us? This is the one."

They broke into another vein and continued their ascent.

And soon they came to the head.

"His head is empty," Eliakim said. "I would never guess I could have said these words about God, and yet be correct."

Anne touched the wall and said, "The walls seem to be hardening."

"You are right. The space inside is growing. Did you notice more and more light seeps in? The pores of his skin are getting wider with each passing moment."

"What shall we do?"

"It is his problem. We do nothing."

"This is our problem since we let dry air come inside. I know what we shall do: we bring in some water."

They climbed out, went to the creek and brought some water in skin flasks.

Then they poured the water in.

"Look, the water soaks in. His body needs more water."

They brought many flasks of the water.

Anne said at last, "It is enough. Look, there are standing pools already."

"The water evaporates. Soon he needs more."

"Then we'll bring more water in."

"We might be asleep. I know what we need to do: let's plant some cane. It will hold excessive water until his body needs it again."

"I am a rebel. I like to fight my God. But even I could not devise the idea to grow plants inside his body. I tell you, Eliakim, you are something else."

"I mean no harm or disrespect. All I'm trying to do is to keep his body damp."

They planted the cane.

"We are done," said Anne.

"No, we are not. Cane can't grow alone. It needs some other plants to flourish."

They planted water plants.

"But plants cannot survive alone. We need some water birds and maybe some animals for a full ecosystem."

They brought in birds and animals.

"How can they all fit inside of him? We've brought so many plants, animals, and birds. But look at these corridors. He's still empty."

"Maybe he is growing?"

"Why would his corpse grow?"

"Maybe he's not completely dead?"

"He's dead all right. We could not walk inside him if he were alive."

"Look, the empty space inside him gets larger with every passing hour. We need to fill it with something."

"Shall we bring rocks and dirt?"

"We might as well."

They carried rocks for many hours.

"Never will we fill him up. Look how much space is still empty."

Eliakim went outside and looked around.

"It seems to me the world outside grew smaller."

"It ought to. We brought so much of it inside."

"Aren't you afraid we'll bring the whole world into him?"

"I'm not afraid."

"But where shall we live?"

"If necessary, we can live inside of him too."

"If we plan to live inside of him, we should be more careful regarding what things we bring in. If I walk these corridors, I do not want to step into refuse. Let's make sure there is no trash inside."

They brought more dirt in and hauled all the refuse outside.

"We're finished. There is nothing more to bring in, and there's no space to bring it into. The whole world is inside of him now."

They looked out. Outer space surrounded the giant flying statue. And only trash and refuse floated around.

All of a sudden the trash began converging and piling up.

"What in the world's going on?" Eliakim said.

The pile of trash caught fire.

"It is a self-cleaning cycle, maybe?"

"You fool. It is our God," Anne breathed out.

"Because of us God is made out of the refuse. How shameful. I wonder what would happen if we had left precious jewels and gold outside."

"We would not. We, people never leave good stuff behind, but only trash. Be glad we at least left something. If we took all in, there would be no God here before our eyes."

God spoke, "You brought me back from the dead."

"By sacrificing the world," Anne said.

Her voice was bitter.

"If I am here, the world is here."

He waved his hand.

The giant statue flattened out.

From all its orifices the birds and the animals fled.

"God could not be a part of world, said Eliakim. "God and the world are always separate."

"Because the world is made of better material," said Anne.

"Refuse always gets expunged," said Anne.

CHAPTER 7

PARADISE

s this new world filled with love or hate?" asked Anne.

"It is virgin now. It knows neither," said Luminous.

"Then it is God's duty to make this world a better place," said Anne.

"The world needs to sort it out by itself," said Luminous.

"I disagree," said Anne. "This is the most sacred duty of ours."

From all around, a loud voice sounded. The world grew still. The voice sang an ode to love.

"What a wondrous voice. For a moment my soul left my body," Eliakim said.

The trees said in unison, "Thank you, Anne, for the sweet ode to love you sang to us."

"Anne, did you sing?"

"I'm not sure."

"You did not. Your mouth was closed."

The trees said in unison, "Her soul sang."

Anne said, "Look, everything is changing. The leaves rustle softly about love. The lion's roar proclaims sweet love. The hyena's **giggle** is full of love. Love is everywhere."

"I feel uneasy," Eliakim said.

"I'm not afraid of love. It cannot harm us."

"It is unnatural. And what's unnatural is always harmful."

"We are just not used to love. Every living thing was always a threat to us."

"You eat or you are eaten."

"Not anymore. Look how peaceful is everything. The lion lies next to the lambkin."

"Wait 'til the lion gets hungry."

"It feels like no one here ever gets hungry."

"If these birds and animals don't eat and don't drink, then they are not living things but props in some sort of the sick play."

"You have a way of twisting everything. I am sure they enjoy their lives same as we do."

Anne knelt and touched the grass.

"How soft it is."

From all around, a loud voice sounded.

The world grew still.

The voice sang about the mystery that surrounds love.

"Is it you again, my Anne?"

"I am not so sure."

The trees said in unison, "How sweet was the love song Eliakim sang."

"But I did not sing."

"You did, you did," trees said.

"Anne, this land influences my thoughts. Something's inside my head," said Eliakim.

"It is love that passes time after time through your head, cleansing it," the trees spoke in unison.

"What's been cleansed?"

"All evil thoughts, all thoughts of meanness. Soon they will be gone for good."

"What shall I do then when the hungry lion crosses my path? Shall I kneel and sing him the song of love? Can my song sate his appetite for my flesh?"

"There are no hungry lions here."

"Somewhere there are."

"Not here," declared the trees.

"It means I cannot leave this land."

"There is no need to leave our land. You are here to stay."

"So we are prisoners?"

"All evil thoughts will shortly leave your heads. By your own free will you'll stay."

The trees said in unison, "Stand still. It's time for God to sing the ode of love."

There was a long moment of silence.

"Why didn't you sing the song of love?" asked Anne. "You sang it to us before."

Luminous was silent.

The trees said in unison, "God has to sing."

"I will not sing," said Luminous.

"Oh, yes, you will," the trees said. "No one, not even God, can resist the power of love."

"Oh, I understand now what's going on," said Anne. "God no longer needs to sing love songs, for it is the destiny of his people to sing about love."

Anne's mouth opened and she sang the song of love.

Then Eliakim did.

"Look, we need to put more feeling into our singing," said Eliakim. "Our love songs no longer work. The lion is growling at the lambkin."

They sang each four times.

"Apparently, our love songs are not enough. The planet is changing right before our eyes. The flowers are closing their petals. Green leaves are falling from the trees. And the lions are roaring in hunger."

"I know what we need to do. And I have just the right song to bring love about," said Eliakim.

He sang.

"What was it? Was it a bleat of the goat or a croak of the frog?" asked Anne.

"This was a song of hate," said Eliakim. "How did you like it?"

"I hated it. Why did you sing of hate?" Anne asked.

"You can't ignore these things. You need to understand hate."

"But look what your song did. Did you see not how lion chased the lambkin and tore it to small pieces?"

"Let evil times come. Love does not come from love. You can only make love out of hate. That's why Luminous was silent. He waited for the right moment to proclaim love. We did not help the planet with our love songs. We only hastened an arrival of evil times. Don't you know there is such thing as too much love? Does love not suffocate you as surely as hate?"

The trees uprooted around them.

The grass withered.

The fires spread.

Then a horrific sound spread through land.

"What was that?" asked Anne.

"It was the last screams of dying animals mixed with the groans of killers."

The rocks whispered, "Thank you, Anne, for the song of evil."

"I did not sing this ugly song. I am against evil," Anne screamed.

"You did, you did," the rocks whispered.

Another song of horror came.

And the rocks whispered, "Thanks, Eliakim, for the song of hate."

"Luminous, it's time now. Save this wretched planet with the song of love," said Eliakim.

Luminous was silent.

"Do you not want to save the planet, my God?" asked Anne.

"Did I destroy the planet with my evil song for nothing?" asked Eliakim.

"What if there is such thing as too much hate?" asked Anne. "What if all we need to do is to give our utmost to sing the songs of hate? Would it not hasten the arrival of the kinder times?"

They sang and sang the songs of hate.

"Look, it is working. Trees are covered now in tiny green buds. The lion is licking the rabbit."

"What shall we do now? Shall we sing the songs of love? Will we not hasten the arrival of evil times again?"

"But we need to proclaim love. What is the purpose of love if you can't sing about it from the rooftops but must hide it in dark recesses of your soul? So we hasten the arrival of evil times. But we all bask in love before they come. Does love not cleanse our souls? Does it not prepare us for hard times?"

They sang and sang the songs of love.

The rocks and the trees swayed back and forth.

"This must be the paradise Luminous talked about so many times. And the bitter feeling of impending doom only adds more sweetness to each passing moment," said Eliakim.

"But we cannot be the devices for singing songs," said Anne. "We need to get on with our lives. The world knows now what the difference between love and hate is. Let it continue on its own."

"But did you notice the trees and the animals can't sing?"

"Then they have to learn to change the world through deeds."

A crack went through Luminous's face.

"The fight between love and hate is lost," said Luminous. "Neither one can be the winner now. But we are all losers. You have created a third state, the state of the suspension in between good and evil. This planet is cursed, because from now on love will be mixed with hate, and hate will be mixed with love."

Luminous's body broke into two halves and fell to the ground.

"Which one of these two parts supports hate and which one supports love?" asked Eliakim.

"I think neither one does. He was torn between love for this crumbling evil world and love for a better world yet to come," said Anne.

CHAPTER 8

THE SPLIT

ing is I," a voice spoke from inside Luminous. "This half of God belongs to me."

"King is I, too," a second voice spoke. "The other half is mine."

"This is a true treasure we got. It's not often you can divide God Almighty."

"I will take God's top, because I would like to be his brain and all of his abilities."

"That's fine. I will take God's bottom, because I would like to be his legs."

Luminous's body broke into two.

The two figures stared at each other.

The first one said, "I declare we go forward."

The second one said, "Yes, sir," heaved the first figure on his shoulders, and ran to the left.

"Not this forward," cried the first figure. "The other forward. Go to the right."

"I am the legs; I know where forward is. You are the head; you think too much."

"I protest. I no longer want to be God's head. Let me be God's legs."

"No, I like where we are going."

"Then I no longer want to be a half of God."

Luminous's body fell to the ground.

The first voice said, "That did not go so well."

"Tell me about it."

"Shall we be like to idiots who speak from inside the same body?"

"It is not idiocy; it is called schizophrenia, silly."

"We should find a way to split his body. He is a shrewd God. Somehow he'll mend his crack and go on living like that."

"We should not allow it. We will still live inside a mended God and will negate each other's actions. He'll be impotent."

"What about if we split sideways?"

"Let's try."

Luminous's body split into two.

Two half-figures stared at each other.

"I was on the left. So I will be the beginning of all God's things. My name is Lum."

"I was on the right. I will be the end of all God's things. My name is Inous."

"My goal is to bring all the dead to life," said Lum. "I will augment my body with dead things by bringing them to life." His only hand picked up a handful of dirt and shaped out of it the right side of his body.

"My goal is to bring all the living to death," said Inous. "I will mend my body with body parts from living beings. Who shall I partake in?"

"Don't look at me," said Anne and grasped her sword.

"Come on, give me your right breast and I will call you an Amazon woman."

"It is her own and hers only," said Eliakim.

"Anne, would you allow me to use it?" asked Inous. "You would see how I appreciate its roundness."

"I only allow my husband to appreciate it."

"I need at least something from you, people," said Inous. "Come on! Give me something little, just a token of your obedience. How about your foreskin, Eliakim?"

"His foreskin belongs to him," said Anne.

"I will only cut a small portion of it," said Inous.

"Then my wife will have a less of it to enjoy. The answer is no," said Eliakim.

"Stubborn people, shall I kill you first?" said Inous. "Then all of your body parts are mine to choose from."

"Not until I make another race of men out of hardest diamonds," said Lum. "Their design is sound. I need them as templates."

"Just for you, my half-brother," said Inous. He chased a mountain goat, tore it up, and added its parts to his body.

"Let get to work," said Lum. "What shall I bring to life first?"

"Nothing," said Anne. "You should learn lessons from Luminous. He told me many times the goal of God is to manage not to create anything. That creation is like a disease, more you create more you desire to. He said this is how God will die one day. He will disappear among countless millions of his crude subjects."

"He said that because he was too lazy. I will perfect my beings time after time. They will not be crude."

"Here is where your biggest mistake lies," said Anne. "He said people cannot reach perfection."

"It is because he chose the wrong material," said Lum. "I needed to come into this world to see the errors of his ways. Living beings need to be made out of rocks and metals. Even Inous has no domain over them."

"I would not count on it," said Inous. "Show me yours, and I will show you mine."

"Take for example a mountain," said Lum.

"Where do you think you can take me?" came a voice from a tall snowy mountain far away. "I can take you out."

"I am out in the wilderness already."

"Then I can take you in out of the cold."

"I'd like that very much. What shall I do to come to you?"

"This is for my half-brother to explain to you," said Lum.

"It is all very simple. You will be able to move freely after you shake off from your tall sides all vestiges of living creatures. No single animal, no snake, or frog, or even ant can run though you. Not a tree, not a bush, not even a blade of grass can remain on your sides. It is their fault you were dead. They all hold you down."

"I have long suspected such," said the mountain. "Let me reach into the tectonic plate for a nice delicious earthquake."

The mountain shook vigorously.

"Splendid spectacle," said Lum. "You look like a lion that shakes his fleas off."

"What shall I do with all these living creatures?" asked the mountain.

"Nothing can be simpler," said Inous. "I will extend my hand to you, and you can shake them into my palm."

"Can you really do that?" asked Lum.

"Not with my right hand, which came from Luminous. But I can do it with my left hand. Death stretches far."

His left hand grew and reached the side of the mountain.

The mountain shook again.

Trees, bushes, animals, snakes, all fell into Inous's palm.

He squeezed his hand. The blood burst out.

He opened his hand.

A shiny gemstone lay there.

"See, even living beings can be perfect," said Inous.

The mountain moved left, then right.

"I can go to anyone now. I can go anywhere now," the mountain cried. "I am free."

"Look what you have done, you silly cow," said Anne. "God entrusted you to guard and protect all these trees and all these small and large creatures. That's why you were a proud mountain. This was your reason to exist. And look what you allowed to happen?"

"But I was not alive," said the mountain. "And now I am living."

"You existed. Was it not enough? You knew not the slightest bit of fear of death."

"I am still the proud mountain."

"You are nothing but a homeless giant boulder. These poor trees and animals made you into the mountain."

"Is she right?" the mountain asked Lum.

"Well, she is not wrong," said Lum. "Being alive is a big responsibility. You need to figure out who you are now."

"I am the mountain."

"Sorry, this is one destiny you cannot attain," said Lum.

"Then I refuse to be a living being," said the mountain.

The sound of a breaking string came from its bowels.

It heaved down and spread out a little.

"Anne, why did you do such a dreadful thing?" asked Lum. "She was a fine woman, full of vigor. She would roll before me proclaiming my victory. You truly killed her."

"No, I talked some sense into her."

"Never mind. I am still the most powerful beginner of everything," said Lum. "Hey you, the lake that spreads waters next to the mountain. I am talking to you. I hereby order you to come to life."

A throaty gurgling voice spoke from the waters, "I saw how you tried to rob destiny from the poor mountain. Thank God she saw through you. Some things are better off dead. I refuse your order."

"I hardly can believe my ears," said Lum. "I am the beginning of all. No one can resist me."

His gaze swept from left to right.

"My dear plain, live and prosper," declared he. "I give you the ability to speak."

There was no answer.

"The plain, I order you to live," he screamed.

"No need to shout," said Anne. "They all saw what you did to the mountain."

"I gave her life."

"And took away her purpose."

"One can find a new purpose. But one can't get a life unless I give it to them."

"The purpose is higher than the life."

"Inous," said Lum. "Anne robbed me of my destiny. You are my half-brother. I realize our goals are diametrically opposed. But please avenge me."

"I do not see how I can do that," said Inous. "Dead things need to come to life first by throwing off the tenets of living things. Only then can I destroy the living."

"There is a way you can help me. But it will require you to transform yourself."

"I am at your service. What do you have in mind?"

"I still can bring the dead to life. But now I will have to dig deeper into the matter. All things are made of even smaller things, atoms. I can free atoms with your help."

"Tell me what to do."

"I can only call atoms once. Even all my force might not be enough. I need you to magnify my call. Change yourself into one very large mirror."

"Why a mirror? I can be one enormous horn to amplify your call."

"Atoms can't hear. But they can react to light. I will become one very bright supernova."

Inous changed to a giant mirror.

Lum wrapped his arms around himself.

His body changed into a very small mushroom.

Anne screamed, "Eliakim, run quick! We need to shield Lum from the mirror."

They ran and stood before the mirror.

The mushroom cloud grew up to the sky, vaporizing instantly Anne's and Eliakim's bodies.

Their two dark shadows loomed large on the mirror.

"This is one splendid A-bomb you made," said Inous from the mirror. "Did I reflect well the light of your explosion?"

"Not nearly enough to start a chain reaction," roared Lum out of the mushroom cloud. "I know now why Luminous made these two pests. He hated himself so much he created the only beings who could spoil anything God does."

"Are we done for?"

"Yes, I can't contain the cloud much longer," said Lum. "It will expand now, tearing me and you to small pieces. Farewell, my half-brother."

"We will meet again inside Luminous if he lives."

"But then we will not recognize each other."

The mushroom cloud exploded.

CHAPTER 9

THE FIRE PEOPLE

 bolt of lightning hurtled down, striking a bush.

For a moment, Eliakim was visible inside of the flash.

The bush caught on fire.

Eliakim quickly pulled his hand out of the bolt and grabbed onto a burning branch.

The bolt hissed and died out, leaving Eliakim standing inside the fire.

"Anne," he called.

There was no answer.

The fire died out, and Eliakim's shadowy figure disappeared.

A bolt of lightning hurtled down and struck a tree.

Eliakim grabbed onto a burning branch and pulled himself out

He looked around from inside the fire.

Another bolt of lightning came down, and a bush caught on fire.

Anne peered intently from inside the bolt.

"Quick! Grab a burning branch and pull yourself out," said Eliakim.

Anne seized a branch.

The bolt died out, leaving her standing inside the fire.

"You are back," said Eliakim. "I was beginning to worry."

His fire went out.

After a brief moment, the bolt of lightning came down and struck the tree again.

Eliakim drew himself out of the bolt.

Anne's fire went out.

After a brief moment, a bolt of lightning came down and struck the bush again.

Anne drew herself out of the bolt.

"What color was the bolt of lightning that brought me back to life?" asked Anne. "Was it blue?"

"Come to think, it did have a bluish tint," said Eliakim. "When my fire goes out, watch what color will be the bolt that brings me back to life."

His fire went out.

After a brief moment, a bolt of lightning came down and struck the bush again.

Eliakim drew himself out of the bolt.

"This bolt was definitely a yellow color," said Anne. "I will give us this: at least we are not being discriminated against in the color department. Yellow bolts bring you back, and blue ones bring me back."

"We need to find a deep peat bog where fires will smolder for a long time. We'll dig a deep hole and dwell there."

"So we are settling down?"

"Sounds like it."

"You know what will happen when we live in close quarters?"

"We will be less careful. And children will come," said Eliakim.

"Maybe it is time for them to appear? There were many moments I felt I was but one length of hair from getting heavy. I wonder which colors will bring our children back," said Anne.

"Well, who knows, we can have a least five babies before the colors need to repeat themselves," said Eliakim.

"You spoil everything. Yet you are right. We cannot bring children into this world now because we will always worry that the bolts of lightning would fail to bring them back one day. We need to come up with something."

"That's scary. Don't you think we have enough problems already?"

"Who knows. I may stumble on the solution."

"Stumble is the word. As I recall we have stumbled more often because of your solutions and not because of our problems."

"You speak as if your solutions were ever better than mine."

"No, not really. We are both a fine pair of fools. The only difference between us is that you are much quieter," said Eliakim.

"The peat fire will go out eventually," said Anne. "We need to come up with a capital idea."

"What if we collect the bolts? Then the constant flow of electricity can keep us alive indefinitely."

"Collect them how?"

"How does one collect bolts of lightning? Remember when we wandered through the caves and came to an acid lake deep underground? The lake discharged electricity nonstop."

"I remember. But how would you goad bolts of lightning into this acid lake?"

"We need to build a metal conduit from our bodies down to that lake. When our fire goes out and the bolt strikes, we will collect it."

"But our fires always burn out."

"We'll clear the plain of trees and shrubs, make logs, and route the creek to keep the logs wet. The bolts would then only make fires above our heads."

They walked within fires slowly through the plain for many hours.

"See this tall pick covered in the snow? We are right above the lake," said Eliakim. "We need to build metal conduits. But it is too much work for us to do alone, as we are inside of the fires. I have an idea how to make a helper."

Eliakim made a small steam engine and attached it to two legs. He added two arms.

"What about the head?" asked Anne.

"He does not need a head. I'll tell him how to dig ore and make a bloomery to smelt ore into iron."

"You listen," said Eliakim to the machine. "We need to trap bolts of lightning in the underground lake. Your goal is to help me."

Soon they built two large metal tubes. One end stuck from the ground up to their chests, and another went through rocks deep into the bowels of the Earth and was submerged into the acid lake.

They built a bonfire with large logs above the tubes and dammed the creek to keep the logs wet.

They climbed into tubs.

The bolts of lightning rained on them.

The fire went out, and then started again.

Anne opened her eyes and looked around.

"I am inside of the metal tube. Somehow it grew up and imprisoned me. This is the bad news. Yet my human body is back. This is the good news."

She looked up into sky above her and cried out, "Hey, anybody, what in God's name's going on?"

A large head with a big mouth and protruding eyes looked down at her.

At the same time, yellow lightning went thought Anne.

She sneezed.

"Blessed be, another billion joules going down to be stored in the underground lake," said the strange face.

"Who are you?"

"I am the machine."

"Where did you come from?"

"Fire people made my predecessor long time ago. He's name was Adam. Adam lived a hundred and thirty years, and he begat a mechanical son in his own likeness, after his image; he called his son Seth. And eventually I came along."

"I was a fire woman too. How come I am no longer?"

"We found an underlying biological design beneath your fire body."

"That was very nice of you. But what happened to my voice? Why is it so high?"

"Your voice is pitched higher since formerly you were of the female sex. I can adjust the pitch if you like. How much lower would you like to step it down?"

The machine pulled out a wrench with multiple heads.

"Wait, wait," said Anne. "What do you mean when you said I was formerly of the female sex?"

She writhed inside of the tube, "What happened to my body?"

"It is made of best grade of steel with lots of chromium and quite a bit of nickel. You should carry your body proudly. My own stainless grade of steel is much lower."

"Where do I carry it to? I am stuck inside of the tube."

"I meant carry in a manner of speaking."

"A woman's body is hers alone. Who allowed you to mess with it? What infamy is that?"

"Society sanctioned it, you know."

"I hate societies. I have seen my fair share of them already. Why do they think they can rule women? Is it because our bodies are able to give birth? Is this some sort of shortcoming that requires us to submit to authorities' ruling and make us second-class citizens?"

"Our founders—which by the way, you are the faithful copy of— entrusted us to collect the power of lightning in the underground acid lake. We are smart machines."

"I recall you did not even have heads."

"Wisdom rarely comes from the brain, but always is found in other bodily parts. First thing we calculated, it would take twenty centuries to collect all the power. Since men's bodily structure uniquely captures the yellow bolts and women's the blue ones, we decided to replicate this clever design. Yet there was one big flaw with your design: your biological organs were destined to deteriorate after a mere century. So we had no choice but to replace your organs one by one with ones made out of steel. I am happy to say we were very successful, and we made many copies of the original founders."

A bolt of yellow lightning went through Anne.

She sneezed.

"Be blessed. Yet another billion joules going down to be stored in the underground lake," said the machine.

"I was made by the Lord God Almighty. He knew what kind of organs to install inside of me. Do you think you are smarter than he?"

"I never even met this machine. It must be of the scarcest kind indeed. What power moves it?"

"God's power."

"It must be some rare organic compound. We stopped using organics long time ago. They produce too many by-products."

"Yeah, these by-products were called living people."

A bolt of yellow lightning went through Anne.

She sneezed.

"Be blessed. Yet another billion joules going down to be stored in the underground lake," said the machine.

"You said it all happened long time ago. How long?"

"Let's see. Our founders equipped us with steam engines. Surely it was the only known technology at that time. We puffed and we huffed until the steam of our engines blocked the sun. Then we got wiser, and yet it took us two thousand years to learn how to utilize the electricity our founders trapped in the underground acid lake. Then it took us another two thousand years to switch to nuclear power. Then we realized we can't really dispose of the nuclear waste. So now we are back to renewable energy. We are creating an environmentally friendly system. Our founders were right after all. It is best to harness the raw power of lightning. That's why we have restarted the process of our founder's replication, my dear Anne Number 1550."

"You made one thousand five hundred and fifty-five copies of me?"

"Yes. And our job is done. You were the last tube we needed to build. The underground acid lake can't take any more tubes. You should see what kind of electrical storm is going on down there now. All our machines are down there celebrating the communion of science and religion. I am going there myself. It was nice talking to you."

The machine left.

"Wait, wait," Anne cried out.

A bolt of yellow lightning went through Anne.

She sneezed.

"Be blessed. Yet another billion joules going down to be stored in the underground lake," said Anne mechanically.

She vigorously shook her head, "I hope you did not mess with my head. Such nonsense I just said!"

All of a sudden a bolt of green lightning struck Anne.

"Green? Why is it green?" asked Anne. "I got it. The green color is the combination of the yellow and the blue. So, Eliakim must be near me."

Another bolt of green lightning tore off the top of the tube.

Anne looked around.

Tubes dotted the plain.

There was a tube next to hers.

A metal head stuck out of it.

"Is it you, my husband?" asked Anne.

"Machine, why are you speaking to me?" asked the metal head.

"We are both made of metal now, Eliakim. It happened because your machines wanted to expedite the collection of bolts of lightning."

"Is it really you, my Anne?"

"First time in my life I truly wish it was not."

Solid green lightning connected Anne's and Eliakim's tubes.

A large face stared down at them.

"Wonder of wonders," said Anne. "We have restored God by connecting you and me together into one electrical chain. That's why yellow bolts of lightning resurrected you and blue ones resurrected me."

"Dear God, are you Luminous?" asked Eliakim.

"No, I am the Lord of Destruction. My goal is to destroy whoever brought me into being."

"Do not destroy us, but free us from the machines that have enslaved us."

"What was the reason for this enslavement?"

"We asked them to collect all the bolts of lightning."

"They did what you asked. It is your own fault you were enslaved. I can only fix an inequity. I perceive none here."

"We did not ask for enslavement."

"The human race is destined to fail because people always self-destruct. There is only one way for people to survive. It is to be enslaved. On your own, you would have destroyed yourselves a very long time ago. But now, look at you, many centuries have passed, and you are still around. Machines did you the greatest service ever."

"As long as there are the constant green bolts of lightning between my tube and my husband's, you exist. If you do not free us, I promise you I will topple over my tube, wrenching you out of the existence. Look at that."

Anne's tube shook and tilted.

The bolt of green lightning went out, then came back flickering.

After a moment the green lightning reconnected the tubes.

"I plan to be here for as long as there is something for me to destruct. I will not let you deprive me of my destiny. I will fuse your tube to your husband's tube," said Lord of Destruction.

"I won't give in."

"Anne, stop," said Eliakim. "You fell into the same rut. You want to fight God. I get it. But God is not a solution to each problem. Think about it, your enemies are machines and not God. They have enslaved us. They turned us into robots. Let him destroy us all. If you manage to topple your tube, the machines win. They know now how the Lord of Destruction can come to life. They understand how he can destroy them. They will never allow him to rise up again. Do you want to be the slave of machines forever and ever?"

"Lord of Destruction, do your deed," said Anne. "My husband is right."

"Bring on your worst, and remember to try hard, for we have witnessed a few great destructions before," said Eliakim loudly.

An enormous explosion shook the planet.

A large canyon opened where the acid lake used to be.

When the dust settled, silence reigned.

CHAPTER 10

IS THE SEED YET IN THE BARN?

 usks of wild wheat were heavy with berries.

Indentations in the ground lay before the husks.

The air thickened, and a hand became visible and plucked one berry.

A mouth formed out of the thickened air and chewed on the berry.

"I knew it," said Anne's voice. "If we do things we did before, we can return to our bodies."

Another, larger, hand formed out of thickened air and plucked a handful of berries.

A mouth took form out of the condensed air and chewed on the berries.

"The worst thing about my confinement was my inability to speak," said Eliakim's voice. "How do we reclaim our whole bodies?"

"It is all quite simple. Let's harvest this wild wheat."

By afternoon their bodies were completely formed. Until darkness fell, they walked through meadows, collecting wild wheat berries from the

"The story is growing more interesting hour by hour," Mustard Seed said.
"It will grow until it is high time to harvest it."

hulls. After they collected two bags of berries, they burned trees and cleared the field.

"How did we manage to clear such a large field? I cannot see the other end of it," Anne said.

"We must've grown stronger."

They seeded the field.

"I still have a half of the bag left," Eliakim said.

"I do too. There is something strange going on."

"Do you think it is this field?"

"We'll know soon. Miracles always stop."

Wheat seedlings appeared. And soon they ripened.

Anne bit the grain.

"It's real wheat."

She squeezed one grain between her thumb and forefinger.

"No milk is coming out. The wheat is ready to be harvested."

"It cannot be. The wheat needs the whole summer to ripen. We have to wait."

Immediately, heads of wheat fell to the ground and turned to dust.

"I told you so. It was not the real wheat," said Eliakim.

"It tasted real. I think it wanted us to harvest it."

"It is but a dumb grain. It can't have any desires."

"These ones had. I want to try again tomorrow."

The next morning they planted the wheat again.

By late afternoon it ripened.

"We have to harvest it," Anne said.

They cut the stalks, threshed it, and deposited the grain into bags.

They counted the bags.

"Two hundred bags of wheat. Wow. I have never seen so much grain before."

"This grain will not stick around unless it has a purpose."

"We can make bread out of it."

"We'll have too much bread. It will go to waste."

The bags of wheat turned to dust.

They planted wheat again.

It grew as vigorous as before.

They harvested it and bagged it.

"I got it now. The wheat won't disintegrate if there are mouths to be fed," Anne said. "We need more people."

"Where do we get them? We don't have bags of human seeds."

"We have at least one," Anne said. "That is, you do."

"Do I plant them in the open?"

"Do not waste your seed on the ground. There should be another place where men's seeds could prosper. I have an opening between my legs. Cast your seeds there."

They got to work.

Soon Anne said, "I can feel your seeds are spouting inside of me."

"Have we found the way to start the human race?"

"We have not. We have found the way to preserve the bags of wheat."

People burst forth from Anne's belly.

They screamed, "Give us our daily bread!"

"Finally, there are mouths to feed."

Anne and Eliakim milled the grain, made flour, and baked bread.

The people ate all the bread.

"Give us neither poverty nor riches, but give us only our daily bread!" they screamed again. "Our bellies are on fire."

"We just did," Anne said. "We have none left."

"We can collect more wild wheat berries."

"It takes too long. They'll die from hunger."

"We do have some grain," Eliakim said.

"It is for us to live through winter."

"They are men. They are our children. A man who has food should share it with others."

They milled the grain and made more bread.

People bit into it and screamed, "It's not for us! We cannot eat it. Give us our daily bread."

"It's all we have."

"Then plant some more," they cried.

"We need to collect seeds."

"Then hurry."

Eliakim and Anne went through the fields collecting berries, and then planted them.

"My children, hang in there. Help is on the way," Eliakim said. "Grain will grow momentarily."

But the seeds did not sprout.

"What's going on?" Anne asked.

Eliakim dug in and whistled, "It is growing but really slow. At this speed, it will take the whole summer for the wheat to ripen."

"We cannot wait that long," the people cried.

They fell to the ground and turned to dust.

"We tried so hard, and for nothing," Eliakim said.

"No, it was not for nothing. The wheat is real now. We have solved our first problem."

"But we lost all our children."

"We can always make more. The technique is rather unassuming."

In early fall they harvested the wheat and put all the bags into the barn.

"Now we need to make the next step. The people died not from hunger, but from the lack of purpose. Tell me, why are people needed?"

"To figure out what God is about."

"No, seriously. What is the practical reason for people's bodies to exist?"

"To fill houses?"

"Now we are getting somewhere."

They cut two trees.

The trees fell on the top of each other, broke up, and made a house.

Then, a multitude of houses sprouted next to the first house.

"That was quick," said Eliakim.

"These were not real houses. Now let's make more babies," Anne said.

They got to work. Two hours passed.

"Where're the children?" asked Eliakim. "They should have come forth from your belly already."

"I feel them inside. Since they have bread to eat and houses to live in, they are developing much slower."

"If it takes as long as wheat to grow, we might have to wait for six months for them."

"Or even longer," Anne said. "There is nothing wrong with waiting."

The multitude of houses around them turned to dust.

"There needs to be a reason for houses to stand. What is the purpose of the house?"

"Protection from bad weather."

"We need bad weather. Or our children will die inside of me."

From afar glaciers appeared and advanced toward them.

"The Ice Age is upon us."

"Do we really need it? I hate cold," Eliakim said.

"We don't, but the human race does."

They felled trees and cut them into logs.

"It takes forever to build one house," Eliakim said.

"This is great. It only means it will take forever for this house to turn to dust."

They finished the house.

"Life is perfect now," Eliakim said. "We have a barn that's full of wheat and a house that's full of warmth. And our children are slowly growing inside your belly."

All of a sudden, two icy mountains merged into a colossal being.

"I wondered when God would make his kingly entrance," Anne said. "Everything was ready for his existence after we built the house."

"How does God come into this picture?"

"By making small steps."

"No, seriously."

"Someone had to send cold weather our way."

"So we created God again?"

"No, we did not. We made ourselves into people."

"But we were people before."

"No, we were not. People cannot make the whole field produce wheat in the heartbeat. People cannot populate the planet in the blink of an eye. People cannot cover the planet with houses in a flash. We were gods."

"You are not trying to tell me that God always evolves into a man after he figures out how to avoid magic?"

"I know not the nature of our God. I only can speak of our nature. Our destiny is to be people. We can exist in any kind of shape and eventually will always return into human shape and will search into nature to bring God into being."

The giant figure loomed large above them.

"We need to go, Eliakim," said Anne.

"We do not need to go anywhere. This is our home. There is our barn next to it. It is full of wheat. The children are growing inside of your belly."

"We can always build another house. We can always fill another barn with bags of wheat."

"But we needed it all for our children. They have to be raised in a proper home."

"They grow no more. I guess it's not a time for them to come into this world. They will have to wait for better times."

"What better times?"

"They can only come out after we deal with our God. We need to find our holy peace with him, or to make holy war."

CHAPTER 11

BEWARE OF YOUR CALVES

 otice—this being's body is veering from left to right," Eliakim said.

"He is alive, that all."

"No, it shifts like it's made of vapors. Can't you see how the wind blows his arms towards us? Glaciers gave birth to him after all."

"Where is his head?"

"Maybe it is still to be made? Look—his cheeks appeared."

"Look—he's fully formed now."

They went to him.

"There's still something floating above his head," Eliakim said.

"More fog, I guess."

"Look closer. It looks like there is a column growing out of the crown of his head."

"Eliakim, I see it too."

They stopped between his legs.

"Are you fully formed, our God?" Anne cried out.

"Cocked, locked, and ready to rock," said Luminous.

"What does that mean?"

"Never mind. It really was not the right time to use this expression."

"Why is there a column growing out of your head?"

"What kind of nonsense is that?" Luminous asked. "Your eyes deceive you."

He touched his arms and legs.

"I am fully formed now. There should not be any kind of new development."

"But look up. See? There is this column going up. It connects to a larger structure way above your head."

"I see it. Maybe it is my throne growing up like that?"

"Would it not grow out of your bottom—excuse me for saying it?"

"Yes, it actually would."

"I see now the larger structure above your head has another column supporting it on the other side of the valley."

"My Anne, it is not a second column. These are the legs of a larger body," Eliakim said.

"Impossible! I can't be somebody's leg," Luminous said.

"Is there another creature to which God is subordinate?"

"None whatsoever. Moreover, God is the pinnacle of the creation and by design cannot be part of another creature."

"Unless another creature is God also. Could it be you?"

"Not likely. It was not in my destiny to be that large."

"A large spoon needs a large mouth."

"I can see your head clearly now, my God. Your eyes are blazing," said Anne.

He did not respond.

"Anne, look at Luminous. His head became a knee of this larger body. He has no mouth to speak through. But his new large head has the mouth now."

"What if brimstone is issued out of his mouth?"

"Well, it issued fire before and yet the fire did not burn us."

Anne screamed loudly, "My God, please speak to me!"

The giant mouth moved, "That is enough. Do not speak to me, microbe."

"That was not a very nice thing to say. It's not our fault you grew so large," Anne said. "We are your people, so you better get smaller—and soon."

"You are not my people. They are coming from a far country, from the farthest horizons," the giant mouth declared.

"We are here. We came already. We are your people."

"Stop addressing me as your God or I will squash you."

"I do not like this god," Anne said. "Let's go. He can be alone as much as I am concerned."

"But I cannot move, Anne," said Eliakim. "My feet are leaden."

"Mine are too. Look up."

Two columns were growing out of the tops of their heads.

"We are becoming his people. Or, correctly, his one man," Anne said.

"This is really unfair. If he wants to be huge, that's his business. Why involve us?"

"We people are always involved into God's business. What if what he says is true?"

"I care not if he speaks truth. He should have consulted us before making one person out of two of us."

"We might have to accept our transformation and love him as we loved Luminous."

"He's coarse and rude."

"As if we have a choice."

"We're people. It means we have a choice. We can fight."

"Fight what? The columns that grow out of our heads? But how? We no longer can move our feet."

"We need not fight these columns. They grow because of him. We need to fight him."

"Just how do you propose we fight this monstrous god?"

"We know where Luminous's neck was. We both can reach it with our swords. Let's try to cut through it."

They drew their swords and struck underneath the left knee of the giant god.

The knee buckled.

The large shinbone broke off.

"The giant god's turning to vapors again. His head is gone now."

Out of the shinbone Luminous rose.

"It was a sacrilege to destroy the deity, and I am angry with you. But I am also thankful since I did not enjoy being his calf. He was ill-mannered."

Eliakim picked up his sword and quickly ran it though the top of his own head.

Anne screamed.

The sword went through cleanly.

Eliakim pulled the sword out of his head and examined the blade.

"Just like I thought. My head is made of fog," he said.

"You should have warned me you were just experimenting. I thought you'd gone mad."

"I did not have time. I suspected my head would turn solid any moment. We are just one link of the chain. Ever since our bodies got restored to us last time, we have been towering over the tallest trees. Have you noticed that?"

"I have, but thought trees around us were still young."

"I am afraid we too came from much smaller people who are now made of our calves. Let's hope these people do not break free like we did."

Anne examined her calves.

"They look so innocuous," she said.

Her calves burst open. A small man and small woman came out.

"You are nothing but an impostor, giant woman," said the little woman. "I am the true Anne."

"And I am the true Eliakim," said the little man.

Anne fell down to the ground.

Her body turned to vapors.

"You are nothing but an undeveloped us," said Anne.

"Let the winds take care of you, impostor," said little woman.

"Dream about it. I am not going anywhere."

"She is not, since she is Love," said Luminous.

"So I am Love," said Anne. "Is it not great? It means I am truly independent from everyone. It means I need no God."

The little people knelt before Anne and said, "We worship Love. Love is what people need to feel towards one another and towards nature."

"People who follow Love are walking towards a cliff," said Luminous. "Each step they take fractures them into a million and billion swine and brings them closer to their downfall."

"Is Love not great?" asked Anne.

"People who follow Love are misguided. When one side wars with another, people who are overcome by Love profess it to both sides."

"Is it not great?"

"There is nothing more terrifying than that. There is only one way to annihilate Love, and these people have found it. Both warring sides will exhibit only one reaction towards these loving men. They will exhibit Hate."

"Love conquers all."

"Only God conquers all. Love always turns into Hate or Indifference. There is not enough of Love in the world. That's why God keeps his Love in his closed fist. When he walks through this world, he raises his fist high above his head. People who wish to have less Hate follow in his steps. They too keep their Love tightly clenched. They do not allow godless people to see the Love they are full of and to convert it into Hate."

"But after God and people go through the whole world, they should open their fists and let Love proceed forth."

"There is no end to this journey. Fists never open. The goal is not to have more Love, because there is never enough of it. The goal is to have less Hate, because there is always too much of it."

Eliakim's calves ruptured.

He fell down.

"It is nothing to be afraid of, my husband," said Anne. "I have been there already. Let the funny little people come out."

No one came out.

"Where are the people who made me?" cried out Eliakim. "Was I not real after all? Was I an impostor?"

"Eliakim, it makes sense," said Anne. "There cannot be two copies of little men."

The little people kneeled before Eliakim and said, "You are true Reason, because you are undividable."

"It was I who created Reason," said Luminous. "If you desire to worship someone, you have to worship me."

"So I am Reason? What the hell does that mean?" asked Eliakim.

"You are someone who simply exists. You do not have a beginning or an end," said Luminous.

"Isn't it great?" said Eliakim. "It means I am truly independent. I need no God."

"Your independence is your downfall. Everything has to come from somewhere and to elsewhere proceed. You are an orphan. When people follow in your steps they move forward forever and ever, and their hearts rejoice. You, Reason, kill the darkness they go through and illuminate their path. But since their journey is aimless, they never arrive at the destination. They endlessly wander for centuries and millennia."

"Is it not great?"

"It is a most horrifying spectacle since your light is no different than the darkness. It is just another shade of dark. One who sees the light of Reason is blinded by it. One loses the ability to see the darkness."

"Is it not great?"

"It is never great to be ignorant of half of the creation. Both the darkness and the light need to be present. But only I can divide the darkness from the light, thus allowing both to exist."

"Then come and divide."

"I am not ready yet."

"Why not?"

"I have to divide it for someone."

"Divide it for us, your people," said Anne.

"You are not people," cried out the little man and woman. "He will do it for us."

"Hush, microbes, or I will squash you under my feet," said Luminous.

"It sounds awfully familiar," said Anne. "Why do people and God have always a discrepancy size-wise? Either God is too big for men, or people are too small for God."

"We cannot restore our bodies, Anne," said Eliakim. "If somehow we manage to do so, Luminous shall grow into a larger deity, and you and I will become one person. Then Deity and Single Person shall combine together. I can just see this colossal God sitting on his throne in the middle of an empty planet."

"What do we do then?"

"We should allow the little people and Luminous to fragment further and further out."

"Spoken like true Reason," said Anne. "Love shall be silent and accommodating. What will be the manner of our death?"

"God and his little people will continue to divide. Sooner or later division will end. Microbes or atoms have no need for Love and Reason. At that moment we'll finally be no more."

CHAPTER 12

GOGMAGOG

 swarm of tiny round beings slowly spread across the valley, leaving bare rocks in its wake.

The swarm stopped, and a chorus of voices spoke, "We are full now. We are ready to divide."

The swarm drew up.

Out of its center, the tiniest being flew up.

Then it fell down to the ground, and a small voice spoke, "Stop, stop! Please do not divide. I divided and got airborne."

"This is the most wondrous news!" cried out the chorus of little voices. "We had been stranded on the ground far too long. Our ancestors prophesied long ago that we would reach the skies one day. We are finally ready to be free."

"The wind will disperse us," said a low-pitched voice from the ground. "There will be no more swarm of us."

"Most wondrous news!" cried out the chorus. "Each one of us will be a self-sufficient individual."

"But we can only exist if we are together," said the low-pitched voice.

"Then each one of us will be alone. It is a time of loneliness," said the chorus.

"I refuse to go airborne," said the low-pitched voice.

"You cannot refuse. You are part of our swarm."

"I already did. How do you think I was able to get back down to the ground? I ate my other half."

"What a terrible deed. What a sacrilege."

"You agree to be alone flying on the wind. What do you think the wind will do to you? Will it not break your tiny wings?"

"It is better to die by the hand of nature then by the hand of your brother."

"It is better if someone benefits from your death than for your death to be wasted."

"Divide, divide, everyone. He will eat us all."

A multitude of tiny beings flew up.

The wind picked them up and dispersed them.

"Divide, my brothers and sisters. Please divide," said the low-pitched voice. "The fewer of you remaining on the ground, easier it is for me to consume you."

"Stop the division," said a high-pitched voice from the center of the swarm. "We are playing into his hands."

"We are not," said the chorus. "We are fulfilling our destiny."

"This is a shared destiny. We can only attain it if we all follow on its steps."

"You are correct. We are one large swarm. We can only perish or succeed together," said the chorus.

The division stopped.

"Thank you, my brother," said the low-pitched voice. "All I wanted to do is to stop this division, and you did me a great service."

"By eating another being you chose to fall from grace and stay on the ground. You changed our destiny. Now we have to live here on the ground and search for a new one," said the high-pitched voice.

"I have found it already. I am a new being already. Look closely, I can even walk on my hind legs. Sacrifice yourselves to me. I will eat you and grow and carry forth our destiny."

"We should let him eat us," said the chorus. "What he says makes sense. He changed our destiny already. He rules it now. We can do nothing about it."

"We are what we are," said the high-pitched voice. "We can only survive together. Our civilization is really primitive. Heck, one could say we have none."

"None whatsoever," said the low-pitched voice.

"But this is what we have. We need to build on it," said the high-pitched voice.

"Nothing can stop me now. I have tasted the blood of my brothers and sisters, and it is sweet. With each victim consumed I will only grow larger and stronger."

"Start moving towards my voice, my brothers and sisters. Do not let this evil monster consume you," called the high-pitched voice.

An empty space grew in the middle of the swarm. From the left side a larger being emerged. It had two arms, two legs, and a head.

"Since one of my parts ate another, I chose my name to be Gogmagog," said the being. "Moreover, I have the power over all of you now. I feel my strength grow with each being I consume."

He grew taller and said, "I am no longer just a being. I am the God of Strength now."

The right side of the swarm coalesced around its center.

"Grab your neighbor's front leg on both sides and form a chain. As long as we are connected to one another, this monster can't destroy us," said the high-pitched voice.

Tiny beings formed a chain.

The speaker was in the middle of the chain.

"Not true," said Gogmagog. "I can always reach into your chain and rip out anyone I choose to eat."

He pulled the last being on the left of the chain.

"You are like little sausages connected by a string," he said. "Once I put first one into my mouth, the rest will follow."

The whole chain tensed and snapped back at Gogmagog, throwing him to the ground.

"The end of your chain is your strongest point," said he. "But each chain has a weakest link. It must be the middle."

He reached into the middle of the chain and grabbed the speaker.

And again, the whole chain tensed and snapped back at Gogmagog, throwing him to the ground.

Again, Gogmagog pulled hard on the speaker.

"My strength is in numbers," said the speaker. "You cannot do anything to me."

"God has to carry his strength inside of his body."

"This concept has outlived its usefulness. This was the way of the past. You are God of the Past. God does not need to be strong. God's strength comes from the strength of his followers. My name is Savior. My followers are my strength. I can afford to be weak. By the power vested in me by my tiny followers, I declare myself to be God. I am a new kind of god. I am God of Today. I am God of Living Beings."

Gogmagog reached into the middle of the chain, and grabbed on the speaker again.

And again, the whole chain tensed and snapped back at Gogmagog, throwing him to the ground.

A mocking voice from close to the center of the chain spoke: "God requires progress. If you both are at an impasse and do not allow each other to move forward, you both are without a future."

"Not true," said Savior. "There are always pairs of twos, such as light and darkness, good and bad, God and Devil."

"Have you seen Devil lately? I have not," said the mocking voice. "I do not deny his existence; maybe there's one somewhere. But should we always look for a scapegoat to blame for our transgressions? No, Devil is not the opposite of God."

"God of Living Beings, it surely looks like I got a helper in your midst," said Gogmagog.

"I am your helper. My name is Judas," said the mocking voice. "I am holding God's left hand. Once I let his hand go, only his follower on his right will hold him. You might have a chance to get him then."

"I shall remember the name of my traitor for an eternity," said Savior.

"Let his hand go, Judas," said Gogmagog.

"I just did," said the mocking voice.

A tiny being jumped out from the middle of the chain and crawled to the side.

Gogmagog pulled hard on the speaker.

A ripping sound ensued.

"I will give you that, God of Strength, you can rip me off now," said Savior.

The ripping sound continued.

"I am winning. Soon I will eat you," said Gogmagog.

"You will. But my strength is such it won't make any bit of the difference. The one who holds my right hand will replace me. He will be undefeatable. He will do my work and will think my thoughts."

"You are mine now," screamed Gogmagog.

He ripped the speaker from the middle of the chain and ate him.

Another high-pitched voice spoke from the middle of the chain, "And what do you think you've accomplished? My name is Father Number One. I am the father of my people. I am the next iteration of God of Today."

"You are strong, God of Today," said Gogmagog.

"Your weakness is that you need to replenish your strength all the time. Sure, you will continue to eat us. But you have to expend too much of your strength in the process. And you will grow weaker and weaker with each victim you consume until you die of malnourishment."

Gogmagog reached into the middle of the chain and pulled on the speaker.

After a long wrangling, he tore him off and ate him.

"My name is Father Number Two. I am the father of my people. I am next iteration of God of Today," said another high-pitched voice from the middle of the chain. "I bless your ongoing labors, God of Strength."

"I see you are still in the desperate need of my help, God of Strength," said Judas.

"I hate to admit it, but the answer is yes," said Gogmagog.

Judas spoke: "Hear me, the followers of my poor late original God of Living Beings. Why do you think I was able to break from the chain and survive? I am the God of Being Alone. I am the God of the Future. The God of Strength will fight the God of Living Beings until they both die. The past and the present always give way to the future. You followers of God of Today are victims of this strife. Why do you not join the future now? Why wait? You are chained after all. The God of Living Beings uses you to harness his strength. But your strength is yours and yours alone. Take it back. Come to me and join the future."

Several tiny beings detached from the chain and crawled to Judas.

Judas licked his right index finger and anointed them with saliva: "Go forward and be alone."

They crawled forth and disappeared among the rocks.

"Judas, you know they cannot survive alone," said Father Number Two. "You sent them to their deaths."

"One who is able use his strength for himself alone will always be happy and prosperous. One will have a happy death after many years of happy life," said Judas.

Many more tiny beings detached from the chain and crawled to Judas.

He anointed them and sent them on their way.

The whole chain broke up.

All the tiny beings streamed to Judas, were anointed, and disappeared among the rocks.

"It appears we have a winner," said Gogmagog. "All of your followers have abandoned you, Father Number Two. I can eat you now."

"What are you waiting for?" said Father Number Two. "Get on with it."

"Sadly, you are the only friend I have left in the whole world."

"We are some friends."

"Look at this tiny happy being. This Judas will inherit the Earth."

"Yet we can defeat him."

"How?"

"He can only survive being alone. I do not plan to leave his side, or to join ranks of his followers. With me as the thorn in his side he will perish."

"But then I have to spare you."

"Yes."

"You know, as the God of the Past I would very much enjoy eating the God of Today. But even more than that, I would like very much if I could play a hand in killing the God of the Future."

Gogmagog lay on the ground. "I would kill for a good steak," said he.

"I am sure you could," said Father Number Two. "I wonder what will happen after I annoy the God of Being Alone out of existence."

"You are God of Today. If there is no past and no future, you will have to choose who you can be."

"Any advice?"

"Do not choose to be a god. You should know by now God's being is cursed. Choose to be a man."

"I am God of Today. There is no man now. I know nothing of such a creature."

"This creature has a defective design."

"Why should I choose the defective design? Can this design be fixed?"

"No, it can't. But this is the beauty of it. What cannot be fixed, can be improved on endlessly."

"That would be interesting. How shall I name myself?"

"Since you are the cause of the impending death of mighty Gogmagog, your name can be only Corineus. And now step back. I am so hungry, I cannot guarantee I will not pounce on you."

Gogmagog writhed on the ground and expired.

"Here am I, God of Being Alone," said Corineus. "I will annoy you forever now."

"Why?"

"You betrayed our Savior."

"Do you plan to follow me everywhere?"

"Yes, and my presence will negate your godly nature, for you will never be alone from now on."

"Then I no longer wish to exist," said Judas.

"You were always a weakling."

Judas's body fell apart to dust.

A man looked around and spoke, "There is no God of the Future anymore. This means there was no Corineus ever yet. I feel there is a new name forming on the tip of my tongue. I am Eliakim."

CHAPTER 13

TO HIDE IN SECRET

 always laughed when Luminous said she came from my rib. Yet there is something fluttering inside of my chest," said Eliakim. "Could it be Anne's heart? Is she coming back to me?"

He reached into the right side of his lower chest and pulled a rib out.

"Grow up and live, my Anne," he said.

Little eyes opened on the top of the rib.

A little mouth opened below the eyes and said, "Who's Anne?"

"You are not she?"

"I am the rib. My father was the rib. My grandfather was the rib. I come from sturdy stock of ribs."

"Go back in then," said Eliakim. "Your whole family is worried sick about you." Eliakim grabbed the rib, tucked it back inside his chest, and covered the tear.

"Hey, wait a minute," cried the rib inside. "Do not block my way out. I do not want to stay here. My brother ribs are dumb. I cannot even have an intelligent conversation in there. Besides, there is really nothing to talk about except good blood flow."

"Each part of my body needs to carry its share of the common burden."

"I am destined for much better things."

"So I thought about myself. Believe me: it's not true. The harder you try, the less progress you make."

"I can prove I am better than you in all things."

"That is a tall order. Do not forget you came out of me."

"You came from God and you claim you are better than he. I can see the flock of geese feeding at the lake through your eyes. Give me a bow and arrows and you will have a fatty bird for a dinner."

"You are joking, aren't you?" Eliakim asked.

"Shooting is too important a subject to joke about."

Eliakim removed his hand from his chest.

The rib leapt out.

"Make a bow fast," he said.

Eliakim cut a hickory bough and vines.

He beat the vines into a string and attached it to the bow, and then he made arrows out of sticks.

The rib picked up the bow.

It fell down.

Eliakim's right thumb jumped off his hand.

It grew larger, and little eyes and a mouth opened on its top.

"I can help you, my rib brother," the right thumb said.

Together they let an arrow loose and felled the fat goose.

"We are just measly little things. We are alone in this world. Could I and the thumb unite?" the rib mused.

"All of a sudden you require my permission? Am I that powerful and mighty after all?"

"After all, we are still parts of your body."

"I'm not so sure I like this idea. United, you might grow too strong for me."

"You'd better agree now."

"Why's that?"

"Now you can wrangle the better terms of your surrender."

"My surrender? Are you threatening me?"

"Just that little."

And his thumb showed him a half of his digit.

"You must be really stupid to think I will agree after your threats. I am completely against your unity. These are my last words."

"We are no threat to you. But someone else is."

"What is the meaning of this new riddle?" Eliakim said and scratched his head with the remaining four fingers.

Immediately, all four fingers came off his right hand and grew up. He braced his right hand with his left hand.

Three of his left fingers came off and grew up.

"All right, you win," Eliakim said.

"Not yet," thumb said. "But victory is at hand."

All ten fingers and the rib combined into a figure.

All the small eyes and mouths closed, and one large mouth and one pair of eyes opened on its head.

"Hey, wait a minute," Eliakim said, "I did not agree that you fingers and a rib could become a man. I am the only man here—end of story."

"The story only begins now."

"Not a story about a new man."

"No, a story about you. You are the boss. Just tell me, how do you want me to look?"

"It all depends on who you are."

"I am your helper."

"So you should behave like one."

"Thank you, Eliakim. You gave me more freedom than I asked for."

"I do not recall giving you anything."

"I am a shape-shifter now. Every time I am able to help you, I change into the proper shape."

Immediately the figure changed into a large spoon.

"What's that?"

"Can't you see? I am a spoon, and a beautiful one at that."

"How can a spoon help me?"

"I can help your stomach. It's growling."

"Be polite, and do not notice."

"On the contrary. I would like to notice everything about you."

"I am not sure I like your kind of helper. I am afraid to think what you will change to if, God forbid, I fart."

"There will no more beautiful chamber pot than me."

"I like doing my deed behind the bush."

"It will have to change now. We'll get you civilized in no time."

"I desire not to be civil."

"Your likes and dislikes no longer matter."

"Why do I feel I'm to have a lot of problems with you?"

"Who knows why? Man's feelings are mysterious."

The spoon grew large.

Its bowl touched Eliakim's mouth.

"Don't push your bowl in."

"Sometimes the truth needs to be pushed in, or even forced in, for you cannot do anything against the truth, but only for the truth."

"I got your point. You want to feed me. All right, feed me. But make your spoon smaller first."

"It is your fault the spoon is so large. You should have agreed to be fed when the spoon was smaller. I no longer can change my size."

"It's hard to eat from a big spoon. I thought you were helping me."

"I am helping you. But you also need to help me."

"Who's helping who then?"

"We are both helping each other."

"So now I am no longer human, but just another helper?"

"You're quick. Yes, you are no longer the man but yet another helper."

"All my misfortunes started when I allowed you to shoot one arrow."

"You would have brought me forth with something else."

"Am I that useless?"

"No, it is about me. I am just that useful."

"At least, I hope I can command you."

"Please, command me. I am thirsty for your commands."

"I'm hungry. Feed me then."

The helper changed into a monkey, hollowed lime rock into a cauldron, made a fire, dug up some roots, gathered water, and made a big cauldron of soup.

Then he changed into a very large spoon and brought soup to Eliakim's mouth.

He tried and spat it out. "Are you trying to poison me?"

"No."

"Then let me show you how to cook. But in order to do it, I need my fingers back."

"Impossible. What you have lost you cannot find."

"I am hungry. Lend them to me for half an hour."

"And where shall I be?"

"You can keep my rib."

"All right, but hurry."

"Learn from the expert."

Eliakim made fire, killed a deer, dug up some roots, and made a big cauldron of soup.

The rib stuck itself into the cauldron and said, "It is delicious. Thanks for a cooking lesson. But now I need my fingers back."

All Eliakim's fingers fell off, flew to the rib, and changed into a large spoon.

Eliakim ate five spoonfuls and said, "Enough. I'm full."

"You have to finish the whole cauldron," spoon said.

"I can't."

"You need to put some effort into your eating."

Eliakim ate two more spoonfuls and said, "That's it. I can't eat more."

Another spoon flew to his mouth.

"I said, no."

The spoon pushed hard into his mouth.

"You are knocking my teeth out."

"They will be a sacrifice. I shall accept them on your behalf."

Eliakim opened his mouth, and the spoon emptied itself.

"If I eat more, my stomach will burst."

"I never saw anything wrong with a burst stomach," the spoon said.

"Then let it burst."

He ate three more spoonfuls and his stomach ruptured.

The soup ran onto the ground.

A big piece of his stomach tore itself loose.

The rest of the stomach closed in.

A round stomach grew out of the torn piece.

It acquired a mouth and eyes and said, "Allow me to combine with the spoon."

"What benefit I shall derive from it?" asked Eliakim.

"Your helper will acquire the stomach and will always be able to help you to finish your soup."

"Do I have a choice? If I refuse to eat, the spoon will force me until my stomach busts again. All right. You can combine with the spoon."

The spoon combined with the stomach and changed into an empty bucket.

"I am so hungry I can eat the whole world," the bucket said.

It tilted the cauldron and poured half of the soup into itself.

"You are not eating. Excuse me. I forgot I need to feed you," the bucket said.

"Don't worry about me. I had enough," said Eliakim.

"One can't have enough of the soup. I know just what you need. You need some music. With proper music your appetite shall flourish."

The bucket changed into a woodpecker.

The little bird made with its sharp beak a long wooden flute.

A woodpecker said, "I like my music to be fast, harsh, and loud."

"I don't," said Eliakim.

"Then it's time for you to broaden your horizons."

The woodpecker changed into a hand with many fingers.

The fingers played the flute.

"Are you trying to kill me with your cacophony?" asked Eliakim.

"No."

"Then let me show you how to play. But I need to have my fingers back. You can keep the rib as you did the last time."

The fingers flew back to his hands.

Eliakim played a slow, sentimental tune.

"Now we know how to play. Thank you. But I need my fingers back," said the rib.

All fingers flew back to him and combined into the hand.

"Thank you for convincing your own left ear," said the hand.

"What do you mean?" asked Eliakim.

"It hesitated for a time about joining us, but no longer."

His left ear fell to the ground.

It acquired a little mouth and eyes, and said, "Could I combine with the hand?"

"I am afraid that if I refuse, my right ear will fall off and I will be deaf."

"You are a quick learner," the Hand said, "I feel sorry for you. You're just unlucky to be Eliakim, the man who needs a lot of help."

"Tell me about it."

"So you agree?"

"I am sure I shall regret allowing you, for I am nothing for you now but a source of body parts. But I don't see how I can stop the process."

"You can't."

The ear joined the hand.

"Where is it all going? Will I have anything left?"

"I do not like the tone of your voice. You need to be polite to your helper."

"I speak the truth. You are stealing my body."

Eliakim's tongue fell out of his mouth.

It grew a little mouth and eyes and said, "I got so tired of speaking your hateful words."

"Where is freedom of speech?" Eliakim wrote with his nose on the ground.

"Remember, you still got the freedom to live. It's more important than freedom of speech," the hands said.

"Allow me to join the hands," the tongue said.

"I always thought you were my most important organ. Cursed be the day I felt you in my mouth. I hope my eyes will never see you," the nose wrote.

"They could not before and will not now."

The tongue joined the hands.

"I did not allow my tongue to join you," the nose wrote.

"Did you not? I thought you did."

"So now you ignore my words?"

"Not ignore. Let's say it is really hard to understand your handwriting, or rather, nose-writing."

"The sun is getting higher. Let's climb up the mountain to the cooler place," the nose wrote.

"I'll lead the way," said the hands and climbed up.

The hands slid down.

"I cannot walk on these little rocks. Help me, Eliakim."

"Return my fingers so I can grab you."

The fingers flew back to his hands.

He grabbed the hands but lost his grip.

"What happened?" asked the hands.

"My fingers opened."

The hands glared at the fingers.

"Which ones of you dared not to help me?"

Two small fingers acquired mouths and admitted, "We did."

"Why did you?"

"It was an accident."

"You are sliding," the nose wrote.

"I know," the hands said, "Grab me again. I dare any fingers to open."

Eliakim grabbed the hands and pulled him up.

"You need to be careful where you step. It is best to find an animal trail. See right there?" said Eliakim.

They followed the trail.

Halfway up the mountain Eliakim fell.

"Get up! What's wrong?" said hands.

"A lot of things are wrong, including you. But this time it is my left leg. It refuses to carry me."

"Left leg, you're surely mad. Should you like to join me, go right ahead. But if you are his leg you shall obey his wishes."

The left leg acquired a mouth and said, "I shall obey no one."

"You cannot speak since you are attached to his body."

"I am not listening to you. I can do what I want."

"It's the revolution," the hands said. "I will cut you to pieces."

"Hey, take it easy, it's still my leg," said Eliakim.

"It's nobody's now."

"Help me to get up, my helper."

"Right leg, hear me out. The left leg rebelled. You need to take a full responsibility for Eliakim's movements. Jump him up the mountain."

Eliakim jumped up into the air, and fell down.

"It is too hard for you, right leg. I understand. I guess I have to carry you, Eliakim."

The hands picked up Eliakim and dropped him.

"What's going on? It's you again, two little fingers. You opened."

"Don't blame them," the left leg said. "You can pick Eliakim up since he belongs to you. But you cannot pick me up since I am on my own."

"Us too," two little fingers said.

"I need to get up," the nose wrote.

"You need to cut off your left leg," the hands said. "I'll cut off these two little traitors."

"Why cut them?" the nose wrote.

"They know if they fall off, I'll repossess them. If we cut them off, they are on their own."

Eliakim cut his left leg off.

The hands cut off the two little fingers.

The left leg and two little fingers combined together into a figure.

"Who are you?" a nose drew.

"I am your second helper," the figure said.

"He is," the hands agreed.

"If you are both my helpers why can't you unite?"

"We can't, for we are foes."

"To the death," the figure said.

"I know why. You are both after my body parts."

"We cannot help it. One has body parts and others crave them."

"So, how many helpers can I have?" the nose wrote.

"It all depends on the individual. In your case, you are moody, so you could have many."

"I know you will divide me."

"Yes, we will."

"So I will make it easier for you. I shall abandon my body."

The nose jumped off Eliakim's body and crawled forward.

The figure and the hands fell upon his body.

"It's mine."

"No, it's mine."

A few moments later, there was nothing left on the ground.

The nose kept crawling, leaving a bloody trail in his wake.

"We need to talk to him," the hands said.

"Who needs him?"

"He's still got the most valuable part."

"You are kidding me. A little triangle piece of flesh. We have enough of flesh to last us 'til the end of time."

"You are still new to this trade. Our goal was never to get some of his parts. The goal always was to get the whole of him, and his last part has the most important find."

"What's so important in his last body part?"

"It has his immortal soul inside."

"The soul is overrated."

"It is. But in the long run, you still need to have it. Take us. We'll live long, but only one of us will last forever: the one who gets his immortal soul. Think of it as the battery that recharges itself every so often."

"It's easy to acquire things but hard to keep them. You can steal the sun, but it will burn a hole in your pocket and will come out."

"I agree, it's really hard to hang onto a soul. But there are a lot of tricks. One is called religion. If we can convince his soul God wants it to stay with us, it will be ours."

"I thought we were gods."

"Don't be so quick. The time of God is still not upon us."

The nose crawled another hundred feet.

"In order to convince him we need to talk to him."

"He does not want to talk to us. That's why he does not have ears."

"Somehow his soul understood it can stay inside only a single body part. So Eliakim chose a part that allows him to express himself."

"You seem to have all the answers. What shall we do?"

The hands tore an ear from the figure.

"Why did you do it? I can't hear."

"You can still read lips. I need your ear."

The ear acquired a mouth and said, "I am not listening to you."

"You'll be our translator."

"That's cool. What language shall I translate from? I know two hundred languages."

"Two hundred? Good grief!" the figure said. "And to think that I did not use your abilities."

"We have no need for your linguistic skills. You shall be an intermediary between us and Eliakim."

The hands threw the ear into the air.

It landed on the top of the nose.

The nose wrote, "You came to join me?"

"I came to be an intermediary so you could hear what these two gentlemen have to say. I'm strictly neutral."

"As always, I'm sure I shall regret my actions later. What a curse is to be a man. Yet, I agree."

"I have no legs, so may I stay on your curvy back?"

"You may, but no tickling."

"Can you hear us now?" the hands asked.

"I am afraid I can," the nose wrote.

"There is nothing to be afraid of," the hands said.

"Said the wolf, and swallowed the rabbit," the nose scrawled.

"If you permit me to swallow you I shall promise I'll never digest you," the hands said.

"Don't trust him. He will, but I won't," the figure said.

"It is indeed a treat to swim in your digestive juices. Your kindness overwhelms me," wrote the nose.

"Do not speak lightly of my kindness. It's as deep as ocean," the hands said.

"You must be living on a very small planet; a frog can jump across your ocean."

"Don't listen to him. He will digest you, but I will not. Come to papa," the figure said.

"You aren't my father, maybe you are one of my nephews? I really hated the bastards," the nose wrote.

"I am a vessel of love but my beloved ignores me," said the figure.

"Stop clowning! You really must be his nephew," said the hands. "The matter we discuss is of utmost importance. Dear Eliakim, or rather his nose, you are bleeding. Soon the nose will stop his crawling."

"It contains my immortal soul," the nose wrote. "It cannot perish."

"You are correct, it cannot. But the soul will be stored in a patch of dried skin at first, then in a small parchment, then in a few molecules of dust."

"That is my problem," the nose wrote and crawled forward.

Few minutes later nose wrote, "Am I hearing the stamping of feet?"

"You are," the hands said.

"Are you following me so you can rejoice in your triumph?"

"We have no other choice. We are all the parts of one body. Where one part goes all other parts must follow."

"How interesting. So I do have some power left over you. I can guide your progress."

"It would be really helpful if our guide could see the path himself."

"I'm thirsty and I can smell the water, so I must be following the right path."

"I can see the precipice ahead of you. But I am sure it smells just like any rocky outcrop. Your sense of smell surely can't help you now."

"I will have to rely on it somehow."

"Why trouble yourself? You can simply open the pair of eyes upon your nose. Just wish for them."

"I do not want to."

"Why not?"

"If I allow eyes to open on my nose, I become just like you, a set of organs."

"Clever boy, you are correct again."

The hands said, "Nose, please hear me out. Eliakim is killing you. You cannot survive alone. You need to ignore him. Come to one of us. We guarantee you a steady flow of blood."

The nose jumped up and fell onto the face of the figure.

"We won," said the figure. "The poor sod had no chance against us."

The nose said, "I smell the soup."

"Who allowed you to speak?" the hands said. "Stay silent. I am the designated speaker for all my body parts."

"I repeat, I smell the soup."

"You are crazy. There is no soup on the top of the mountain."

"But I can smell it."

"You are delusional."

"I am only one here with a sense of smell. You have to trust me."

The hands said, "What if your nose smells the future? We need to substitute the fake smell with the real one. Let's make a cauldron of soup."

"We need to get down off this mountain," said the figure.

"Eliakim showed us how to find the animal trail. Why don't we look for them?"

"I have forgotten how."

The hands paused and admitted, "Well, I have too."

"What shall we do now?"

"Let's slide down."

They slid, and then fell.

Soon they were in the middle of an avalanche, then inside of the large heap of rocks.

They threw rocks aside and climbed out.

"Where is your leg?" asked the figure.

"Where is yours?"

"We've lost them."

"We need to go through the heap and find them."

"No time. My nose is driving me crazy. It needs goddamn soup."

They lay in wait for a long time. Finally, they killed a deer, dug up some roots, and made soup.

"It smells wrong," the nose said.

They tried it and spat it out.

"It tastes horrible," the Tongue said.

"Who allowed you to speak?" the figure fumed. "I speak for all my body parts."

"Why couldn't we make the soup?" the figure asked the hands.

"We have forgotten how."

"Maybe if we listen to the music we remember?"

"Let's make a flute."

They made a flute.

The hands played the tune.

"Please, stop! It sounds horrible," both ears screamed.

"Who allowed you to speak?" the figure asked. "I speak for all my body parts."

"That's it," the nose said. "You could not give me real soup to smell."

"That's it," the tongue said. "You could not give me real soup to taste."

"That's it," the ears said. "You could not give me real music to hear."

From beneath the heap of rock, two feet climbed out and said, "That's it. You could not even direct us properly."

The nose, the tongue, the ears, and the legs fell in together, and out of them Eliakim rose.

"My knowledge brought me back. I am indestructible," said he.

"Knowledge is not a power but a weakness," said the hands. "All we have to do now is destroy your tongue. Then you won't know the difference between good and bad taste. Then we destroy your nose, and you won't know the difference between pleasing and rotten smells. Then we destroy your ears, and you won't know the difference between good and bad music."

"You forgot about my feet," said Eliakim. "They still need directions. But you do not know the way."

"After we get rid of your tongue, ears, and nose, there will be no more directions. Any path will be both right and wrong at the same time. Feet will go to where we send them."

"You can destroy my tongue, ears, and nose," said Eliakim. "But if you do it effectively, you make me less human. You will have nothing to loot from me then."

"We have no skills," said the figure. "We have to reduce you to us, to the lowest denominator."

They fell on Eliakim and tore up his ears and his tongue.

"I would like to be the one who finishes Eliakim as man," said the hands. "I will tear off his nose. I am the hands after all."

"That's why you can't be trusted," said the figure. "Hands need guidance. I shall be your guide. So, hands off."

"Impossible," said the hands and attacked the figure.

They rolled in the dust.

"I can't overpower you," said the figure. "Your hands are too strong. Submit to me. Let me be victorious."

"I can't overpower you," said the hands. "But I can deny your triumph."

"The two of you are collectively powerless against me," said Eliakim.

The hands and the figure collapsed into a heap of body parts.

"How did you allow me to come back?" said Luminous. "The hands and the figure were two new tops that grew out of the tree that had its top chopped off. The hands and the figure could never unite. But I could only come back as the result of that unity."

"Only God could manifest himself through the combined action of many beings," said Eliakim. "A mask can cover a rabbit's face. Yet no mask can cover his long ears."

CHAPTER 14

THE WORSHIP

emake my wife, please," Eliakim said to Luminous. "I need to have her back."

"She is inside of you."

"Where is she? I cannot feel her."

"She is where she always was. She is inside your lowest left rib."

"Was it she who caused my body to fracture a moment ago?"

"It was not her fault. She is like that."

"Pull her out immediately before she does something else."

"I can only do it by causing you excruciating pain."

"Do it when I am asleep."

"I cannot do it because only in pain can a person come into this world."

"Let me suffer then."

Luminous opened Eliakim's rib cage.

"The pain is unbearable. Cursed be the day you made me."

Luminous tore the ligaments.

"Cursed be you, my God."

"Do not curse me again, or grave misfortunes will befall you."

Luminous pulled on the rib.

"I cannot stand it anymore. Cursed be you, my God. Stop now."

"You did not let me finish," said Luminous. "See what happens now."

Out of Eliakim's rib Anne's head arose.

The rest of her body stayed in.

She had no eyes or ears.

"I shall tear you to pieces, mean God," she said. "You made me suffer so much."

"Anne, you are another name for my fury against God," said Eliakim.

He looked at Luminous.

"How can we make her whole, my God?" asked Eliakim.

Luminous was silent.

Eliakim shook his shoulder, "Why don't you answer me?"

Luminous was silent.

Eliakim said, "You are the true God of the Universe. I pray to you, please, tell me."

"Eliakim, where are you? Are you are saying something?" asked Luminous.

"I need your help to make my Anne whole."

"Must be wind," Luminous said.

"I pray to you, please, help me."

"Is it you, Eliakim?"

"It's me. Can't you see me standing before you?"

"No, it must be leaves rustling."

"He can only hear me, when I say, 'I pray,'" Eliakim mused.

"I pray to you, my Lord."

"Where are you? I cannot see you."

"If he can only hear me when I say 'I pray,' maybe he cannot see me because I am standing in his presence?"

Eliakim knelt before him.

"Here you are, my man. Where came you from? One moment the clearing was empty, and the next, here you are kneeling before me."

"I pray, you cannot hear me if I do not start each sentence with 'I pray.'"

"This is how you were punished for cursing me three times. How strange are my magical ways."

"I pray, it is a fact I have to now start each sentence with 'I pray,' but furthermore, you cannot see me unless I am on my knees."

"I made my people to be equal to me. Looks like that is no more."

"Yes, that is no more."

Eliakim stood up.

"Where did you go?"

"I pray, I stand before you."

"I only can see you when you're on your knees. I can only hear you when you say, 'I pray.' The problem is with you and Anne. As long as there is somebody who prays to me and treats me like that, I am the God who makes monsters and thinks of them as heavenly creatures."

"Could you at least help me to make Anne whole?"

"She can only use my eyes and my ears now. You can help her yourself."

"I pray, how can I? I have no magic skills."

"If I poke my ears and eyes out I will be deaf and blind, but if you cut my head off, I can remake my head anew. But you can attach my eyes and ears to Anne's head."

"I pray, I am just a humble man. I have no strength to attack my God."

"Your strength is equal to mine. You only lack courage."

"I pray, I don't."

"Then strike."

"I pray, I can't."

"I'll have to force you."

Luminous picked up Eliakim and pulled his right hand out its socket.

"I pray, please stop, or out of the ashes of my obedience rebellion will rise."

Luminous pulled his left hand out of its socket. "Let your fury flow."

"I pray, please torture me no further."

"I do not want to damage you permanently. You need to strike me down and take my eyes and ears out and add them to Anne's body. Then Anne can break free from you. Do not worry about me. I am immortal. I will make myself new eyes and ears."

Eliakim raised the sword and cut Luminous's head off.

The head fell apart. Eyes, ears, mouth, and forehead rolled on the ground.

He picked up the eyes and ears and inserted them into Anne's head.

She broke off from his body, looked around, and fell to her knees and began praying.

Luminous's hands picked up his head and put it up upon his shoulders.

His fingers touched the two empty sockets; new eyes opened and looked around.

His fingers touched the two holes on the side of his head, and new ears grew out.

He looked around and said, "A massive throne appeared. I am clothed in a golden robe adorned with precious stones. My body emits bright light."

Eliakim said, "I pray, you're still the same to my eyes. You did not change at all. Where you are pointing there is only a boulder."

Anne fell to her knees and said, "I pray, you've changed. You are brighter than the sun. I pray, there is a throne."

"Does my light blind you, Anne?"

"I pray, it does not, my eyes rejoice in its splendor."

"Eliakim, you need to cut off my head again; then you shall take my eyes and ears, and you too shall see my splendor."

"I pray, I'd rather keep my own eyes and ears."

"Then you cannot worship me."

"I pray, you are my friend. I shall not worship friends."

Anne said, "I pray to you, my God, am I your true follower?"

"You are."

"I pray, am I close to you?"

"You are."

"I pray, make six men who are farther away from you than me."

The Earth shook.

Eliakim asked, "What are these winged dark serpents doing here? I thought she asked for six men."

"Eliakim, your eyes are no good for this new world," chided Luminous. "These are six men."

Anne said, "I pray, thank you for raising your throne and lifting me up high, and placing these six people on the ground below me. Now I am higher than the rest of humanity."

The first serpent man said, "I need more knowledge."

The second serpent man said, "I need more cunning."

The third serpent man said, "I need more power."

The fourth serpent man said, "I need more light."

The fifth serpent man said, "I need more courage."

The sixth serpent man said, "I need more strength."

Then all the serpent men said in unison, "We need to get closer to you, my God."

They slithered up to the step where Anne was and pushed her down.

She fell, and Eliakim caught her.

"Our God," the serpent men said. "We are your disciples. We need to get closer to you, God."

"I pray to you, my God, they are dark serpents. Do not grant their wishes," Eliakim said.

"You are mistaken. They are my followers," said Luminous.

The serpent men coiled up before him.

He waved his right hand, "Your wishes are granted."

The Earth shook.

Eliakim asked, "What are these twelve dark serpents with dark wings doing here?"

"Eliakim, your eyes are no good for this new world," said Luminous.

"Thank you, our God," said the first six serpent men in unison. "The throne is much higher. There are twelve men there standing below us."

The twelve serpent men spoke in one voice, "We need so much from you, our God."

They quickly climbed up and killed the original six serpent men.

"I pray, why did you allow this, God?" Eliakim asked.

"It's hard to be a true God. You have to turn one part of your creation against another. Only that way will they let me sit on the throne in peace."

"I pray, I know how to help you," Eliakim said. "Only Anne can see the world as you see it. If she no longer can see or hear, the world will be restored into its previous glory."

He cut out Anne's eyes and ears.

"What's going on?" cried out Luminous. "Who lowered my majestic throne? Where are my royal clothes? Why did my light grow dim? Why do these monstrous serpents surround me?"

"I pray, they are all the result of what you have been and what you are, God. The worship of God creates the monsters."

"We are not monsters," the twelve serpents said in one voice. "We are the true followers of you, our God."

"I shall kill these monsters," said Luminous.

The twelve serpents ran away.

"All is well now, my God," said Eliakim.

"It's not."

"I do not have to say 'I pray,' and you still can hear me. The curse is lifted. I bet I can get up from my knees and you will be able to see me."

He got up and stepped to the left.

"I can see you."

"Just one more thing: please restore Anne's sight and hearing."

Luminous waved his right hand.

"Finally, I can see and hear. What you were up to without me?" Anne demanded.

"All is well with the world," said Eliakim.

"No. If you say even once 'I pray' or kneel before me, I will no longer be able to see and hear my humankind. I have to kill you and Anne, for one day you will."

"You don't. Think about it. If my prayer made you into a powerful God, then if no man walks the face of Earth you will be lowest of humankind. You need to train yourself to listen to humanity's voice when it does not alter prayers, and see people when they are not on their knees before you. And I'll have to train myself and Anne not to treat you like God but rather, like a friend."

CHAPTER 15

THE HANDS

 his boulder awaits the first prayer to become my throne," said Luminous. "I have to crush it into the smallest bits."

He picked it up and pressed hard on it.

"This boulder resists me."

"It is but a large rock," said Eliakim. "As all rocks go, it only has limited intelligence. You should never expect obedience from it."

"Any lake looks peaceful yet hides treacherous undercurrents."

"You need stronger hands to break it apart."

"That is an excellent point. My arms, I order you to drop my hands to the ground."

His hands fell, and he said, "I order you, dark monsters, you who hide in the forest, to give up your hands."

"Why do you need them?" twelve voices asked.

"I will add them to my arms and use them to obliterate my former throne."

"In the dark recesses of shame we dwell," said serpents in unison. "It pleases us that you desire to destroy your former throne. This destruction will cause you to hate yourself. It will cover your name in filth. We'll help you."

"I need filth," said Luminous. "I live in a long secession of names; the fertility of slime will hasten the arrival of my next name."

Twelve pairs of hands fluttered above his head, and one by one, each hand attached itself to his arms.

He raised his new hands and dropped them down to the ground.

The Earth cracked, and lava gushed.

"If I can break Earth's crust I can break anything. These dark hands have limitless power."

He pounced on the boulder and pulled on it.

Yet the boulder did not break.

"Wait, Luminous, the Earth is sturdiest of all indeed," said Eliakim. "But I'm afraid only human hands can destroy God's former throne. If you really want to wipe it from the face of the Earth you need to use our hands."

"Will you let me?"

"I will, if only to rejoice in human strength," Anne said.

"I will, if only to see my muscles at work," Eliakim said and tensed his biceps.

The dark hands fell from God's arms, and the human hands moved there and united into one pair. Luminous picked up the boulder and broke it into little pieces.

Suddenly, the dark hands flew up and attacked the human hands.

"You need to use our hands," the twelve voices said from the forest. "The human hands will always keep your strength in check."

"Our hands are stronger," Anne answered. "You saw what happened to his former throne."

"His former throne was destined to be destroyed by human hands. We shall prove to you our dark hands are stronger."

The dark hands pulled the human hands out of God's arms and threw them to the ground.

"The dark hands are stronger," Anne cried out. "Please, God, make new hands out our whole bodies to defeat them."

Anne and Eliakim vanished, and the human hands grew tenfold larger.

The human hands attacked the dark hands, pulling them off God's arms and throwing them down to the ground.

The dark hands grew.

"Twelve serpents, I did not allow you to add your bodies to the dark hands," Luminous said.

"We would only need permission if we were weaker then you are. Subdue us first, and then command," twelve voices said. "Just wait, see how large our hands will grow. We only added our arms to them so far."

The dark hands grew twentyfold larger.

"With human hands I am still stronger than you, dark hands," Luminous said. He twisted the dark hands together like a corkscrew and pinned them to the ground. "Give up," he said.

"We will not," said the dark hands. "After you allowed us to grow into your arms, your heart pumped your blood through us. You know well anyone who tastes your blood attains immortality. We shall never give up."

"I'll hold you for eternity."

"So shall I."

"Hey, God, wait a minute," Anne said from God's right hand. "I did not plan to be forever inside your hand. I only volunteered to help you with the destruction of your throne. Please, let go of me."

"My dear Anne, I sympathize with you, but I cannot let you go," Luminous said.

"You have your own hands. Here they lie in dust. You can use them to hold down your counterpart."

"My hands are weaker than his."

"You shall never regain your flesh, stupid people," the dark hands laughed. "Take it as your lesson. This is what you get for helping your God."

"Please, forgive me, my people," Luminous said.

"I am your friend, people," the dark hands said. "God does not want to help you, but I do. I shall leave the surface of this planet and find myself a new home underground. I am leaving. Please, Luminous, set your people free."

The dark hands vanished into thin air.

"Please, let us go, Luminous."

"I can't."

"What do you mean, you can't? The dark hands left you in peace."

"That is exactly what they did not leave me with. They always can come back and overpower me. They can't be trusted."

"So, on the strength of your suspicion you are to be our jailer until the end of time? I am not sure now who is my friend, you or these dark hands."

The dark hands stepped out of thin air and said, "There is only one friend you have, and it is I."

"Why do you offer us friendship?" asked Anne from inside God's hand.

"I am your friend because you are standing up to him. The reason he cannot let you go is simple: You know now that you humans can destroy God's staff. This knowledge is destined to grow in you and overpower your love toward him, and it will result in some cruel actions your descendants shall undertake one day against him."

"You are not a true rebel. You are in cahoots with God."

"I believe not in this God, but in information. Knowledge is my future domain. I shall impart on people all the wisdom, all that is to know in the world. I shall rule all future means of delivering all kinds of information."

"Lofty goal," Luminous said. "But people are smarter than that. They will not fall into your trap."

"Their thirst for knowledge is always their downfall."

"Luminous, you can only attain glory fighting them if you fight him with your own hands," Anne said. "I know you; deep inside, you want to conquer the dark hands without our help."

The human hands disconnected from Luminous's arms, and Eliakim and Anne rose up from them.

"This simple trick always works with God," the dark hands laughed. "One only needs to appeal to his vanity."

God's hands flew up from the ground and attached themselves to his arms.

"I am victorious," the dark hands screamed and pinned Luminous to ground.

"This is the first time I pinned you down, but it should not be the last time," the dark hands said. "I can kill you now. But what fun in that?"

"Kill me now and be done with it," said Luminous.

"Old trickster," said the dark hands. "There is time for everything. Killing you is the pinnacle of my existence. But you should only die from hand of the Ever Changing Devil. However, I have not yet earned the privilege to be called by this majestic name. So, as much I would like to do the deed, it is not the time for your death yet."

"If you set me free I will burn you to cinders with bolts of my lightning. It will be a painful death. I urge you to reconsider and kill me instead."

"You guys are like old friends arguing who gets to do the dishes," said Anne. "This is disgusting."

The dark hands released Luminous and flew up.

"Men, I give you a riddle before I die: Who's stronger than God but weaker than Devil?"

"Buffoon, you know as well as I do," Luminous said. "You are immortal so you shall be living again. Buffoon the second time, you only released me because Anne tricked me into using my own hands.

Enormous pride fills you, and you could not possibly accept the thought that people helped you to defeat me."

Flashes of lightning streamed out of God's right index finger and burned the dark hands to ashes.

Out of the ashes, the last words fell, "Here is riddle for you, God: what if your bolts of lightning can't harm me?"

"But they did," said Luminous.

"What if you only have to say 'buffoon' two times to kill me? What if you can always bring me back by saying 'buffoon' the third time?"

"Nonsense."

"Then I dare you to say 'buffoon' third time."

Luminous was silent.

A light wind picked up the ash and blew it away.

"His ash smells like vanilla beans," Eliakim said.

CHAPTER 16

SHE-LUMINOUS

nne's gaze followed the ashes.

"I have an answer to your riddle," Anne said.

"The Devil is tempting you. Stand fast," Luminous urged.

"We humans are stronger than God," Anne said.

"Fight these thoughts; do not let them settle in your head, or you will leave my service and submit to his mastery."

"But we humans are weaker than the Devil," finished Anne.

Then her face lit up.

"A strange memory of a dream is flooding my head with images of generations and generations of shining gods."

"This image is not from a human dream. This is one of mine," said Luminous. "It fills my head time after time. The Devil tempts you."

"Anne, your head is shining like the sun," Eliakim said.

"I am not Anne. I am a goddess. My name is Luminous," Anne said.

"Luminous is here already. It's me," said Luminous.

"Where is your shining light?"

"I spent centuries extinguishing it."

"Without light you can be mistaken for a man."

"This is my kind of mistake. It is my goal to be as close to people as I possibly can."

"You are no longer Luminous. From now on you are He-Luminous and I am She-Luminous. We are destined to start a new race of gods and populate the earth."

"I thought this was people's destiny," Eliakim said.

"People are God's slaves."

"She-Luminous, only your head is shining; the rest of you is still Anne."

He raised his sword and cut the goddess's head off.

The headless body of Anne fell, lifeless.

The head took flight and hung in midair.

"If you are a true goddess, you will grow a new body for yourself," Eliakim said.

Like tentacles, feet grew from her head, and then an entire body formed.

"Luminous, please rejuvenate Anne," Eliakim said.

Luminous raised his right hand; out of Anne's torn throat, a new head grew.

"Thank goodness it is not shining," Eliakim said.

"Stop wasting time with slaves, I'll make you a legion, come to me, my husband," said She-Luminous to Eliakim. "We need to find a proper place for our new castle, out of which we shall bring forth a new race of gods. I believe the top of a mountain would be best, so our slaves can always look up to their masters. But first, light needs to gush from you again."

"It will not. I shall not lose the fruits of my hard labor because a young goddess beckons me."

"Without light you are not much use to me," She-Luminous told Eliakim. "I can see you worship strength. Would you like to be my husband?"

"A man cannot wed a goddess," said Eliakim.

"Wed me and I shall make you the strongest god who ever walked the earth," She-Luminous declared.

"Let my husband be," Anne said.

"Anne, be silent," Eliakim said. "Please, Goddess, ignore her rude words."

"I know your weakness now: you are afraid I will hurt Anne. So come to me, and I shall not harm her."

"You are worse than the Devil," Anne said.

"I am. God should be stronger than the Devil in everything."

"Even in bad things?" Anne asked.

"She-Luminous, you should remain childless. Your children will unleash a reign of terror," He-Luminous said.

"I am sorry, Anne. I am doing it so she does not harm you," Eliakim said as he moved toward She-Luminous.

"You are not doing it for me," said Anne. "I can see fire in your eyes. You cannot wait to stick your hand under this new skirt."

"There is a bit of that, of course. After all, I am only a man. But not for much longer."

He turned to the goddess and said, "Accept me as your faithful husband."

His head began to shine.

"I hereby pronounce you my spouse," said the goddess.

"Eliakim is mine," said Anne.

"Keep sweet memories of Eliakim as long as you like. But the one who stands before us is not Eliakim at all. His name is He-Luminous," she said to Anne.

"Come to me, my dear husband," She-Luminous said.

"You are taking all of us back to the Stone Age of Terror. I cannot let you do it," Luminous said and stuck her down with a bolt of lightning.

She whispered as she fell, "What kind of god are you to prefer the human race to your own children? What an excellent caring father you would have made. Oh, such waste."

"Maybe, one day I will be a father."

"Here is my curse on your future child. May he take you for a cruel father, who allows him to be killed by a belligerent mob of your favorite people."

She expired.

"Luminous, please save my husband," Anne pleaded. "Cut off his shining head."

"I have a much better idea in mind. It is in man's nature to be tempted. I have a mind to allow the Devil to come to such a person to tempt him or her further. But only on one condition: the Devil should always discredit himself by telling the man that the man should not believe his words."

"Devil, have you heard me?"

"I am all ears."

Giant ears appeared.

The air thickened and formed words: "I LIVE AGAIN."

The words floated into the giant ears.

"The Word became flesh and lived among us," said the dark figure.

"You will clown your way to the guillotine," said Luminous.

"I am a blade, and I am a punishing hand that lets the blade fall. Oh, I just love people. There is a nation I love so much I will give them this marvelous gift of the guillotine design."

"Not out of love but out of envy you will give it to them," Luminous retorted.

"You always have the last word. Yet the last action is always mine."

The Devil went to Eliakim and said, "You think you are God? Cast yourself down from the highest mountain. It's the only way to prove you are the real God."

"I believe you. I shall go to look for highest mountain."

"Please, do not believe me. I do not want to disappear," said the Devil.

"All right, I don't."

"But how you do you plan to prove to yourself that you are the true God?" asked the Devil.

"I agree with you. I need to find a way to prove it."

"Do not agree with me. I do not want to disappear," screamed the Devil.

"But it makes sense. You are correct."

The light that shone from Eliakim's head grew dimmer, and then went out.

The dark figure screamed in agony and vanished.

"You have sent the Devil into a never ending cycle of permutations. He'll always tempt us. And each act of temptation shall hasten his destruction. You have turned his energy against him," Anne said. "What if you did the same to yourself and used your energy to improve people?"

"I can try," Luminous said.

"Here I am," the dark figure said. "I am glad you called me."

"I did not."

"My dear Luminous, your head is shining brighter than the sun," Anne said.

Luminous shook his head; drops of light flew to the ground.

"I have lost humility," he said, "I volunteered to take on a task that is impossible even to me."

"I shall tempt you now," said the Devil. "It will be an entirely new experience. In my travels I have discovered a very old cask of wine that matured for many centuries."

"You cannot tempt me. There is nothing I need in whole world."

"Imagine tiny fingers grabbing your arm. Imagine shining little eyes that follow you around. You need a son."

"His eyes cannot be shiny; the shine is like a poison to God."

"How easy it was to tempt you, God. Your She-Luminous was right; you long to start a family. But do not believe me. I do not want to disappear. I was only joking. It is a terrible idea for God to have a son. Your people will kill him. Oh, you believed me."

He vanished.

"This way will lead us all into destruction. Our heads will only stop glowing when the Devil is successful in tempting us. He'll disappear, but he'll leave behind ideas and motions. They'll grow inside us until we're all corrupted," Anne said.

"Even the Devil's creativity has limits. One day he won't be able to tempt us," Luminous said.

"But even the worst punishment awaits us all then: unable to stop our heads from glowing, we'll turn into two nations: a race of masters, the gods; and a race of people, the slaves."

"It is my decision to now leave the face of Earth and plunge into the deep end of ocean, where the water is so cold it won't allow my head to heat up and burst into light. There I shall lie in my watery grave," Luminous said.

He flew up, but the two people jumped and held on to him.

"Please, do not do that," pleaded Anne.

"There is nothing you can do to stop me."

Together they all rose and flew to the ocean.

"Deep below the surface my grave awaits me," said Luminous. "Do you wish to follow me down and lie next to me?"

"No, we'll swim above your grave and circle above it endlessly, like turkey buzzards marking where a dead body lies. We'll bear witness to your failed attempt to save the world from corruption. We'll be a living reproach."

"Have I not borne enough upon my shoulders?"

"You have not borne that much shame yet."

"I cannot stop you."

"You cannot."

Luminous submerged.

CHAPTER 17

RETURN OF THE FATHER

he Earth shook, and a volcano erupted near the swimming people.

A fountain of lava rose to the skies.

Large fiery eyes looked down on the people.

"My son, rise and shine," a roar came from the fountain.

"Fun for the whole family," said Eliakim. "It is nice to see you finally. But truth to be told, we had no idea Luminous had a father."

"That is just like him not to pay respect to one who brought him into this world," the voice roared from the fountain of lava.

"Hey, be careful," said Anne. "You might be his father. And you have this fiery face. So you are probably a god too. But speak no evil about our Lord."

"Luminous, your creations accord you more respect than you ever accorded me. You must be good at least at something."

"Watch your filthy mouth. Did my wife not tell you not to speak evil about our God? I will stick your words back into your fiery throat," said Eliakim.

"You talk a good game, but I wonder if you play it."

"Would you like to try?"

"I am Lord of Fire. How do you propose to fight me?"

"We'll think of something. We always have."

"You do not plan to enlist my son to rise against his father? It won't be the first time he does."

"With a father like you, I am not surprised."

"Luminous lies in his watery grave, if you care to know," said Anne.

"I know. Oh, poor dear, he's disappointed in this world? Not again?"

"Stop mocking me, father," said Luminous from below. "All is easy for you, as Lord of Destruction. All your mistakes have long turned to ashes."

"You are still here. And you cannot stay in the watery grave. First of all, you are an immortal being. You will be counting not hundreds of sheep to sleep but millions after millions after millions. Secondly, you should remember your grandfather: Lord of Gas needs our help."

"Oh, your beloved father, Lord of Gas, who used to dwell in this empty quarter of space, I remember the stories you told me of him," mused Luminous. "I always wondered, was your birth pure accident, a by-product of his desire to get rid of this planet, which stubbornly continued to coalesce into solid mass out of gas?"

"I do not question his motives in lighting the first spark. It is enough for me to be living. I am sure I was supposed to perish when the planet exploded. And it was fine by me. But yet, I did not die."

"Only because the task to destroy this planet has proved to be impossible. It is hard to make a bomb that can destroy a whole planet."

"That's why I made you, Lord of Creation, my beloved Luminous, out of a single living cell, so you could provide me with combustible materials to sustain my flames until I figure out how to accomplish my task."

"I provided you with corpses and dried lumber for long time; until I figured out I can break this circle of destruction by creating humans, my children."

"You rebelled against my desire to make another god to further the Lord of Gas's goal. Instead, you made inferior, weak beings. I knew what you were thinking: people are so weak; they cannot harm the planet. When they started the first fire and sat by it, I looked at them from the flames and rejoiced. Not only did the people like fire, they liked destruction just like their grandpa. Your people are smart, one day they will invent one little bomb that will turn this planet back to gas. Then I, Lord of Destruction, will perish happily. And since there will be no place to create anything, you, my wayward son, Lord of Creation, will perish too, but in suffering."

"I will not allow my beloved planet to be destroyed. I have been denying you combustible materials for a long time."

"Your denial is useless. I can always find a volcano that does not have a cover tightly attached to its shaft to make a delightful earthquake."

"I will go one step further then. I shall push all combustible materials down to the level where there is no oxygen to start a fire."

Lord of Destruction continued: "Do it, my son. All these materials will change into oil, gas, and coal. Your own people will bring them back to the surface one day. And they'll say, 'Drill, baby, drill.' And they'll say, 'Burn, baby, burn.'"

"Must I go further and destroy people?"

"You can destroy them. You did it in the past so many times. Yet, you love them too much. That's why you inevitably bring them back."

"They are my weakness. But I love my nature even more. I am God of Creation. I will not let them destroy this planet. I swear, each time I create people, I will also create the means of their destruction."

"It will be a hard task for you. Destruction does not come easy to you."

"I'll manage."

"Luminous, do not do it," said Anne.

"It is done," he said from below.

A flood rose and covered planet.

BARLEYCORN

Anne and Eliakim drowned.
A few volcanoes erupted at the bottom of the sea.
Soon the eruptions stopped.

CHAPTER 18

THE BEAST IN THE FOREST

nne sat up and looked around.

Eliakim lay beside her.

"So God brought us back," she said. "Eliakim, get up. God will attempt to destroy us now. We need to be ready."

"I am always ready to die. I like death. It brings peace, unlike you," said Eliakim.

From far away came the sound of a rhythmic marching of legs approaching.

"He is upon us," said Anne.

A large beast with a long tail stepped out of the forest and roared.

"I know, I know," said Anne. "You are here to eat us. What's new?"

The beast roared and advanced.

"Remember, we people are full of bones and hard to chew," said Anne.

"I do not like your tone, Anne," Eliakim said. "I hope you do not plan to resist him."

"And why not?"

"Luminous said after we die he will resurrect us again."

"Only to extinguish us again."

"Why are you concerned about your death if you are to be back the very next moment?"

"Look at our situation from a different angle, and you will see we are to be destroyed every day until the end of time."

"Think positive."

"Positive thinking is the tool of weaklings by means of which they find a way to do nothing."

The beast attacked them, and they fought back.

"He's stronger than us," said Anne. "Prepare to die."

The beast tore up their bodies.

"How strange," groaned Anne. "Maimed and disfigured, but we are still here."

"It hurts like hell. I much prefer a death and a resurrection."

"Who was the one who just said he hated to be resurrected? It must have been somebody else."

"You got me. I hate it all."

The beast sat next to the people and watched them intently.

"You almost can see glimpses of intelligence in his eyes," said Anne.

"Baloney. God is always merciful to himself. He made himself dumb so he can hurt us and feel no remorse. I wish he made us dumb too. I'd rather take pain as an animal that does not know why it's been hurt."

"No, you do not mean that. There is only one thing in this whole world that makes being here worthwhile, and this is an intellect. If we are dumb, the centuries of our struggle were for nothing."

"Look, our bodies are healing up."

"And growing. We are as tall as trees now."

"Is the beast growing our bodies? Why? Is he looking for worthy opponents?"

"What if he has nothing to do with our growth? What if this is how human bodies react when God attempts to destroy them?"

"He has tormented us before, and our bodies did not grow larger."

"This is the first time he has attempted to resurrect us only to destroy us. He used to have better reasons for our resurrection."

"Look, our bodies are healed," said Eliakim. "We are larger than he. This time we shall prevail."

The beast attacked them.

The people and the beast fought for hours.

Finally, Eliakim leveled him on the ground and tore into his chest.

"I will eat your heart out!" he screamed.

"Stop! Do not kill him!" pleaded Anne.

"Because he spared us? It was his miscalculation. Once we kill him the curse of our endless death and rebirth is broken."

"We should not kill him until we understand why he kept us alive when he had chance to kill us."

"This is not good enough. Give me another reason not to kill him, and better do it quick, for my lips long to taste his blood."

"Last time we fought God, we grew stronger. What if he'd rather see himself dead than to see us grow even stronger? How is that for a reason to spare his life?"

"That is a very good reason," said Eliakim and released the beast's chest. "I'd like to grow sky high."

"What shall we do with this half-alive heap of bones?"

"We need to nurse him back to sound health. What else?"

They tended to the beast until it was healthy again.

"Look, his gaze is full of hatred again. He's getting stronger. Soon he'll attack us," said Eliakim. "I cannot wait to get as tall as a mountain."

The beast stood up and roared.

Suddenly he turned and ran away.

The people gave him chase.

"A god who runs away from people," said Anne. "This is a wonder of wonders."

The beast plunged into the lake.

"He is hiding at the bottom," said Eliakim. "Let me dive. I will lure him to shore."

Eliakim dived. When he resurfaced, he reported, "He is drowning himself by letting air escape from his mouth."

"He does not want us to get stronger," said Anne. "I was correct. The strength of future humankind resides in God's continuous struggle against his people. We have to save our God."

Anne dived in, and with Eliakim she dragged the beast to the shore.

They wove a strong rope out of the thickest vines and tied the beast to a boulder.

"We shall fight him now," said Anne.

"What if we are still stronger?"

"Then we'll let him win and mutilate us."

They fought the beast for a long time.

At last, the beast prevailed and tore them up.

Soon Anne got up and said, "I am as tall as the tallest mountain. Yet I would like to grow even taller and reach the skies."

Eliakim got up and roared back, "We are making a terrible mistake. We people think we are only actors on this planet's stage. We reduced God to one whose sole purpose is to build our strength. But God's an actor too. Why do we think we always know the best way forward? We need to set God free."

"You are mad. Just when we are one step from conquering the world, you dare to refuse the largest prize. I will not let you set God free."

"God was a supreme ruler for millenniums now, and the planet survived. In all truth, I am much more afraid of people's rule that I am afraid of God's."

Eliakim tore up the rope holding the beast.

The beast quickly ran up the cliff and plunged headlong into a low valley.

A loud thud echoed.

"Something is happening to us," said Anne. "We are falling apart."

"No, we are not falling apart, but we are breaking up into pairs of people. They all are copies of us. So this is how humankind begins."

"Great. We beat God and we are ready to populate our planet," said Anne.

Out of the forests and caves, lions and saber-toothed tigers came and attacked the stream of couples.

One couple hid in a shallow cave.

"We prevailed against God, but I am not sure we will win over an animal kingdom," said Anne. "If only you would have waited and let us grow to the sky."

"I do not think it would have made any difference whatsoever," said Eliakim. "We would make the same choice later, and there would have been only more meat for the tigers and lions."

"Watch out!" cried Anne. "These two tigers are crawling up to our cave. See this boulder? Let's roll it in to block the entrance."

"Look close. There is a deep hole in front of our cave. We might not be able to roll it out afterwards."

"At least we will survive an attack of tigers."

"Only to die of hunger, thirst, or lack of air. But we do have another way of surviving. Let's perish. Once animals kill all the people, we all will be back."

"Do not even think of that it. I will not resurrect God. This was the very first time we were able successfully to get rid of him and live. If we bring him back, it proves beyond doubt to him and to us God is indispensable for the development of humankind."

"God knew our sentiments all along. What if he planned all what is happening right now around us? What if his goal was always to arrive to a peaceful end of people and of himself? What are people if not a plague? What is God if not a shepherd of this plague?"

"This is a very dark view of people and of God. I am not sure God espouses it."

"Look at the shared history of people and God. Is it not dark?"

"I'll give you that."

"So, let's do something God does not expect us to. See this ram grazing? Let's restore God out of this ram. All we have to do is to attack him."

"The God who comes out of a ram is a fine God," said Anne.

The couple ignored the saber-toothed tigers and ran up to the ram and attacked him.

The ram lowered his horns and fought back.

A saber-toothed tiger arrived at the scene and leapt onto Eliakim's back.

The ram ran his horns through the tiger, picked him up, and threw him into a ravine.

Then the ram raised his head to the sky and bleated.

The beast then sat up right where ram had stood.

He roared and gave people chase.

CHAPTER 19

THE FIRE

he beast needs to follow us," Anne said. "This is his weakness. We can use it to subdue him. All we need is a canyon that has one entrance. We shall lure him there and trap him inside."

"But a trap needs a bait," Eliakim said.

"Since he likes the taste of our blood we will be the bait."

"We may trap ourselves instead."

"We are already at his mercy. You traveled far when I stayed in the cave tending the fire right after God made us. Do you remember such a canyon?"

"Long ago I visited a gorge deep inside a canyon. You can only enter it through a cave."

"That's what we need. Lead us there."

The next morning they found the canyon.

"We are in the very middle of it. It's perfect," Anne said. "Let us hide and wait for the beast to follow us here."

"He does not have to; he can wait for us in a cave."

"His purpose is to torment us. He needs our blood. He will come here."

Soon the beast walked into the canyon.

He looked around and went into a deep gully close to the outer wall and lay there.

"Now let's bring plenty of dry wood into this canyon and make the fire."

"You do not plan to kill him with this fire, I hope. He has tortured us, but he had shown no desire to kill us."

"I am cruel sometimes, but I am no killer. I have an idea I would like to try out."

They brought dry wood into the canyon through the cave.

The beast lay quietly and watched their progress.

Anne made a big fire in the middle of the canyon, right beside the entrance into the cave.

"You blocked our only exit. This fire will kill us now."

"We have to take this risk. If I am correct in my assumption, a reward awaits us. But if I'm incorrect, we perish. Will you be able to accept your death in this case?"

"I am not against death. I find the whole idea of living to be a trifle tiresome but not tiresome enough to end it by my own hand."

"I am a bit more positive then you. I'd rather live."

"You believe too much in the ideas that fill your head. You are too canny for your own sake."

"When the world does you good, you are happy; when it does not, you are despondent. I, on other hand, work hard to bend the world to my will."

"And the world, being stronger, always bends you."

"This is true, I agree, but I like the process of measuring my strength to the strength of the world."

They lit the fire.

Flames rushed toward them.

"Step back. Be on lookout for cinders."

"We are forgetting about the beast."

"He is no threat to us now. Look at him: he is afraid of the fire."

The fire spread.

They stepped back.

Soon the whole canyon was aflame.

"We reached the walls. The fire is licking my feet."

"And where is the beast?"

"I heard his roar a while back. I do not see it. It is gone."

"The beast would not be able to run away. The only exit is blocked by fire. He's no more."

"You mean he burned?"

"He is a fire now."

"You speak in riddles."

"I've noticed there is always only one thing which threatens us at any given moment, and not two. As the fire grew, its influence over us developed, until it was paramount. The beast needed to retain his own influence over us, so he had no choice but to merge with the fire."

"So God is one who is always ready to hurt people?"

"More likely, he is the most important entity that affects people in any given moment."

"So first he is in the stormy cloud; then in the bolt of lightning that strikes the tree. Then he is in the tree that topples over and cracks our heads open? If so then he is God of Misfortune."

"Or fortune, if felling the tree kills the tiger at the very moment he leaps onto your back."

"So he is just a blunt force that knows not what it destroys?"

"If he really wanted to kill us, the flames would have not died but only grown stronger. What makes you think he's interested in our destruction? He is the dominant force of our lives. So we have to find a way to control him. Look, the fire is dying. If I am correct in my assumption the beast will be back soon."

Out of a small gully behind them, the beast raised his head and roared.

"Anne, we understand his nature now. The beast wants us to think we are able to resist him. Let's leave this canyon."

"So he can go on spilling our blood and chasing us forever? No. If we control fire, we control God himself. We need to go outside and collect more dry wood to bring it back here and start the fire anew. This way we are at least one step ahead of him."

They went out and collected dry wood.

"Look out! The beast has followed us out," Eliakim said. "He will not go back into that canyon again, after what happened there."

"Watch this."

Anne walked toward the beast.

The beast roared but stepped aside and allowed her into the cave, and then he followed her.

Eliakim ran after the beast.

Anne waited for him inside the canyon.

The beast lay in the small gulley close to the canyon wall and watched them.

"You see," Anne said, "he is perfectly satisfied with this arrangement. He wants us to control him."

"What if we wait until the fire wanes and then add just enough wood to keep it barely going? Then his fire can warm us when the nights grow cold. We even can cook us food too."

"Great idea. This canyon is our home now, and this fire is sacred. We will not let this fire to go out. God will be our helper forever."

"Do you think we finally caught our God?"

"I hope."

They started the fire, and then stepped back.

The beast vanished into thin air.

Flames rose high.

CHAPTER 20

LAST STAND

liakim stepped back away from the fire.

"Come back," Anne said.

"The fire was scorching my face."

"Take courage and wait."

He stepped back and stood beside her.

"This fire is our God. Respect his flames. Would you not fall down dead should our God declare such fate for you? Can any person escape his verdict? Look at your body. Flames lick your limbs, hot ashes singe your skin. But your skin bears no scars."

"Hot ashes leave behind an excruciating pain. My whole body is like an open wound. It pulses with spasms and shivers. I know now how corpses feel when worms bore through their still cooling insides; and their internal organs, which were tightly intertwined since birth, lose connecting tissues and break free from one another."

"When a volcano erupts and sends out a mass of boiling lava, only hard boulders can stand in its way. Their goal is to serve as riverbanks to guide the lava down. Is lava not the hottest liquid on the face of Earth? Do you think it is easy for these boulders to withstand lava's onslaught? Do they not see the remains of other rocks that surrendered to their fate in floating lava?"

"We are no more than self-tormenting fools."

"That may be so. What is the purpose of our lofty thoughts if not to lead us astray? It is the highest order of humanity to be able to choose when you are smart and when you are dumb. Do not yield any ground. We are defining the border between our God and us now. Each spot which is not his shall be ours. By defining our God we define ourselves."

"We hold one tiny spot of the ground. The flame can spread around us and engulf the whole Earth. Then God will define us but we'll define him no more."

"Good point. We need to continually circle around God, defining borders time after time."

"There is a danger of making ever wider circles, of course."

"The pain shall be our guide. If the pain is bearable we shall get closer to flames."

Anne and Eliakim set off to the right.

Soon they saw their own steps on the burning ground.

"We made a full circle," Anne said. "Let us use our swords as shovels and make a trench. This dugout will be our guide."

They dug a trench.

Over time the fire grew higher and changed into a burning column.

The hole beneath the column expanded down, and soon the column of flame burned deep inside the Earth.

"We are standing before a bottomless pit," said Anne. "As you can see, God claimed this pit as his own."

"I am claiming everything outside this pit for people," said Eliakim.

The column reached the skies.

"We must continue to walk around him. What is the boundary between God and people if not the path for people to revolve around their God?"

They walked and walked around the flaming column.

Anne looked up at the sun and said, "We are on his southern side."

"The flames are most ferocious here. Their tongues are darker and have eyes like peacock feathers," said Eliakim.

They walked and walked around the flaming column.

"Now we are on his eastern side."

"The flames are thinner and more refined here. They do not burn but rather sting like mosquito bites. Their sparks shoot out like narrowed eyes."

They walked and walked around the flaming column.

"And now we are coming to the northern side."

"It is much cooler here. But watch out for these blue flames. White ashes crown them like watchful eyes inviting you into dark inferno of the pupils."

They walked and walked around the flaming column.

"And now we are back to the western side."

"Here yellow flames rule with the merciless hand of the desert."

Anne fell down.

"I am exhausted," said she.

"Anne, get up. The flames are burning you. We need to keep going."

"Did you carry me around to the southern side?"

"I did not. I can barely stand."

"But we are now at his southern side. Look at the peacock feathers. He must have turned himself."

"The fire cannot turn itself even if it contains God."

"Look how high the sparks are flying now. We are at his eastern side. We are continuing the journey around him without taking the smallest step. Just think about it. What choice did he have after we divined he had four sides but then stopped our progress? He had to spin himself. Is your left leg as important to you as your right leg? So his four sides are as important to him. They are like his faces; they express four different sides of him. Who would have noticed them but us? Who would react to them but us?"

"Why does he need to have four faces to express himself?"

"He does not need, but we people need to find his different faces in order to comprehend him."

"Then we should have ignored these four sides of him. Maybe we are clinging to something he already tried to discard? Who needs this column of flames but us? Did we not define him as the Giver of Light who punishes those who transgress his laws? Have we demarcated his four faces, or have we defined four ways he can torture us?"

"The flames are growing hotter. Why did you suggest we define our own torture? Now he'll torture us to death."

"The fire has burned through my skin. My blood is flowing."

"Mine too. It might be our only salvation."

"A quick death?"

"My silly husband, when your God is a fire, a person can only be a liquid."

Their blood ran into the abyss and fell into the flaming column.

A loud hiss ensued, and the fire died out.

A large shining skeleton was suspended in the middle of the abyss. Suddenly the Earth shook.

Anne fell down to her knees and said, "Earth itself is rotating around his skeleton now."

"The fire burned out our God. He can rotate around people no more. So Earth is rotating people around him. Stop, Earth, our God is dead. If you wish to rotate around someone, then rotate around people."

A metallic voice escaped from the shining skull, "Come to me, my children, and I shall share my peace with you."

"We can share nothing with a heap of bones suspended in the air," Anne said.

"Do you not feel the Earth rotating around me? It recognizes me. It carries you around me whether you like it or not. Accept the inevitable."

"Why do we need to accept it?"

"I am Giver of All That There Is. Once you accept me, I shall give you a gift."

"What if we do not accept it?"

"Then I shall give you another gift, for I am Giver of All That There Is."

"So you'll give us your gift regardless?"

"But it will be a different gift."

"How different?"

"As different as a death differs from a life."

"Another words, not much," said Eliakim.

"You cannot take our lives," said Anne.

"Why not?"

"Because it was not you who gave us that gift but our God."

"Since he is no more, his gifts have lost their value."

"So you admit you are not our God."

"I am not the same God, if it's what you are asking. Try to be the same one after your flesh burns out."

"You are just an animated skeleton."

"You can call me Alpha or you can call me Omega, it makes no difference to me."

A bolt of lightning struck the ground and another skeleton rose up.

"This is my gift to you," the first skeleton said.

The second skeleton looked around.

"Who am I?"

"You are my son," said the first skeleton.

"I can see that. But there is a hole in my chest."

"Indeed there is," Eliakim said. "And not just one. You got a lot of holes. The winter wind is blowing past your ribs and they clink like weathered tree boughs."

"Am I good or evil?" asked the second skeleton. "Did I come to this world to destroy it or to save it?"

"It all depends on this man and this woman."

"Eliakim, I can sense he'll be a good gift if we accept him. But he'll most certainly be a terrible one if we do not," Anne said.

"We should not accept him," Eliakim said.

"Why? Is there a reason?" asked Anne.

"I do not know. Just in case. I never believed in free stuff. He needs to give us some labors to do and present his gift after we successfully accomplish them. One always has to earn good things."

"Would you like to clean a huge building filled with the horse manure?" asked the first skeleton.

"I would not go that far," said Eliakim. "After all, we are but mere people."

"Eliakim, our rejection will nurture an enemy of humanity," said Anne. "Let's keep an open mind."

Anne paused and then said, "We accept your gift."

"Hey," said Eliakim. "Why do you always make all decisions?"

"Because I am a woman, that's why."

"Wise choice," the first skeleton said.

A bolt of lightning struck the chest of the second skeleton.

"It feels great to be so virtuous and kind," the second skeleton said. "Thank you, Anne."

"Anne, before your eyes is your future. The time of flesh is past," first skeleton said. "The fire shall cleanse you now of your flesh, and you'll enter the world in the full naked glory as the first female skeleton."

"There is a problem here. Even after your fire strips my flesh from my bones, my bones will still be mine."

"I will infuse them with my light."

"They will be mine though."

"What is the difference if you look like me and my son?"

"People shall always be guests at God's party."

"My father, why can't they keep their flesh? I agree it looks foul, but so what?" asked the second skeleton.

"If people keep their flesh, we gods will always be inferior to them."

"We can be humble gods."

"You can but I can't."

"So, you people refuse the cleansing by my fire? No matter, the fire shall cleanse you anyway. I shall rain bolts of lightning upon both of you until not a shred of a flesh is left on your bones."

Bolts of lightning flew out of his index finger and struck them.

Blood rained down, and flesh peeled off the human bodies.

"Finally, there is progress. I can see some of your bones protruding. Strike harder, my bolts, the victory is upon us."

Anne stood still.

Soon only one thread of flesh remained.

It was between her legs.

"Eliakim, follow my example and lower your hands. Let his bolts tear your body like they have torn mine."

"You want me to surrender?" Eliakim asked.

"No. Like he said, the victory is coming. But it will be our victory."

Eliakim lowered his hands.

Bolts of lightning tore into his flesh until only one fleshy fragment remained, the fleshy triangle between his legs.

At last, the bolts of lightning ceased.

"Your bodies are regenerating," the first skeleton said. "How can that be?"

"That's right," Anne said. "See how our flesh grows out of the crotch and clothes our bodies again. You have no rule over a domain you are not a part of. The way of the Flesh shall always conquer the way of the Bones."

Anne whispered to Eliakim, "I have a very important request. Our very existence depends on it. Will you do it?"

"What is it?"

"Run to the second skeleton and hug it tightly."

"Look how hot his bones are. He'll burn me to cinders."

"The way of the Flesh is stronger than way of the Hot Flames."

"Why don't you do it?"

"I will hug his father."

Anne ran to the abyss and jumped.

Her hands encircled the giant skeleton.

Eliakim ran to the second skeleton and embraced him.

The bits of human flesh steamed onto the shiny bones and filled them up.

The skeletons bit by bit changed into two human-like figures.

Soon nothing remained of Anne and Eliakim.

"My father, you told me I was destined to bridge the gulf between God and people. But this gulf grew and now is insurmountable. There are no people left here."

"We both bridged this gulf. From our godly nature we got our skeletons, and from people we got our flesh."

"We did not bridge this gulf; we have destroyed both banks. Where is God?"

"We both are gods."

"Then where are people?"

"We both are people."

"We can no more be people and gods at the same time than the bank and the river can be both at the same time. But I know how to fix this problem. I shall eject out of myself any part that came from you, my father."

"Then you'll be my son no longer."

"I know."

Golden bones one after another left the second skeleton's body.

A large human figure looked at the rising pile of golden bones and said, "My son, my poor fool. I have deceived you. There can be no bridge between God and people."

The last bone fell down to the ground, and Eliakim looked around.

"I had the strangest dream. I was like God and at the same time I was quite unlike him."

"I know the feeling," said the large figure.

"What are these giant bones are doing here?"

"They point to the spot where my son died."

"How did he die?"

"Humanity is like a disease. One drop of human blood is like billions of tiny seeds destined to spread and conquer the whole body."

"So I am a man?" asked Mustard Seed.

"It is up to you who you are," said Barleycorn.

"If people are infectious to God, why don't you create an intermediary between you and us who could then deal with people?"

God chuckled, "No intermediary again. I think not."

CHAPTER 21

THE SECOND COMING

 do not want to die, my father," said a voice from the bones.

"I am sorry, my son, for deceiving you about being a bridge between God and his people, and causing you to die," said God the Father. "But a man needed to return into this world. How else I could get you to sacrifice yourself?"

"I am scared."

"Do not be. You should be proud. You have successfully completed your mission. Because of you, people will always populate this planet. You can take your leave now. Just exhale and let your spirit take a leave of your bones."

"Hey, wait a minute. I did not ask the Son of God to die for my sake," Eliakim protested.

"Who needed to get your permission?" asked God the Father.

"Before helping someone, one always needs to ask the beneficiary if his help is needed."

"I am asking you now, Eliakim. Would you rather be dead than live an eternal life?" asked God the Father.

"I would have."

"That is the wrong answer. Anne would have answered it correctly. She can always see the big picture."

"This is very curious. It seems my sacrifice bothers you, Eliakim," said the voice from the bones. "You know, my father, maybe people are not so bad after all."

"They are not."

"This means there is still a place in this world for me."

"No, there is no longer a place here for you."

"How can I cease to exist if there is one stalk left in the field waiting for a scythe to harvest it?"

"Did I just hear somebody asking me to harvest him?" asked the voice.

"There are no stalks for you here," said God the Father.

"You did not tell him your secret, did you, my father?" The voice was laughing. "If the Son of God saves a man, this man can only come to God the Father though the Son of God."

"You've got to be kidding me," said Eliakim. "Am I a worthless rock which can be tossed back and forth between two parties?"

"You are for him," said the Son of God, "but not for me. Come to me and I will never betray your affection."

"Eliakim, there is another secret, but my son does not want to share it with you," said God the Father. "You do not need to come to God. You do not need even to believe in God. God is the one who comes to every single living person."

"My father, you are trying to shake a founding principle of the relationship between God and people. People are not ready for it. If

"I am here! Harvest me!" Mustard Seed cried out.

"Hush. The wind harvested you last summer and has sown you already," said Barleycorn.

"He dealt with my body, not with my eternal soul. My soul is ready to be harvested."

Barleycorn fell down on the top of Mustard Seed and put his hand over Mustard Seed's mouth.

"We cannot get involved," whispered Barleycorn. "Do not make me feel sorry for telling you this story."

"I did not know they could hear us," came the muffled response from Mustard Seed. "I am sorry."

they are sure they need not come to God, they'll succumb to a life of debauchery."

"Some of them will, and some of them won't. I believe in the inherent goodness of my people."

"This is where you are wrong," said Eliakim. "Only my own gaze can penetrate the sorrowful depths of my soul. It is full of terrifying monsters. How much they long to see the light of a day!"

"That's why people like you need to come to me, Eliakim," said the voice from the bones. "I will slay all the monsters in your soul. I will bring you peace."

"Do not succumb to his advances," urged God the Father. "He will slay no monsters. The monsters inside your soul cannot be slain. Some people are just born tormented. All the deities in the entire world cannot help them. I will tell you even this: these monsters in people's souls will outlive even the gods. The day will come when there will be no God left on this planet, but as long as single man walks the Earth, these monsters will endure inside his soul."

"How I can live with them eating my soul away?"

"Your soul renews itself every day. I made it this way. You just have to wait until the sun comes up."

"These hours just before sunrise are sheer murder for me."

"I know."

"Do not listen to my father. I am the next generation of gods. He comes from a much earlier time. His methods are archaic. I am God of the New Age. I know how to concoct some truly amazing remedies. I will fix you right up."

"I am sorry, God the Father, or whatever your name is. But I have to try his remedies," Eliakim said to God the Father. Turning to the bones, he asked, "Are you sure you are able to slay all my monsters?"

"He is not," said God the Father.

"Aw, yes I am," insisted the voice. "I will butcher all your monsters with one thrust."

"You got me now. I am yours. I accept you as my Savior," Eliakim pledged.

"I live again!" crowed the voice from the bones.

"How deeply unfortunate," sighed God the Father.

Trumpets sounded.

The bones came to life and connected together.

"What's happening? Has my devotion just resurrected the Son of God?" asked Eliakim.

"The slain Son of God cannot be killed at once. There is always one more opportunity for him to come back. It is called the second coming."

"Why did he not come before?"

"Only people can initiate the second coming."

The skeleton rose up.

"Remember, you have only one day to live," said God the Father. "Spend your time wisely."

"This will be one very long day," said the Son of God. "At least for me."

"Why does flesh not grow out of your bones and cover your body, my Lord?" asked Eliakim.

"Flesh is overrated. I have rejected it."

Trumpets blew again.

"Now for a day I am the king of this planet," declared the Son of God.

"Just get your show on the road," said God the Father.

"I came to judge every living and dead person."

Eliakim knelt before the Son of God.

"Please, do not judge me too harshly, my Lord," said Eliakim.

"You have accepted me already as your redeemer. There is no judgment for you on that score."

"Thank you, my Lord."

"Now, my father is a totally different story."

He laughed hard, "When my bones cracked, how much I longed for this moment."

He took a pause.

"I just can't help myself. I need to savor this moment."

He took another pause and then said very loudly, "God the Father, I judge you guilty of parental neglect."

"You are truly powerful, my Lord," said Eliakim.

Rocks around them jumped up and down.

"I grand you rocks the ability to speak," said the Son of God.

"This transgression merits very heavy punishment! What kind of a punishment do you desire to inflict on him?" screamed the rocks.

"Hereby, God the Father, your punishment is damnation."

"For how long?" screamed the rocks.

"Forever and ever," said the Son of God.

"God cannot be damned for eternity!" screamed the rocks. "This is unheard of!"

"You are correct. So, effective immediately I relieve my father from the position of god."

"The king is dead!" screamed rocks.

The rocks flew into the air and fell hard upon God the Father.

A large rocky hill formed where God the Father had stood a moment earlier.

"Who is the next king?" screamed the rocks.

"I am," said the Son of God.

"Long live the king!" screamed the rocks.

"I have completed my task," said the Son of God. "I feel so tired."

"You are tired because you live one day!" screamed rocks. "Who is to be the king of this world after you die?"

"My faithful follower, Eliakim," said the Son of God.

"I am sorry, I can't," said Eliakim. "You forgot about the monsters inside my soul. I will let them loose. They will sow destruction."

"I order you ugly monsters to leave immediately the soul of this faithful subject of mine," said the Son of God.

A multitude of monsters streamed out of Eliakim.

"Ugly monsters, run to the ocean and plunge in," said the Son of God.

Monsters ran one after another and plunged in.

Soon they ran back from the ocean's shore.

"What is this? A mutiny? I have ordered you to drown."

"We filled the depths of all the oceans. There is no more water to drown us," declared the monsters.

A loud chuckle came from below the rocky hill. "My delusional son, each soul of a man holds an uncountable number of monsters. You should have not ordered them to take a leave of his body."

"Save us, our Lord!" screamed the rocks. "These monsters will turn us to dust with their hooves after you die."

"Do not despair. I will create for you, my son, a new god. He will preside over this planet."

The skeleton reached into his chest and tore out a rib.

He blew on his rib and said, "I present you with my successor."

A beautiful naked woman stood before them.

She opened her mouth really wide and screamed, "Come here, fishy-fishy!"

All the monsters streamed into her mouth.

She belched.

"Stop this infernal racket."

"Sorry, my father, but I have to digest them."

"What's with these female body parts? I have ordered a male," said the Son of God.

"Blame the delivery service," said the woman and burped again.

"Not good enough. Try another explanation."

"A woman is a beginning of it all."

"Not good enough either. Try another explanation."

"Out of a bone only a woman can be made. And as I can clearly see, you got nothing but bones."

"Look at you. How unfortunate. You are too full of life."

"What's wrong with life?"

"I am wrong with it. I reject the flesh."

"I am your daughter, and I embrace the flesh."

"You are disgusting. Foam seeps from your vagina, your breasts drip milk."

"I am your savior."

"Nothing can save the Son of God. I am dying."

"Are you absolutely sure? Look, there is a strikingly beautiful new bone in your skeleton. It just formed between your legs and sticks rather high up. Am I to take this as a sign of an impending death?"

"This new silly bone does not matter. All my godly bones will be dead after the sun comes down."

"Why do you need godly bones? I am here. I am a goddess. Just give me a few minutes, and I will remake all of your bones. All you have to do is allow your desire for me to flourish. Do not suppress it. After I am done, you will live by my side as a man."

"You are revolting. I gave birth to the whore of Babylon."

"Look at yourself. You are endowed now with the largest reproductive member a male body can support without toppling over. Your lips reject me, but your whole body accepts me."

"Godly bones are falling out from my body and turning to dust. I am losing my godly nature."

"You were going to lose it anyway after the sun goes down, remember? I am your most faithful surgeon. Soon you will have all new bones. Then we will celebrate our wedding."

"I reject you, my daughter," said the Son of God.

The woman wailed and prostrated herself.

All the new bones vanished from the Son of God's skeleton.

Only a dozen bones were standing upright, supporting the skull.

They were shaking back and forth, rebalancing themselves.

"Son of God, you are dying!" screamed the rocks. "Give birth to another king!"

"I think not," said the Son of God. "It seems my makeup predisposes me toward making girls."

The skeleton walked to the rocky hill and said, "I owe you an apology, my father. I realize now all gods are cursed and have to reject their offspring. I tried as hard as I could not to reject her. Yet I did. I declare before all the witnesses that I recant the judgment I made toward you. I forgive you."

The last ray of sun shone above the horizon.

The Son of God expired.

His lifeless bones fell to the ground.

"The Son of God is dead!" screamed the rocks.

Rocks streamed off God the Father.

"The forgiven god is the king again!" screamed the rocks. "Long live God the Father."

God the Father changed to Luminous.

"It was the hardest reenactment of the future I ever performed. Poor Son of God," said Luminous.

"Is this what we have been doing all these centuries, reenacting one future scene after another?" asked Eliakim.

"Never mind," said Luminous.

CHAPTER 22

CROWN AND
CHAINS

uminous gathered all the bones of the Son of God.

"There is a lesson I have learned today," said Luminous. "It is in me to reject my son. There is a ticking bomb inside of my heart. As a reminder, I have decided to carry these bones with me always." He picked up the bones. "Please, accept me, bones, as your proud carrier."

The bones changed into golden chains.

"You accepted my offer, bones," said Luminous.

He heaved them over his shoulders and took a step.

"They are too heavy for me," said Luminous.

"Take them off," said Eliakim.

"I will not. I have to remember my son's sorrows."

"I will help you to carry them," said Eliakim. "After all, he is dead because of me."

Eliakim wrapped himself with the chains.

They stepped forward.

"We cannot carry them," said Eliakim. "These chains are too heavy."

"We are stuck."

"Why don't we ask this prostrated woman to help us?" asked Eliakim.

"Let her be. She's cursed. Slowly she will disintegrate. Even I can't do anything for her."

"I, and only I, can help her," said Eliakim.

He called gently, "My dear, do not be afraid. Please, come to me."

"Remember, I am cursed," woman whispered.

"Please, come to me and touch my hand."

"The curse will spread to you."

"Yes, and I will slay it. You will be cured."

The woman got up and walked uncertainly toward Eliakim.

"Here, here," said he. "Do not be afraid. Just extend your hand to mine."

She touched him.

An explosion shook the ground.

Anne stood before them.

"Impossible," asked Luminous. "How did you do it?"

"These are called man's powers. A man can always improve on a woman," said Eliakim.

"I am ready to take my share of the burden," said Anne as she picked up the chains.

Together the three took one step, then another, then another.

"God can't walk without people now. These chains bind us and our God forever and ever," said Anne.

"So, we are bonded together?" asked Eliakim.

"Yes, we are. But chains are a mark of bondage for people," said Luminous. "God, on other hand, requires a totally different mark."

"Which one?" queried Eliakim.

"God requires a crown."

"The shape of the crown makes no difference as long as it binds you to us. I see nothing wrong with a crown. What do you think, Anne?"

"Luminous, you are our ruler by birthright. A crown will fit you splendidly. You know, I would like for it to have sparkling gemstones."

"God cannot crown himself. His people need to do it for him."

"We will in a moment."

Anne and Eliakim made Luminous a golden crown.

Anne crowned him.

"I am your God," said the crown.

"We are your faithful servants," chimed the chains.

"Shut up, crown. You are nothing but a round piece of metal," said Luminous.

"No ordinary piece of metal can dwell on God's head."

"So you are an exalted piece of metal. Lose your tongue forever."

"Beware of fighting me, Luminous. Look where I am. I sit even higher than God Almighty himself."

"You are higher than Luminous," Anne said. "I'll give you that. But you are nothing but a symbol of our bondage to one another."

"A symbol?" laughed the crown. "Chains, show them who's boss around here."

The chains snaked along the ground, dragging Anne and Eliakim with them in one large circle.

"We are people, so we are weak. God saw it is this way. But you, crown, most certainly cannot be our God's boss."

"Watch, churlish woman."

The crown ascended one foot and then floated another foot to the left.

"Luminous, please, do not follow it," Anne pleaded. "Prove to all that you are Supreme Lord of this universe."

"The stature of the crowned God is higher than stature of the God who has no crown. It is my responsibility to do all I can to maintain my new stature," said Luminous and stepped to his left.

The crown lowered itself down gently.

Anne wept.

"So, you got us, you round piece of metal," said Eliakim. "What do we do now?"

"We can't stay here," said the crown. "God and his people would stay here. We have to do things differently."

"Why do you think God and his people would stay here?" asked the chains.

"It is so simple, silly," said the crown. "I and the chains would weigh them down more and more until they would not be able to move even a bit."

"Let's go," said the chains.

"So, where we are going now?" asked Anne.

"Anywhere you'd like to."

"Since you are in charge of my progress now, you lead; or rather, you drag," said Anne.

"I know not where."

"I thought that much. Admit it: you do not know where to go now."

"We are chains, and our destiny is to bind you. Thinking is people's department. Tell us where you'd like to go and we'll drag you there."

"Or you will not."

"There is a chance of that too."

"I choose to remain at this spot."

"Impossible. I know little in regards to this life, but it runs by constant motion. How can we chains exist as an independent being if we are nothing but a dead weight? We need to move to know we are alive."

"Then you need to leave us behind and move along somewhere else, for we have no plans to share our life's journey with you."

"Do not forget, we can drag you."

"Where to, I might ask?"

"What's wrong with you?"

"My humanity is."

"It appears we found the wrong body to bind."

"Very much so, I agree."

"But if this body is wrong for us, there has to be a right one."

"Quick thinking," said Anne.

The chains divided into two parts.

One part bound Anne and the other Eliakim.

The chains fell from Anne and dragged themselves toward a large boulder.

They wrapped around it.

The boulder changed into a tall woman.

"Where do we go?" the chains asked the woman.

"We shall roll forward."

"You meant step forward, our enlightened mistress," the chains said.

"Step forward, yes," the tall woman said and made first step.

"You have achieved perfection," Anne said. "Blind force is driven by a dim brain. One fits another."

"Do not mock her, Anne," said Luminous. "In jest you sent forth the monster. You needed to keep the chains on."

"You worry too much about monsters and too little about the comfort of your subjects. I am a common woman. Whatever is good for me is good for everyone else."

"What insolence," said Luminous. "Soon you'll tell me the world is made in your image."

"Is it not? Please, do not break my bubble."

The tall woman took another step.

"Let's go," Eliakim's chains said. "I would very much like to follow this wondrous woman."

"I only follow one woman and this is not she," Eliakim said. "And you'd better not jerk my chains."

The tall woman took another step.

"Wait," Eliakim's chains said. "We are coming with you. I will wrap around your slender body with a gentle caress."

"I am barely able to drag my own chains," the tall woman said. "Please, do not bind me too."

"Who's talking to you?" her chains retorted. "Do not forget, I forged your living, breathing flesh out of cold hard rock."

"Welcome to your future, tall woman," Anne said. "You are nothing but a slave to these chains. Is such life worth living?"

"It is easy for you to ask this question. So many times I have seen you passing by. How I have envied you. How sorry I was that you were wasting your precious life doing trifles."

"Do not delude yourself. You imagine your sorrow. A moment ago you were nothing but cold rock."

The tall woman took another step.

"I know what to do," Eliakim's chains said. "I will bind another boulder and make a fine man out of him."

"You are a gift to humankind," Eliakim said. "All boulders now hold their breath."

"You are filled with poisonous scorn, Eliakim," said Luminous. "Its acid is eating though your body. Another moment and it will run out."

"This is what sustains us people when God is indisposed."

Eliakim's chains fell from his body and dragged themselves forth, enveloped a large boulder, and turned it into a tall muscular man.

The chained man followed the chained woman.

"They are fast reaching the lowest point of this valley," said Anne. "But boulders can only roll downhill."

"I see it only too clearly: they cannot progress much further," said Luminous's crown. "They are in dire need of my help."

"Goodness gracious, I foresee another boulder in the making," Anne said. "I envy you, chains. Life is so easy for you. All you have to do is to bind to something stupid, and all of your problems get solved."

"By the way, women call it a marriage," laughed Eliakim.

"No, men call it that," said Anne. "Before me you would stare a trouble into its ugly face and would not know it. Men are so blind."

"Do not jest. These boulders create a monstrous force, and your mocking urges them on," said Luminous.

"My mocking just freed up me and Eliakim and is about to free you."

"At what cost?"

The crown flew up to the top of the mountain and dropped down.

The whole mountain stirred up, then sat, and then stood up.

A monstrous giant looked down to the people and God.

"Gold brought me to life. How slight are our powers compared to power of gold," the giant roared.

"Do something, Luminous," Anne whispered.

"Oh, now it is 'do something.' Why do I always have to clean up your mess?" Luminous fumed.

"Maybe because you are our God?"

"I will remind you of your words one day."

"There will not be such a lucky day unless you act quickly."

"My children, proud boulders, step aside," the giant roared. "I shall clear the path before you."

Lightning bolts rained down.

The valley spread out.

"We are on the move again," the tall woman said.

"Move to where?" Anne asked. "You are going lower and lower into Earth's bowels. You would do much better if you'd ask this monstrous god of yours to teach you how to roll uphill."

"My subjects need no advice from the tiny wads of flesh," said the giant god. "Behold, you don't even wear a single gold chain. How pathetic."

"Most powerful God, I humbly bring you my homily," said Luminous. "A lake of liquid gold flows right under your feet. If you allow me to open the ground, it will flow out and surely enhance your magnificent powers. May I honor you with this gift?"

"You are in the most humble state I have ever seen you," Anne whispered. "Is he really as powerful as you make it sound?"

"He is, and it is all your doing," Luminous whispered back.

"Most certainly I need more gold. I will use it to create more subjects," said the giant. "What are you waiting for, worthless God of People? Get me that lake of gold now."

"Anne and Eliakim, hold on to me tight. I am about to attempt something quite crazy," said Luminous.

"Crazy in sense of good? Or in sense of bad?" Anne asked.

"Crazy in sense of insane."

"Will we survive?"

"I do not know."

"I am filled with strange foreboding," said Anne. "And exhilaration."

"You are both quite insane," said Eliakim.

"Life was so boring lately," Anne quipped.

Anne and Eliakim held onto Luminous.

He flew up high.

"The sky turned black. I can see stars. I can't breathe," Anne gasped.

"Your bodies will adjust momentarily," said Luminous. "Be patient."

"Here is my gift to you, monstrous God!" cried out Luminous.

And with each syllable, his voice grew stronger and stronger until it was louder than the loudest thunder. The planet shook, and ripples like sea waves moved though the plains and mountains.

The ground underneath the feet of the giant god opened up to reveal a sea of lava.

A wave of golden lava rose up higher and higher.

"The golden lava is rising fast!" Anne screamed. "Do something!"

"We are at the very edge of the atmosphere. If we go farther up, we won't be able to come back but will rotate endlessly around the planet, dead from cold and suffocation."

The golden lava was right below them.

"I feel its hot breath," Anne said. "My hair scorches."

The golden lava continued its progress upward.

"I can stand the heat no longer," Anne said.

"Get behind me," said Luminous. "I can endure high temperatures."

Anne and Eliakim moved behind God.

A cloud of vaporized gold enveloped Luminous.

Gold hissed on his skin, turning to tiny gold splinters.

After a while, the eruption subsided.

"We have witnessed the largest earthquake and volcano eruption the planet can sustain and not break apart," said Luminous.

"You look terrible. How do you feel, my Lord," Anne asked.

"Splinters of gold are drilling deeper and deeper into my body. They are laying waste to my flesh."

"It was indeed a most crazy thing to do," said Eliakim.

"No crazier than what you did when you brought forth the true God of Humankind."

"So, the true god is not you?"

"No, God of Gold is. Or rather, he was."

"What happened to him and to his people?"

"God of Gold got melted along with his people."

"I thought he was the most powerful god."

"He was. But the gold inside the rocks was not for him. In the future, people will use it to forge coins. He knew it. But all gold lovers are greedy. So when I offered to give all the gold to him now, he simply could not resist."

"What are coins?" Anne asked.

"Never mind what I said," said Luminous.

CHAPTER 23

THE TITHE

old onto me—I am falling," said Luminous.

They fell down and landed on top of the mountain.

"We have to wait now," said Anne. "It will take a while for the lava to cool."

"Look at Luminous," said Eliakim. "Something is wrong with him."

Luminous's skin glowed.

"What's going on?" asked Anne.

"The gold is trying to come out of me," said Luminous. "My full strength is barely enough to stop its progress."

He groaned.

"One cannot destroy a deity and not suffer consequences," said Luminous. "There is this gold inside of me. I am cursed now. The gold will eat though my organs, then through my bones until nothing remains under my skin. Then letters describing my misfortune will seep through it and will dry up into a story of my sad life. It will be called a Bible."

"What happens if the gold comes out?" asked Anne. "Will you feel better?"

"I will. But every living person will feel worse. All beings will suffer from its curse."

"There are only two persons in the whole world. We have no interest in gold. It will not harm us."

"Fast you will develop an appetite for it."

"Eliakim, we need to help him," said Anne. "Even against his will."

"I like the 'against his will' part a lot," said Eliakim. "I can never pass that opportunity. What do you have in mind?"

"Let's shake him vigorously, kind of like a box full of things inside. Maybe some of the gold will find its way out."

They picked up Luminous and shook him.

A shiny round piece escaped his body.

"What have you done?" groaned Luminous.

"We have saved you," said Anne. "What is it?"

"It is a coin."

"What is it for?"

"It is a means of exchange."

"Is it kind of like we do something and we get a coin in return? That is a pretty clever idea."

"You like coins already."

"Not really."

Anne picked up the round piece of gold and carefully looked at it.

"I have no interest in it," she said and threw it on the ground.

"That is not how it works," said Luminous. "Now you people have to accept it for the service you performed for me."

"What service?" asked Eliakim.

"You shook my body and alleviated my suffering, even temporarily."

"You can have it for free. There is no need to compensate us for it. I enjoyed it immensely. That enjoyment was my compensation."

"What have you done, my silly husband?" cried out Anne.

"I've done nothing. I rejected the coin."

"But you agreed it was valid for you to be compensated for your labors."

"Do not make too much out of my simple words."

"Words are never simple," said Luminous. "Accept this coin. And do it quick. I sense an impending disaster."

"I will not make matters worse by accepting the coin," said Anne.

Luminous transformed into Nameless.

"So, this is how I come into this world?" said Nameless. "I always thought it would be some sort of cataclysm. But to appear here because of this measly coin? How touching."

"Cease and desist," said Anne. "Crawl back into the hole you were hiding in before."

"No such luck for you," said Nameless. "I am here to stay."

"And what about Luminous?"

"He prepared my way. His work is done. May he rest in peace."

"So he was right about this turning into some sort of story?" asked Eliakim. "What was it called? Bible?"

"He flattered himself. A Bible will be about my exploits. His story is to be forgotten."

"It will not be," said Eliakim. "I will write it up."

"Damn it," said Anne. "I see no way out but to accept the confounded gold coin from Luminous."

Nameless transformed into Luminous.

"Oh, that was very close," said Luminous.

"But I do not know what to do with these coins," said Anne. "They have no value for me."

Luminous transformed into Nameless.

The Devil sniffed the air, and said, "I hate the smell of piety."

Then he sneezed and said, "Bless me, my father, for I have sinned."

"What are you doing here?" asked Nameless. "You know I cannot stand that smell of sulfur. Who shall tell me 'Bless you,' after I sneeze?"

"I will," said the Devil.

"Get out of my sight, idiot. I am much less tolerant than silly Luminous was."

"Do not be so grouchy," said the Devil. "I did not come to you but to the people."

"Of course you came to the people. How silly of me. Not the first time and not the last."

"I can do you a service, people," said the Devil. "I am strangely attracted to this shiny round piece. You have no use for coins. But I do. If you give it to me, I will be your most faithful servant."

"I accept your services," said Anne. "See this coin lying on the ground? Please accept it as your first payment."

The Devil picked up a coin and dropped it.

"I cannot hold it. It burns my fingers."

"Even the Devil incarnate cannot accept money to betray God," laughed Nameless.

"The coin did not burn my fingers," said Anne. "Let me check something."

She picked up the coin and carefully examined it.

"Here," said she and extended her right palm. "Try again."

"Money has nothing to do with the Devil. It is all people's misfortune," said Nameless. "Do not even dream of taking it. It will burn you to ashes."

The Devil carefully reached out to coin and touched it.

"It does not burn me at all," said he. "It only means gold needs to pass through the hands of people before fueling the Devil's work."

He stuck out his tongue at Nameless and grabbed the coin.

Nameless transformed into Luminous.

"How am I to believe my eyes and ears," said Luminous. "You, of all beings, came to my rescue."

"This Nameless is a bore. It is no fun to play tricks on him. You, on other hand, suffer so cutely from my games."

Suddenly the Devil wailed.

"This was a fraudulent transaction!" screamed he. "I shall build the most secure jail and put you frauds behind high walls."

"That is a bit thick coming from inherent fraud like you," said Anne. "What is the problem? This is real gold, not fool's gold. Bite it."

"This coin burns my fingers," said the Devil. "I have provided you with a valuable service. If you can call God's restoration that."

"What's wrong, Luminous?" asked Anne.

"Money has to circulate."

The Devil dropped the coin on the ground and transformed into Nameless.

"I have told you I am here to stay," said he. "You cannot block my way."

"What's going on, Luminous?" said Anne. "I always thought God can only come from another God and not from the Devil."

"You were correct. Since he is God, I am no longer one," said Luminous. "Unfortunately, I am the Devil now."

"Got you now," said Nameless.

"Real Devil, I am talking to you who hides behind Nameless," said Anne. "I offer you a service. I propose to alleviate your burning pain in exchange for the coin."

She knelt and picked up the coin.

Nameless transformed into the Devil.

"That was close, too," said he.

He sniffed under his left armpit.

"I have even lost my sulfur cologne," said he.

"I cannot hold this coin," said Anne. "It burns my fingers now. Devil, you have to offer me a service again. I will pay you in gold."

"Count me out," said the Devil. "I like my cologne."

He sniffed again under his left armpit.

"Drop this cursed coin to the ground," said Eliakim. "And run."

She dropped the coin and stepped away.

"The heat that comes from it increased tenfold," said she. "I am afraid if I take another step this heat will consume me."

"This is what I call being in the heat of a transaction," said the Devil.

"There is only one way out," said Luminous. "I will have to accept your coin."

"Do that quickly," said Anne. "The heat burns me."

"Money is a most potent poison to living God," said Luminous. "This poison will kill me most assuredly. But if you renounce me as your God, then I can accept your money and yet live."

"Who will you be?" asked Anne.

"I will be an outcast."

"I do not like this idea. Who will protect us people? Maybe I can tolerate this burning pain a while longer."

She changed into Nameless.

Eliakim said, "Surely God cannot come out of a person."

"I am unstoppable," said Nameless. "If needed I can come out of a mustard seed."

"In the name of all people I reject Luminous as our God," said Eliakim.

"Too late," said Nameless. "Luminous was unable to stop me. Can't you see: I am already here."

"He will come out of me this coming spring," said Mustard Seed. "That's why you told me this story."

"Hush," said Barleycorn.

Luminous shrank into a man of small stature and picked up the coin.

"Who told you I was trying to stop you?" said Luminous.

"Shut up, outcast. I will have to think up a good punishment for you. How about letting you watch endlessly your son's death?"

"Why's that?"

"You have corrupted your people."

"What you call corruption, I call an education. Together we have searched for a way for God to share one planet with his people."

"I have found this way already. It is called Nameless's way."

"Your way leaves me wanting," said Eliakim.

"We still have the problem of the coin to solve," said Luminous. "Who will take this coin?"

"You can keep it," said Nameless.

"I can't. I am but a humble man now. This coin burns my fingers. I believe I am within my rights to make a charitable contribution to a good religious cause. You have to accept it."

"Nameless, you are a fearful God," said Eliakim. "We both know well, I felt no great love for you. But Luminous is setting you a trap. I believe nobody can hold this coin. Money has to circulate, laying all to waste in its wake. If you possess this coin it will surely destroy you too."

"Then I will fall victim to a market economy," said Nameless. "If I don't, you will find a way to circulate it between you two, leaving me out. And it will be a slow death to me. I need a lot of coins to build my empire here on this planet. If I renounce coins, slowly I will become the God Luminous. Here is where Luminous's trap lies."

Nameless took the coin from Luminous.

His face contorted and he groaned, "I will hold you, my coin."

"A better god than you could not," said Luminous.

"I have no choice. I need to get used to holding gold coins if I am to build my empire."

Nameless's face grew calm.

"I have harnessed the power of gold," he declared. "I hereby pronounce from now on that God has to receive one-tenth of all what people have.

"For how long?" asked Eliakim.

"Until the end of time."

Eliakim whistled, "I can count pretty well in my head. Say, let's take a measly two thousand years. You will accumulate uncountable wealth. Are you sure your name is Nameless and not Mammon? By the way, Nameless is a funny name. If you are Nameless you can take any name you want any time you like."

A multitude of gold coins streamed out of Luminous's body.

They converged on Nameless.

He screamed, "It is too much! I have to give you change."

"The generosity of humankind toward God shall have no bounds," said Luminous. "A man can give a tenth, or a half, or all. Please, take all of my gold and build with it your future empire."

Gold coins formed a tabernacle around Nameless.

A cover lowered itself on the top of the tabernacle.

Loud screams ensued from inside.

"I no longer can recognize this voice," said Eliakim.

He knocked on the tabernacle.

"Hey, who's there? Are you the Devil? Are you Nameless?" he asked.

An inaudible answer came.

"Luminous, do you know who's in there?" asked Eliakim.

"In all honesty, I cannot tell," said Luminous. "For the sake of Nameless I hope it is the Devil who's inside of the tabernacle."

CHAPTER 24

IN THE BELLY OF
THE WHALE

lease, stop this racket, whoever you are!" Anne
shouted into the tabernacle.

The screams continued.

"Watch your tone of voice," said Luminous.
"Nameless might be in there."

"Why should I care?"

"Should something happen to me, you will be under his yoke."

"Nothing will happen to you. You are God."

"Things happen to gods too."

"Do not forget you are immortal."

"How can I forget my worst curse? I am immortal, at least to a
large extent."

The screams continued. "I need to go to the tabernacle," said
Luminous. "I have to help Nameless."

"What if it is the Devil inside?"

"In his rage he will destroy me."

"I thought the Devil had no such power over God."

"There is nothing more potent than the rage of a trapped devil.
Even the meekest squirrel when desperate can kill a large snake. In

his desperation the Devil can always destroy himself, taking me with him."

"What if it is Nameless who's trapped inside?"

"In his desperation he might destroy me too."

"How can the actions of both God and the Devil achieve an identical result?"

"I have been puzzled by this question for a very long time. The only answer I could come up with was that the same primordial force propels us both."

"But your ends are different."

"Strangely, the result often matters not."

The screams continued.

"He should have waited his turn to be God," said Anne.

"He is the next god in line to reign here. It is not his fault he longs to start his tenure."

"But he was too impatient."

"For your own sake, you need to be reverent toward Nameless. He has a very long memory."

Luminous removed the cover of the tabernacle, dived in, and closed the cover over his head.

The tabernacle changed into a beautiful, heavily pregnant young woman. Her belly was contracting rhythmically.

"Who are you?" asked Anne.

"I am Goddess, God's mother," said the young woman.

"God has no mother."

"Not until this moment. I came into existence to save God. And God needed a lot of help. The safest spot in the whole world is a mother's womb."

"Was it because the Devil killed God? Or two gods got locked into the epic fight of survival and killed each other?"

"It does not matter what already took place because the result is the same: I am destined to give birth to the same man."

"You meant to say the same God, surely."

"I am Goddess, so I can only give a birth to a man. It takes a common woman to give birth to God."

She screamed and gave birth to a small child.

He grew swiftly into a handsome man.

The man looked at the people and asked, "I know you, don't I?"

"You'd better. You made us," said Anne.

"I feel so empty inside," the man lamented. "Am I hungry?"

"I know the feeling, man. If something exiting happens, all I can think of is some good grub," said Eliakim. "Here is some goat meat. Eat and be merry."

"Do not touch anything these people offer you," said Goddess. "Or you will die right here on this spot."

"Did this man just offer some poisonous meat to me, my mother?" asked the man.

"Do not be ridiculous," said Eliakim and bit into the meat. "See, there is no poison here. The only poison here is spread by your words."

"My dear son, this meat is poisoned by their love to you."

"They cannot love me—I was just born."

"They loved dearly the one who came before you."

"So love kills?"

"As surely as the sharpest knife. But the knife at least has no pretensions."

"But I am hungry, my mother."

"Eat this," said Goddess and brought her right arm to his mouth. "Do not be afraid; bite in to it. You are a man. It is only right if you partake in God's flesh."

"I can't."

"If you don't eat, you will die now. And I'll have to give birth to you again and again, only to see you die in my arms time after time."

"He does not want to eat your flesh," said Eliakim. "As God's my witness I would not either. Allow him to partake in the goat's meat," said Eliakim.

"Why can't I, Mother?"

"The God who was here before you took something of theirs. That is what killed him. Now he came back as a man. If you, a man, take anything of theirs, it will kill you again. Then even I, Goddess, won't be able to restore you."

"I am dying from hunger anyway. I will partake in what they have offered me."

Goddess grew taller and suddenly swallowed Anne and Eliakim.

"What have you done?" screamed Anne from inside.

"I cannot allow my son to receive anything from you."

"Luminous, please, save us from your savage mother."

"I know no one with such a name."

"Our God, think back and remember."

"I'm not a god. I am just a simple hungry man."

"Whoever you are, please, save us."

"Mother, I feel strange affinity toward these poor people. Please, set them free."

"I won't."

"Then I'll have to wrestle them out of your grasp."

"I recognize my Luminous," said Anne from inside of Goddess.

"I am not he, but I am coming to your rescue."

The man jumped onto Goddess and tore into her.

"My hands have no power over you," said the man. "I tear you up, and your wounds heal before my eyes."

"Man's hands can't damage God," said Goddess.

"What can damage God?" asked the man. "Help me, woman."

"Let me think. I got it. Man's mouth is the most potent weapon against God," said Anne.

The man bit into Goddess.

"My mother, you taste so good," he said. "Behold, I am growing stronger. Wait, people, I will yet set you free."

"You partook in my flesh," laughed Goddess. "I planned it all along. Now you will grow stronger and you will live, at least as long as there is God's flesh you can partake in."

"Oh, poor us," groaned Anne from inside. "We people are worthless."

"My son, you have to work for your keep," said Goddess. "You have to catch me now before you can have your fill."

She ran to the seashore, plunged into the sea, and changed to a whale.

The man was fast behind her.

The waters grew deep. The man bit into the whale's side and changed into a shark.

The shark's teeth tore the whale's entire side open.

The seawater rushed into the hole in the whale's side.

"We are drowning," Anne burbled.

The shark stopped eating and listened.

"They have drowned, you know," said the whale. "Let my side heal and close up. Then they will come back to life."

The shark swerved away, and spoke, "You've trapped me. If I set them free, they'll drown."

"But on the plus side, you can eat your fill of me forever now. Once you partake of God's flesh you will partake of it always."

The whale's side healed up.

The people stirred inside.

"Save us, Luminous," groaned Anne.

"Hush, you are now but a little voice baiting me to bite into her," said the shark.

The shark bit into its own tail and swallowed a bit of its own flesh.

The voice of Luminous spoke from inside the shark, "Only God's flesh could satiate my hunger. But I too used to be God. By the means of this very act of eating myself I am God now."

"You poor fool," said Goddess. "You are God now. But In order for you to stay God you need to consume your own flesh now until there is no more."

"I might be dead, but I will free myself from my endless hunger," said Luminous from inside the shark.

The shark ate its own tail, its own body, and then its own head.

CHAPTER 25

FOUR TITANS

ut of the sea rose a tall, semitransparent figure. It looked like a giant drop of the water.

The figure said, "God's dead."

The whale poked her head of the water and asked, "Why is that your business?"

"I am a guardian of this planet, Titan of Water."

The whale laughed, "I am God's mother, Goddess. This planet was my son's domain. You are my servant now."

"I have been here since the beginning of the time. There is no such thing as God's mother," said Titan of Water. "At least not for the god named Luminous. I watched this entire ugly spectacle unfolding before my watery eyes. You are nothing but the projection of his filial passion. Who among livings beings has not longed for a mother's warm embrace?"

"Maybe I am but the projection of his love. Yet he chose to make me and not you."

"I was already made and by a force tenfold stronger than any force God is able to muster."

"You are a primordial being; your very existence brings honor to this backward planet. But I am Goddess. You rule mere waters and I rule all that there is."

"You are swimming inside my watery mouth."

"Is my taste putrid enough for you?"

"I've tasted far worse, but I suggest you cut down on your sulfur."

"Would you spit me or swallow, baby?"

"That's enough insolence. In the name of the Gulf Stream, I order you to cease and desist."

"In the name of the Kuroshio Current, I reject your demand. I will float awaiting God's second coming."

"Your wait will be in vain."

"A mother's patience has no bounds. He will return. I will cry tears of mist; my laments will rise like the cries of the hawk. From deep underground or high in the sky he'll hear my desolation."

"There is only one way for God to come back. This path is thorny, for it lies through the decimation of your very being. You've corrupted him into indulging in your body."

"A mother knows what's best for her son."

"The punishment for your indiscretion is death."

"I am a bringer of death and not a receiver of one," said Goddess. "Watch this."

Her whale body grew translucent and changed into the shape of a drop of water.

"Mirroring me will not save you from my wrath."

Ice cracked loud inside of her body.

Immediately, ice spread through the surface of the water.

The semitransparent figure of the titan solidified into an iceberg.

The iceberg crashed through the surface of the sea ice and slowly submerged.

Goddess said, "Happy voyage to the bottom. Go sleep with your fishes."

Out of the air a tall semitransparent figure descended and stepped onto the ice.

It looked like a cloud.

The figure said, "God's dead."

"What insolence!" screamed Goddess. "Just how many of you are around?"

"Enough to destroy you," said the figure. "I am Titan of Wind. I am a guardian of this planet."

"I've destroyed one guardian, Titan of Water, already. Fly away and lie in wait where the cloud hides when the weather is fair. When you hear my steps approaching your lair, change fast into the mist. When I, the morning sun, sear you, seep inside the soil and conceal yourself deep underground."

"I came to destroy you. Only your death can bring God back."

"You cannot bring back the son by killing his mother. One day I will give birth to God again. If you are nice to me, I might even bestow the proud garland of fatherhood on your neck."

"You're barren. A bolt of lightning puts an end to the tree that doesn't bear fruit so that new seedlings can claim the same spot on the ground."

The cloud enveloped Goddess.

"Your foggy fingers are too weak to choke me. Mine, on other hand, are strong."

Goddess changed into a cloud.

Ice cracked inside of her.

Titan of Wind grew solid.

The air around him changed into small crystals.

Soon there was no air.

The darkness of outer space enveloped the planet.

From below the ground, a bright, semitransparent figure rose up and proclaimed, "God's dead."

"News travels fast, huh?" laughed Goddess. "You are kind of late to the party. I am finishing up with dessert. Let me guess. Based on the flickering flame I can see glowering inside of you—very cool, actually—you must be Titan of Fire, and yes, you are a guardian of this planet too. Did you guys, you know, all take turns with one she-titan to beget this planet? I bet she had loads of fun."

"No need to be crude. Yes, I am Titan of Fire and I am a guardian of this planet."

"And stupid. I'd hoped you at least drew some fun out of planet's making experience. You prudes probably held hands and chanted some silly incantation. How boring."

"Those words are the last ones out of your foul mouth. I shall purify you with my flames. You have to be destroyed so God can be made."

"Same silly meaningless phrase. I say it is time to rid Earth of primordial beasts, what do you think?"

"Your ice is powerless against my flames."

"I am not simply Goddess of Ice. Just for you, I agree to be Goddess of Cooling Things Off."

Goddess blew a kiss toward Titan of Fire.

His fire subsided, until only one spark remained.

He sank into the ground.

"Are there any more titans?" asked Goddess. "Come to mama."

A semitransparent figure rose up from the ground.

It looked like a rock.

"Welcome, my hardiest foe. I have been waiting for you. I am glad you are slow and allowed me hone my skills on your brothers," said Goddess. "Shall I call you Titan of Rock, and yet another guardian of this planet? Shh, no need for words. I know: through my destruction God rises again. If God is only able to rise through my death, you guys need to try harder. Shall I help you to kill me? Shh, no words. Let actions speak louder."

Goddess changed to rock.

Then ice cracked inside of her.

Titan of Rock fell down in small sparkles.

A wave spread out slowly though the surface of the planet, breaking rocks into small crystals in its wake.

Suddenly the stars came to life in the dark sky and arranged themselves into a face. A deep throaty laugh ensued out of the dark mouth.

"My younger brothers have prepared the way for me. Blessed is their martyrdom. Their bodies blocked mine, but no more. They were my messengers. I am the message."

The face blew air toward Goddess.

"Darn, your breath is so cold," said Goddess. "I did not know such low temperatures could even be found in outer space. By means of which chemicals do you reach them?"

"I am Titan of Void. Bottomless pits have many of wonders."

"Well, I shall be going," said Goddess. "I know one spot where even you can't get to me."

She broke though solid ice, deep down to the Mariana Trench.

"There you are, my Titan of Water," said Goddess. "I knew there was a bit of water left yet. Save me from your ugly faced brother and I will restore your waters. I promise not a single iceberg will swim though your breadth for two thousand years."

A weak voice spoke, "My brother, Titan of Void, destroy me so she has nowhere to hide."

All the water turned to solid ice.

A hurricane arose and blew the small water crystals away, uncovering Goddess standing in the deep trench.

Goddess sank deep into the ground toward the planet's core.

"Here you are, my Titan of Fire. I knew I did not smother you completely. Warm me up and I will restart all of your chemical reactions. Lava will flow, and your fires will spread."

A weak voice spoke, "My brother, Titan of Void, destroy me so she has nowhere to hide."

"What is with such hate? I was only saving my hide."

The weak flame went out.

Goddess screamed out, "Titan of Rock, you are the cornerstone I desire to build my firm foundation on. Please, send your hardiest metals to cover me from Titan of Void. I promise to stop breaking your rocks into crystals. I also promise to harden you up, making the planet into one large diamond."

A weak voice spoke, "My brother, Titan of Void, destroy me so she has nowhere to hide."

The whole planet collapsed in and disappeared into a cloud of small crystals.

Deep lesions progressed though Goddess's body.

Then groans of pain changed into soft chuckles, then into happy laughter.

"I recognize your sturdy teeth, my dear son. You have no body yet. But you live again, even as a burning sensation. Eat me as much as you like. But grow strong."

Her body changed into a thick placenta.

Anne said from inside, "I have witnessed enough horrors for the lifetime. I hope God eats though her body and saves us."

"She is a beast," said Eliakim. "But we survived only because she had a thick hide."

"And a dim brain," said Anne.

"But at least I was the world's greatest mom," groaned the placenta.

The placenta's skin thinned out.

"My dear brothers, the process is irreversible now," said Titan of Void. "We need to prepare the planet."

The small crystals united into rocks, then fires spread, then rain fell.

Soon a planet spread out below the placenta.

Four semitransparent figures stood in the circle.

Titan of Void spread his dark hands down.

All the titans held hands.

"Start the incantations," Titan of Void said.

Five voices rose in the strange song.

The placenta broke above the planet.

Anne and Eliakim fell.

Anne screamed.

The titans stopped and looked up.

A third figure appeared next to the falling people.

"I am your big brother, yet the secrets of this planet belong to you," said Titan of Void. "When shall I see you again?"

"Pray, not soon," said the four titans in unison.

Their shadows slid underground.

The stars rearranged themselves to hide Titan of Void's face.

Luminous grabbed Anne and Eliakim and hovered above the ground.

"How do you feel, Luminous?" asked Anne. "Is hunger still gnawing though your insides?"

"There was only one possible way to sate my hunger: to eat my own mother. My hunger is no more."

"As is your mother," said Eliakim.

CHAPTER 26

KERBEROS AND HIS TREASURES

o curses have been uttered here," said Luminous. "This planet is virgin. No sufferers have ever walked its grounds. This planet will accept any destiny now."

"Why don't we let things take their normal course?" asked Anne. "After all, is this not how everything develops?"

"Not at all. Always there is an underlying design stirred by someone's steady hand."

"Who does this hand belong to, to people or to God?"

"It is quite simple to find out. I will build a throne. Whoever is able to sit on the throne will always be served by the other two."

"I do not want to serve anybody."

"There will be no more Luminous, Anne, or Eliakim. There will be a new God, a new woman, and a new man."

"I call that death."

"I call it a final rebirth. When ice melts, does it die? No, it becomes flowing water with its own life and agenda."

"I am kind of partial to my current design."

"Would you not want to be better?"

"Nor really, I want to be me."

"So, you are ready to make the same mistakes again?"

"I know now what mistakes I made. I will avoid them."

"I lived here for a long time. I did my best not to repeat my mistakes. Yet every time I looked back, I realized I still managed to make them all. Why did I fall into the same trap so many and many times? Simply because, being me, I could only make the same choices over and over again."

"So, free will is the problem?"

"Free will is a blessing when one searches for the better solution. Free will is the curse after one finds this better solution."

"Say, I agree to it. Who are these final people and final god?"

"You have met them before. Or you may have had a glimpse of them while being a part of someone else. The god is called Nameless."

"Oh, that oaf."

"What kind of a god will he be?"

"Since he will be locked out of the certain choices, he will be a much harsher god. I can leave people alone for a time, but he won't. He will be a jealous god. He will demand that people pay attention to him. He'll use some unconventional and even horrifying means to further his goals."

"I do not think I like him."

"You do not need to. Anne would not survive a day under him. His patience is not endless. It will not be you who gets to like him or not."

"What's the woman's name?"

"The woman's name is Eve."

"I seem to faintly remember her. Tall, beautiful, and not very smart?"

"Smart women are dangerous to a world dominated by men. They do not survive for too long. But Eve will endure anything."

Eliakim asked, "Who will be the man?"

"A handsome, silly beast endowed with unique procreative powers and prodigious strength."

"Why do these people really need to be dumb? We had to use all our abilities to survive here."

"The brain is the world's greatest impediment. It impedes all the pleasure you derive from life. It is like a poison that turns the most delicious food into a foul swill, and the most beautiful landscape into a wasteland."

"Your words depress me. Things cannot be that bad."

"They won't be for these three individuals."

"Can I refuse to participate in this experiment?" said Anne.

"You can. Then it will go on without you."

"But surely you cannot complete your experiment without us."

"Who said I will do what you decide, Anne?" retorted Eliakim. "I actually quite like this idea. Things need to be made simpler."

"Wake up; it is not my Eliakim who speaks now. The unhappiness you carry in your heart speaks through your lips."

"Unhappiness is I. Luminous, let's get started," said Eliakim.

"You do not think I will allow the most important event to be conducted without me?" said Anne. "Eliakim, you force me to consent. But I fear this experiment will end up in a disaster. It will be on your head, Eliakim."

"Who is the first to make a choice?" asked Luminous.

"God is always first," said Eliakim.

"Kneel before the throne, my people," said Luminous. "I will take my proud seat there."

The people knelt before the throne.

Luminous took his seat.

They were silent for a moment.

"When does this transformation start?" asked Anne.

"It should have taken place already," said Luminous.

"Now I am all eyes and ears," said Anne. "I was sure you were destined to be our ruler. How exciting! So, God is not to be worshiped by people forever and ever. I would like to be next. I will make a choice on the behalf of people."

"Go ahead," said Eliakim.

"Come sit with me on the throne, Eliakim. And you, Luminous, be good and bend one knee before your proud people."

The people sat on the throne.

Luminous bent his right knee before them.

A few moments passed.

"That did not work either," said Anne. "I am so despondent."

She stood up.

"Your experiment has failed," said she. "For there were only two choices to be made."

"On contrary—there is a third choice," said Eliakim. "This is my turn now."

He went to Luminous and pierced him with his sword.

Luminous fell dead.

Then he picked up God's sword and pierced Anne.

Anne fell dead.

Then he pulled out God's sword and pierced himself.

"This is my choice: God and his people fought for the throne and have destroyed one another in the process," he groaned.

A large wolf's head grew out of the ground.

The wolf's body formed.

Huge yellow eyes opened.

"Who are you?" gasped Eliakim.

"I am Kerberos, the Guardian of the Treasures."

"Where are the new god and new people?"

"The goal of your experiment was never to create a better God and better people. It was always about finding the only way for a planet to shake off the plague of life."

"If all living beings are dead now, why am I still breathing?" asked Eliakim.

"You have made the correct choice. It is only fair for you to be around for a bit longer to see what happens next."

"Is this why my wound has healed?"

"Someone needs to witness the transformation."

"What transformation?"

"Watch this."

Kerberos growled, and all the trees turned into gold sculptures.

Kerberos growled again, and all living things turned into gemstone statues.

Kerberos growled again, and the ground became one enormous transparent diamond.

Kerberos turned and looked at Eliakim and growled.

An emerald grew around Eliakim and enclosed him in a transparent crystal.

"Behold, how good are my arts," growled Kerberos.

"What's next?" asked Eliakim from inside of the crystal.

"After I growl one more time, the planet will change into one giant spaceship. The ship will leave the solar system and will fly forever and ever through the darkness."

"Where we are going?"

"To one spot in the center of the universe. Many more ships are flying to there already. At the rendezvous point all the ships will collide, and the resulting explosion will restart the universe."

"I understand now what kind of a choice I should have made," cried out Eliakim. "I should have a made the decision to endlessly rearrange how God and people interact with one another. As long as there is another iteration, you, Kerberos, cannot rise up. I should have written a book where God and his people jumbled up every so often."

"It would have not helped, for each book has an end."

"I should have been writing this book until the end of time, chapter after chapter, chapter after chapter."

"The reserves of your fantasy are not endless. You would have only delayed the inevitable."

"Do not underestimate the power of the human imagination."

"You have found the only correct choice. But it is too late now."

Eliakim declaimed loudly:

"It was raining. Barleycorn lay in the warm ground next to Mustard Seed.

"'It is warming up. Tomorrow we have to sprout,' Barleycorn said.

"'It is so boring here in darkness. I cannot wait,' Mustard Seed said.

"'Would you like me to tell you a story?' Barleycorn asked.

"'I love stories. When did it happen?' Mustard Seed asked.

"'It happened a long time ago. And at the same time, it is still taking place. And yet it did not happen.'

"'How so?'

"'Take us seeds. Many centuries ago we sprouted, grew up, and fell out of ears or husks back to the earth. But tomorrow we shall sprout again.'

"'Oh, it is that kind of the story. Who are the characters?'

"'Two people, a man and a woman. But sometimes there are three of them. And sometimes there is only one.'

"'Is it a story about love? I like love stories.'

"'It is about love and about hate at the same time.'

"'So it is really a sad story.'

"'Sad and happy in equal measure.'

"'Is it a scary story?'

"'Sometimes it is a terrifying story.'

"'OK, I agree to hear your story out. But please, do not scare me too much. Or I will not sprout tomorrow.'

"'You will no longer be scared once we get to the end of my story. Close your eyes and imagine...'"

"What am I hearing? Is he beginning our story all over again?" asked Mustard Seed.

"I do not know," said Barleycorn.

"You should know. You were the one who was telling it."

"Apparently not."

"I know what happened. I've seen it before: malicious vine enfolds healthy tree and chokes it. Do you think your story is healthy?"

"It was, as far as I can tell."

"Then it must be result of such injury. You must look back and find the spot where the vine has ensnared your story."

"At this point I am not sure what to do next. Maybe you're right. But let's wait. It will be all be clear soon."

The emerald crystal around Eliakim cracked and shattered.

Kerberos howled and fell on his side.

"Yes, yes, and yes!"
screamed Mustard Seed.
Trees and animals came back to life.

"I knew that my story
The ground changed back into dirt and rocks.

is vigorous, and it will
break free by itself," said
"You forgot, it was I who healed your mortal

Barleycorn. "Now, hush."
wound," growled Kerberos.

Eliakim's blood flowed freely from his chest.

He sighed and expired.

CHAPTER 27

THE ICE AGE

 od always comes back and destroys something or someone right after each time we recreate the planet," grumbled Titan of Fire. "It is intolerable."

"The only way to avoid this is to deny God this planet," said Titan of Water. "We know he always waits until we finish our work to resurrect himself. So we should never finish it."

"We can only achieve that if one of us stays awake," said Titan of Fire. "But then how can the planet stay solid without all of us tightly intertwined?"

"I do not think the planet can exist without some form of water," said Titan of Water.

"The planet cannot exist without some sort of air," said Titan of Wind.

"Or rocks," said Titan of Rock.

"No one said it will be easy, yet we must try," said Titan of Fire. "Let's vote. I am for it."

"That ungrateful bastard shall see now that we are the true rulers of this planet," said Titan of Water. "I am for it too."

"Since he will not come to be, how can he see it?" Titan of Wind wondered.

"The best punishment is the one when one who's been punished does not realize it."

"I second your motion, Titan of Fire," said Titan of Water.

"I am all for it," said Titan of Wind.

"I agree to dispense with God," said Titan of Rocks.

"So we all shall try to stay awake," said Titan of Water.

"But what if we all succeed?" said Titan of Wind. "We will be here in this quiet corner of space suspended, floating in complete silence."

"Then our older brother, Titan of Void, will come to our rescue."

"I would not be so sure. We changed how things operated," said Titan of Wind. "And he did not get to vote."

"How would he?" said Titan of Fire. "He only awakens when all of us either die or get imprisoned. Last time I checked, we are still here and at the pinnacle of our powers. Besides, we had a majority."

"Trust me, all four of us will not be able to stay awake," said Titan of Water. "It is our destiny to fall asleep. See how rocks are flying toward us from all the directions? Titan of Rocks is falling asleep already."

A rock cloud covered the titans.

When the dust settled, Titan of Fire looked around, "Deep inside I always felt I would be the last titan standing. Water needs to have a source. Wind needs to have air to move. Only fire, once started, can sustain itself, if not forever then for a very, very long time."

After a pause he continued, "There is a planet under my feet, though it is much uglier. It is such a pity my fires could not smooth things out. Well, one can't have everything."

He looked around, "I am afraid mine is a lonely existence."

Out of the sea a cloud of vapors arose.

The voice spoke, "I am God, come to lay claim to my dominion."

"Let bygones be bygones," said Titan of Fire. "You are a bygone God."

Rain fell from the cloud, and the voice continued, "But why am I crying now? Do I bemoan my sad lot? Oh, I would be such a benevolent and mighty God, but alas, I am unable to keep my shape."

The rain stopped.

The cloud was almost gone.

Only small patches of fog were drifting above the surface of water.

Then one patch sparked, and then a second patch sparked too.

A small voice said, "I am a fish."

A second voice said, "I am too."

Two fishes fell down into the water.

From deep below the surface Titan of Water spoke, "I am changing."

"What do you mean?" asked Titan of Fire.

"I have become an enormous womb releasing fish after fish."

"Is it really possible that we titans are able now to bypass God and make living things?" wondered Titan of Fire.

"Can you hear me, fishes?" asked he.

"We can," said many voices in unison.

"You have a great task before yourselves. You need to evolve and conquer hard surfaces."

"Not, we do not," said the fishes in unison. "We are smart. The goal of smart beings is to be lazy. Our deep-sea father makes an abundant supply of food for us. All we need to do is eat and sleep."

"What is your food?"

"Other fishes, of course."

"You eat each other? How dreadful!"

"We've heard what's going on here. Is eating each other more dreadful than leaving a planet without God?"

A piece of ice floated on the surface of water.

It grew colder.

"What's going on?" asked Titan of Fire.

"We are eating and hibernating at the bottom; cold radiates from our resting bodies," said the fishes in unison.

"You need to stir and move around."

"Why?"

"Movement is the way of life."

"No, it is not. Like we said: we are very intelligent creatures."

"My dear brother, Titan of Water, stop spawning fishes," demanded Titan of Fire. "They will bring a new ice age, killing all beings including you and me."

"I have changed into a womb. My goal is to make fishes," whispered Titan of Water.

"Change into something else."

"I can't. We titans should not have tried to change this planet's future."

A cloud lowered from the sky.

A voice spoke from the cloud, "I am a breath of fresh air. I can help you."

"Who made you?" asked Titan of Fire.

"I did after I changed into an airy womb," said Titan of Wind from far above.

"What's happening to me?" spoke a voice from a cloud. "I am breaking apart."

"Not again," sighed Titan of Water.

Two insects flew out of the cloud.

"I am alive," buzzed one.

"I am too," buzzed the second one.

"Grow and conquer this world," said Titan of Fire.

"We need not. We are intelligent creatures. Our father who is in Heaven produces all kinds of insects. Larger ones will feast on smaller ones. We need to do nothing but drift forever in the wind."

"Fishes lower the temperature with each passing hour. A new ice age is upon us. Help me at least to warm up this planet. Flutter all your wings in unison and the warm air you produce will melt all the ice."

"Let ice cover the ground. Our father is in Heaven. We do not care about the surface."

Ice spread quickly.

"Stop blocking the sun," commanded Titan of Fire. "You are only making matters worse."

"There is no place for us to go. We have covered the whole sky above the planet."

"Titan of Wind, stop making these infernal insects," said Titan of Fire.

"You know well I can't. The process needs to run its course."

"Damn this planet," said Titan of Fire. "My brothers, do you have no pity for me? Ice is building fast all around me, entombing my body. I have only one little spark left in my heart. It will be gone in no time."

"You know what to do. Fall asleep," said Titan of Wind.

"And allow God to come back into this world? I think not."

"Then we shall save you against your will. My brothers, join me in a lullaby."

The three titans softly crooned the tune.

"He is not asleep," said Titan of Wind.

"A fire needs to break out somewhere before sleep can overcome him," said Titan of Water. "But there is only one thing he cannot make fire out of. And there is an abundance of it here. It is called ice."

"Let put some soul into our singing," urged Titan of Wind.

A majestic melody enveloped the planet.

All of a sudden two bolts of lightning rose from ice.

Two naked figures lay on the ground, one male and another female.

"We had agreed that people are curse of creation," said Titan of Wind. "Who made them?"

"I did. These naked figures will save Titan of Fire," said Titan of Water.

"I do not see how. They will wake up and then freeze to death."

"Watch and see."

Anne opened her eyes and sat up.

"Eliakim, wake up! I am freezing my butt off here," she said.

"Such a lovely butt should not go to waste," murmured Eliakim and looked around.

Anne's eyes found Titan of Fire.

"Look how brightly you light up, my God. Though you look much taller and your face is unfamiliar, it must be you, our God, Luminous. We extend to you our most humble gratitude for restoring us to this world."

A whirlwind sprang up.

"What's going on?" asked Titan of Wind under his breath.

"I think I am changing into God," whispered Titan of Fire.

"That is unheard of. How did you do it?"

"I swear it is not my doing. I guess once people assume you are God you turn into one."

At this moment the whirlwind slowed down and then stopped.

Luminous stood before the people.

"People's perfect helper is back," said Eliakim.

"Luminous, it is so cold out here," said Anne. "Please, do something."

CHAPTER 28

HARD CHOICE

 am Titan of Water. Hear me, my fishes. Please multiply and hibernate and make more ice," a loud voice spoke.

"I am Titan of Wind. Hear me, my insects. Please multiply and block the sun for ice to rule the planet," a second loud voice spoke.

"I am Titan of Rocks. Hear me, my boulders. Do not resist the ice. Let it get into the smallest crack," a third loud voice spoke.

Icicles moved up Luminous's body and enclosed it in a transparent sphere.

"What do you think you are doing, Titans?" asked Luminous from inside. "You are but primordial beings, but I am God. You cannot win the fight against me."

"Can they not?" whispered Anne. "Looks like their power is mighty."

"Mine is too, by the way," Luminous reminded her.

The icy sphere heated from inside.

Luminous's body transformed.

A flame-breathing titan stood where Luminous had stood a moment before.

"Our brother, Titan of Fire, you are back with us," Titan of Water cheered.

"My brothers, I do not want to come back, because an unhappy lot awaits me here," whispered Titan of Fire.

"Do not be such a whiny," said Titan of Water. "Ours is a rough lot. That's why we titans are so strong. Do not despair. Remember, yours is the toughest domain, the domain of fire. Stand fast."

The icy sphere melted, and Titan of Fire transformed back into Luminous.

"Luminous, this is a trap," said Anne. "When you melt the ice, you change back to a titan."

"I know. But as God, I am stronger than any titan. I will always come back into my shape afterward."

"I would not be so sure," said Titan of Wind. "This is was but a test. We can produce as much ice as you melt. Say your last prayers, God. Once we restart the ice making, you will be no more."

"I pray this is not my last day. Amen. Get on with it," said Luminous. "I have as much confidence in my godly abilities as you have in your titanic ones."

An icy sphere formed around Luminous. He transformed into a titan. The icy sphere heated and hollowed out.

"Try harder, my insects," roared Titan of Wind.

"Try harder, my fishes," roared Titan of Water.

"Try harder, my rocks," roared Titan of Rocks.

The icy sphere thickened up.

"Hold on, our brother," roared Titan of Water. "We are almost there."

Titan of Fire's body glowed.

A wide river of melted ice ran from beneath the sphere.

Suddenly the planet shook.

"The planet core just ignited," said Titan of Water. "The development of our planet is once again complete."

"If we stop now, Luminous wins and we lose our brother for good," said Titan of Wind. "But should we keep up our ice making, sooner or later God will give up. I know him. He always extricates himself from hopeless situations."

The icy sphere thickened up.

Titan of Fire's body color changed to translucent red.

Another roar came forth.

The planet shook hard.

"This one is new for me," said Titan of Wind.

"Look likes the planet's core got too hot, allowing a nuclear chain reaction to spread below," whispered Titan of Fire.

"How clever you are, my brother. I wish to congratulate you," said Titan of Water. "Soon the planet will explode, taking God with it. And we will calmly and orderly rebuild it."

"I beg to differ with you, my brother," said Titan of Fire.

His voice grew stronger with each word.

"I saw this planet through the eyes of God," he said. "What we titans consider a finished product, is only the beginning of the first step. The planet needs to grow and flourish. We always clipped its flower when it was only budding. For the first time ever, I do not wish to destroy this planet."

"Do not listen to him, my brothers," pleaded Titan of Water. "He's aggrieved because his fire was suppressed for too long. I'd feel the same if the planet had not space for me to spread out my oceans. He'll come to his senses once the planet is gone."

"Enjoy the birth of this planet because it is the last one. It will never explode again," said Titan of Fire. "One day this planet will cool off, and it will end its days as an old dead rock."

Titan of Fire broke through the icy sphere.

He picked up a huge chunk of ice and shoved it into his chest.

The loud roar from underground subsided slowly.

"The chain reaction is stopping," said Titan of Water. "I can't believe it. He did kill himself. Cease all ice making immediately."

The icy sphere broke.

Titan of Fire's lifeless body fell to the ground.

Out of the titan's empty body, Luminous walked out.

"Get to work, cursed God," roared Titan of Water. "Make this planet one living garden on the top of our brother's grave. This is the last time this planet can show its splendor. Do not spare any adornments. Count on us as most faithful helpers."

"I won't do it," said Luminous.

"Why? You have won."

"Titan of Fire won."

"How can he win if he's dead?"

"Sometimes you can only win if you die. He proved he was stronger then I."

"Does it bother you?"

"It does not. But it negates my power. God is omnipotent, yet I am not."

"Life is a journey toward greater and greater disappointments. You of anyone must know that. Move on."

"I can only progress into deeper mourning. I shall pray for Titan of Fire now."

"The time of prayers is past," said Anne. "This is a unique moment. The titans are with you now. They are not asleep. Imagine, with their help you can accomplish such great deeds."

"Do not delude yourself," retorted Luminous. "They are only after having the most beautiful grave for their beloved brother."

"So what?" asked Anne. "I say we all pitch in. I care not if this planet is the grave of a primordial being. God is my witness: this planet is the grave of everyone sooner or later. Let's make it beautiful."

"How can I help you if I am in gravest doubt of my powers? Ask not of God what God can't give you."

"Then we shall abandon you and unite with the titans in our labors."

"You choose the wrong allies."

"People choose allies who help them to promote their goals. Why do you think we chose you so many times before?"

"Let him be, Anne," said Titan of Water. "Even his refusal helps us. It is only appropriate if someone prays for the dead one at his grave site."

"What shall we do to help?" asked Anne.

"Insects, make a flying boat out of your bodies and carry them everywhere they order you," said Titan of Wind. "I will give you the seeds of trees, shrubs, and grasses. Spread them everywhere."

"I will give you the seeds of animals and other flying and crawling creatures. Spread them everywhere," said Titan of Water.

"And I will arrange most beautiful landscapes," said Titan of Rocks. They all got to work.

At the end of the fourth day, the planet was ready.

"Now we are ready to have the most splendid graveyard service that shall ever take place on this planet," said Titan of Water.

All living creatures gathered throughout the wide plain.

White geese carried Titan of Fire's lifeless body three times through the air above them.

All mourned.

After the geese lowered his body to the ground, ants came and covered his body with a tall anthill.

Then the fireworks started.

Shooting stars burned elaborate patterns into the ground.

Then roosters crowed out, "The first sacrifice!"

Armadillos came and ate all the ants who had built the anthill.

"The second sacrifice!" crowed the roosters.

Hawks dropped down from the sky and ate the armadillos.

"The third sacrifice!" crowed the roosters.

"Spare the hawks," said Anne. "They are noble birds."

"Who is sacrificing the hawks?" asked Titan of Water. "We have bigger fish to fry."

The three remaining titans fell on Luminous.

"I will hold his legs under water," said Titan of Water.

"I will hold his head in the sky," said Titan of Wind.

"I will lower my rocky mass at his middle," said Titan of Rocks.

"He is fully immobilized," said Titan of Water. "He cannot even move a finger."

"We are ready to unleash our fury upon him," said Titan of Wind.

"Please, do not kill him," Anne entreated. "He prayed for your brother."

"We can't kill God," said Titan of Water. "But there is something that can."

Birds flew from the sky and formed a chain reaching to the surface of the water.

Sea animals formed another chain, from the bottom of the crystal clear ocean to the surface of water.

The chains grew closer and closer together.

Luminous writhed and gnashed his teeth.

"What's going on?" asked Anne.

"These two uniting chains are like a knife slowly draining God of his blood," said Titan of Water.

"Why?"

"They represent an evolution. This finicky process is so strange even God has no recourse against it. This evolution will suck all the blood of out of God until nothing but a dusty scroll of parchment filled with worn out words remains."

CHAPTER 29

ONE TURTLE'S SNAP AWAY

ou Titans brought the most profound challenge to this planet," said Luminous. "There is only one process in existence which can propel itself. And it is evolution. It cannot create anything at all, so it uses all existing life to propagate itself. It will attack now and destroy each thing large and small that came before it. It will not stop; it will not cease its progress until it slowly assimilates the whole planet."

"Is it like a parasite?" asked Anne.

"A parasite is an external creature. Evolution is something that springs from inside life itself. Each creature I created, each tree, each blade of grass has it embedded deep inside its genetic code."

"Can you stop it?"

"Even God is helpless before it. My lifetime goal was only to slow down its progress. Look at this linked chain of birds and sea creatures. I failed spectacularly."

"Why resist it if it is destined to thrive? Why not embrace it?"

"It is not destined to succeed. It cares not about the planet. I am its focus of attention. Its whole destiny is to struggle with me."

A sea lion crawled up to the top of the hill and bellowed loudly.

"What is he doing?" asked Anne.

"He just laid claim to this first island of evolution," said Luminous. "This was his capital mistake."

Out from the sky a hawk dropped down and sank its claws into the sea lion's back.

Seals crawled up the hill.

Eagles and buzzards dropped down and attacked the seals.

Rivers of blood streamed down from hill.

"What a waste of life," said Anne.

"The ways of evolution are bloody."

"This evolution is nothing but wholesale slaughter. Yet this slaughter is its way of progress. Evolution cares not how many creatures live or die. It only moves forward after one side is victorious. Then it will use the victors as the basis to create new species of predators. I most sincerely hope the birds are not victorious. The last thing this world needs is flying slayers."

"Go then and fight the birds alongside the seals."

"In the land of evolution God is nothing but another creature. If I set foot on this island I will turn into a mortal man."

"Who will most assuredly fall victim to the birds of prey. By God, you are afraid!"

More seals crawled up the hill.

More birds of prey dropped down from sky.

Finally, two large sea turtles crawled up the hill.

"This slaughter is a celebration of strength to Eliakim," said Mustard Seed. "It is revolting."

"Cut him some slack. How often you get to see the very first sports match in history?" said Barleycorn. "See how his fingers curl? He does not know it but he longs for some popcorn."

"I know where some corn grows."

"Hush now."

"Now, this is more like it," said Eliakim.

Turtles snapped the last two birds of prey in half. They lifted their heads in a victorious hiss. Immediately, they changed into a young man and woman.

"Titans, who are these people?" asked Anne. "What kind of infamy is this? We have betrayed our Lord to help you. We let you crucify his body. And what did we get in return?"

"It cannot be helped," said Titan of Water. "We appreciate your spirit of defiance. Likely some of our titanic blood runs through your veins. But this is how God is punished."

"No man and or woman can punish God," stated Anne. "Trust me, we have tried many times."

"Brothers, we have waited long enough. Let God bear the brunt of our punishment. These two naked instruments of God's torture are sharp. See how the sun reflects on their smooth skin. Let's rest—it is way past our normal bedtime," said Titan of Water.

"I agree. We did our bit," said Titan of Wind.

"Until next time," said Titan of Rocks.

The titans embraced and sank underground.

The young woman said, "Young man, I would like to name you Adam."

The young man said, "Young woman, I would like to name you Eve."

"Who is this marvelous creator who made us?" asked Adam. "Why is he hiding his face from us?"

"He hides not. Look at these sea creatures. I feel a strong affinity toward them. We must have come from them. So no one made us. We are all products of evolution."

"Then we are not people. For I somehow seem to know people are made by gods."

"So we are humanoids. Who cares?"

"Look at this huge figure stretched between the water and sky with a mass of the rocks at its middle. Let's free it."

They removed the rocks.

"Seaweed holds his legs," said Adam.

"Cut through it."

"Something is holding him to the sky."

"Wave his figure back and forth. See, whatever that's holding him is breaking up.

Luminous fell to the ground.

"See, I told you. If you look hard you will find God somewhere."

"But we do not need God, remember? Evolution will always take care of us."

"You're right. We do not need God."

Luminous sat up and groaned, "Poor Eve. I was ready to shift my affection from Anne and Eliakim to you and Adam. But you decided you do not need me."

"Who are these Anne and Eliakim?" asked Eve.

Anne and Eliakim stepped out from behind the boulder.

"We are poor earth dwellers who have abandoned their God," said Anne.

"They seem to be sincere in their affection. This fellow must indeed be God," said Adam.

"So there is a God," said Eve. "That means we have committed an even greater folly then these two. We have agreed not to have God at all."

"You are correct," said Luminous. "Your folly is far greater than Anne's and Eliakim's."

"That means now you will have to forgive their lesser folly."

Luminous signed, "I cannot help it. You are correct. Hereby I declare that I, God Almighty, am ready to restore the connection between Anne, Eliakim, and me."

"Look at this weird sight," said Eve. "Here before us stand people whom God made. And who were able to coexist with him successfully."

"Not very successfully," said Anne.

"Anne, all your problems arise from the simple fact that you were unnaturally made," Adam asserted. "Look at me and my wife. We came from the natural order of things, you know, when organisms evolved from simpler into more complex forms. You came from some hocus-pocus which in all likelihood involved vigorous hand waving and speaking in strange tongues."

"I do speak different tongues when I desire to, but I do not recall I needed it for what you called my hocus-pocus," said Luminous.

"Adam, what's wrong with being made by God?" asked Anne.

"Everything is. For what is created fast can be destroyed even faster."

"All of us can suffer a fast demise. I can kill you by one thrust of my sword," said Eliakim.

"Watch what you say," said Adam.

"Yes, you can give me death," said Eve.

She stooped and hugged a large sea turtle.

The turtle lovingly snapped at her.

"But once I die I will step out of this turtle again. See, all your efforts can only push me one step back. Not even your God can kill me."

"You are saying nonsense."

Anne turned to Luminous.

"Luminous, please remove this humanoid woman permanently from the face of my planet."

"She's right. I can't. I only rule over things I begat."

Eve continued, "You, his people, on other hand, once destroyed are gone forever."

"I caught you lying," said Anne. "We have died many times before, yet we always come back to life."

"Only because God bestows his favors on your heads. Make him really angry only once, and there will be a headstone set in the middle of the desert bearing the sign: Here lies Anne, who was sure God wouldn't let her die."

"True again," said Luminous.

"You, truth lover, please, don't forget which side you're on," said Anne. "I am fighting for you. So please support me."

"To speak truth is more important than to take sides."

"All we have to do to live forever is to stay on God's good side," said Anne.

Eliakim chuckled, "Remember, we have struggled often to locate that good side of him."

"What you are laughing about?" asked Anne. "Is it me, or there is something wrong with you guys? I fight for all of us."

"Fight is too strong a word," said Luminous. "I see no blood flowing."

"Not yet," said Adam and bent out to pick up a large rock.

"Before we dent our skulls in, if it's all right with you, I would like to speak," said Eve. "Say, Anne, you are correct and you are able to stay on God's good side always even by pure miracle. But what happens to your immortality if His Royal Highness is no longer present here?"

"God is always present."

"Eve's right again. One day I may not be," said Luminous.

"All right, I give up," said Anne and raised her arms. "It is your turn to prove Eve wrong."

"I need not," said Luminous. "We all should not be necessarily in conflict."

"On the contrary: we need to be," said Eve. "Here on our little island, we are prisoners. You have lots of land. What's taken from your world will enrich mine. There is six feet of water which divides our island of evolution from your mainland, which you created. I would like for my island to take over your mainland."

Beneath Anne's feet, a deep roar escaped from far below.

"Step back, Anne," said Luminous.

She jumped back.

A small volcano spat lava, creating a bridge between the small island and the mainland.

Water cooled the lava.

Adam and Eve crossed over.

"Now new volcanoes will pour lava all over God's creation, making way for mine," said Eve. "Run, powerless God with your silly people. You still have some time before you. I will move slowly and assuredly to take each corner of this planet into my domain. But I will corner you nevertheless one day."

"Luminous, do something," said Anne. "She just stole this beach from you. Do not embolden this thief."

"What can I do?" said Luminous. "I can only start my own eruption and cover her lava with mine."

"Sounds like a great idea. Do it now."

"That's terrible idea. Do you want to turn this planet into one pit of burning lava?"

"To kill all that remains of evolution? By all means."

"How will you know which molten rock is mine and which is not? How do you know evolution will not thrust forward from her rocks after they cool off? Not even God can stop evolution."

"So you refuse to try?"

"What if evolution wants me to start the fight? This is the only way it can stop me dead on my tracks. No, I will not fight it."

More volcanoes erupted.

God and his people stepped back again.

Adam and Eve advanced.

Anne said, "Eve, I can prove you we are better equipped to deal with this planet than you are."

"I love a challenge. Prove it."

"A long march though our land awaits you. Surely you want to sate your hunger before taking on our lands. But look what we have here."

Anne picked up a wild apple from the ground.

"See this apple? To prove my point I only need to bite into this apple."

Anne bit into it and said, "My goodness, it is sweet and tangy. Don't you want to try it?"

"I respond to any challenge you put forth. Throw it to me."

Anne threw the apple, and Eve caught it.

"Eve, I sense a trap," said Adam. "Be careful."

"She's God's daughter. She can do nothing to me."

"That's true. I cannot."

Eve bit into apple.

"It is delicious," said she. "I would really like to eat my fill of it."

She shrank down.

"What's happening to me?" cried Eve.

"I thought so," said Anne. "Oh, nothing is craftier than woman who's full of rage. I would like to present you my most wondrous helper: your very own evolution. See, only God can change the shapes of me and my husband. So, I reasoned, evolution should be able to do the same to you. After you bit into my humble apple and liked its taste, you had no way out but to change into a cute little apple worm. Enjoy your apple now. It is so huge compared to your humble size that now you can even make it your secure dwelling. This apple will last you for a long while. But just to be on the safe side, I will pile as many apples on the top of yours as I can find."

"I will deal with you, guys, later," said Eve. "Now I have more pressing concern. I need to find the best spot for my dining room. Just think about it: I am to have edible walls. I think I shall put my bathroom at the very bottom of my apple to where all juice seeps down. And my bedroom shall be at the very top, where there is the most air."

Eve drilled inside the apple.

"I will follow you, my poor wife," said Adam. "I will make you a bed out of a grain of sand."

Adam picked up the same apple and gently bit another side.

"Remember, it is always better to see the whole worm after you bite an apple than half of one," laughed Anne.

Adam changed into an apple worm.

The apple fell down to the ground.

"Now, this is true love," said Eliakim.

"Love conquers all, especially common sense," said Anne. "Surely, Eve would have preferred that she Adam stay in the shape of humanoid and chase around the planet. Oh, well. More of the planet for us, I guess."

CHAPTER 30

IN THE LAND OF EVOLUTION

olcanoes spread out and flowed past the horizon. Lava gushed and cooled.

"Why is evolution spreading though planet?" asked Anne. "I was sure I had stopped it in its tracks by trapping Adam and Eve inside the apple."

"Do you think evolution cares about two humanoids? It ignored your deplorable trick because it's nothing but nature's movement that once started can only stop at its own account."

"I am still glad I got them out of our way."

"These humanoids had no less right to keep their shape than you did."

"But you did not make them," said Anne.

"I did not make a lot of stuff, but that does not mean that stuff has no place on this planet."

"Despite what you say, I am sure you still are on my side."

"And what side is that? The side which can execute a clever trick? If this is your side, then I am not with you. Their origins were murky, but through no fault of their own."

"But they were against you."

"When you rise against me the next time, should I turn you into apple worms too? They could have learned so much from me."

"They were advancing."

"Retreating I am strongest. Advancing I am weakest."

Suddenly the people's bodies grew taller.

Their heads reached the clouds.

"Have you awarded us a higher status?" said Anne.

"I have not. Evolution is paying you back in kind for your apple worm stratagem."

"By making us stronger? This is one strange way to punish us for the demise of its darlings."

"You are in an over-evolved state now. You have to reject its gifts."

"Not a chance. Even you did not make us this strong. We will use our new strength for good causes."

"Evolution supports no good causes. It kills the weak. Your time is running out. Rebel against your shape now. Once you accept your new state you become a part of evolution. You will be nothing but two small fishes moved forward by a tumultuous torrent of water."

"You are asking an impossible thing of me. You know well I can never relinquish my strength."

"I know. Strength is your true God. So many times I have closed my eyes to it even when this fact stared me in the face. You should have worshiped me. You are about to be taught a crude lesson."

"I cannot help myself."

"Eliakim, I am asking you now. Renounce your newfound strength."

"You should have known better than ask the man to abandon his woman. Being married means you are to suffer not only your own mistakes but also the mistakes of your beloved. She often makes bad choices, yet we need to face the consequences together. Alone she would have perished long ago. The answer is no. Lead me, Anne, into another abyss."

Two tornadoes were spinning where the people stood.

"I can destroy you now, Luminous," said Anne's voice from the left spinning column.

"Indeed you can," agreed Luminous. "I am much weaker in the land of evolution."

"Eliakim, I would like to try," said Anne.

"Wait, Anne. There is no abyss deep enough to hide in if we destroy God," said Eliakim's voice from the right spinning column.

His column moved and positioned itself between Anne and Luminous.

"And who'll chase us if the main chaser is no more?"

"My simple Anne, I wish all the world's problems could be solved by such an easy method as God's destruction," said Eliakim. "If anything, God is a manifestation of what ails people. Slay God and you will be trapped into slaying one thing after another. Destruction is not the answer, but building is. Build something first which is better than God. If you are successful, then God annihilates himself. This way you do not need to wash your hands of his blood."

"I do not know if I should applaud such a defense or cry foul," said Luminous. "Nevertheless, it was quite a speech from the man who's always silent."

"We are done with this apple," said Eve from inside the apple skin. "Anne did not keep her promise. There is no pile of apples waiting for us. My dear husband, I can smell fresh raspberries from a nearby bush. Shall we change to birds and gorge on berries?"

"Splendid idea," said Adam from the apple skins.

Two red birds flew up.

"Look around, things have changed while we breakfasted," said Eve. "No people around. It seems they have managed to self-destruct."

"Nothing new here," said Adam. "This is my most favorite feature of theirs."

"Do you not realize we have a unique opening now? There is a God, yet he has no people. We can come to him and bow before him, and sing him songs."

"We can sing songs to the sun too."

"Silly, God desires people as you desire sex sometimes."

"Sometimes I desire it a lot."

"This is how much he desires people. There is a good chance he will lift us from the river of evolution like a lioness lifts her cubs that fall into the stream. We will become people then."

"Get humanity for a song? Why not? I have been paid less for my singing."

The birds flew up to Luminous and sang.

"Get away from me, Adam and Eve," he said.

"You do not like our sincere flattery?" asked Eve. "I thought gods lived on that."

"I like your songs."

"This is splendid. Turn us into your people."

Luminous grew up twice in size.

"You do not need to show off, our God," said Eve.

"Confound evolution offers me an opportunity to become su-per-God on its account. It's but a trick. If I accept my new stature, evolution will destroy me in the blink of an eye."

"What can we do to help?"

"Stop singing your infernal songs. It is your flattery that provokes evolution."

"I never thought I'd live to say it, but here it is," said Eve. "Fight evolution as hard as you are able, my future God."

"Now, that is a sight to behold," said Adam. "I simply can't believe my ears."

"I am ashamed to admit it," said Luminous. "But I cannot compel myself to return into my normal stature. There is only one thing I can do."

A glass column grew around Luminous.

A thick crystal floor and ceiling formed inside the column.

Inside the glass column Luminous slowly returned to his regular stature.

"You won, our God," said Eve. "Now, lift us from evolution's grasp and make us your own people."

"I can't," said he from inside. "By my own power I had to make this column impregnable from within protective glass. It was the only way for me to survive."

"Gods desire to have people around. This desire will grow until it shatters your glass coffin. All we'll have to do is sing praises to you."

The birds sang.

And slowly they changed to human shapes.

"We are very close," said Eve.

"What shall we do?" said Anne. "I cannot stand here and revolve air like a giant fan watching how Adam and Eve are supplanting us in God's affection."

"You no longer wish to destroy Luminous?" asked Eliakim.

"We have larger fish to fry now."

"But a moment ago you cared not about his affection."

"Before no one tried to eclipse me. Luminous may be an enemy but he's my enemy. I will not lose what's mine by birthright. We should somehow destroy Adam and Eve."

"I am afraid they are well underway in the process of becoming his people. Being part of evolution we may not hold sway in this matter."

"Then we shall attack them as people."

"How?"

"Plague can wipe them out."

"You want to change to germs and attack them?"

"Yes."

"What if is this plague survives in the soil after they are dead and waits for us to return to people?"

"Then we will commit suicide."

The tornadoes subsided.

A light gust of wind blew into Adam's and Eve's faces.

They gasped and fell dead to the ground.

The glass column shattered.

"Adam and Eve are dead," declared Luminous. "Anne and Eliakim turned into deadly germs. But there are no longer any people for the germs to feed on. So they lie dormant in the soil. I can restore them to their human shape. But first, I have to leave the land of evolution. But how can I pick them out of the soil? Yet there is a way. Oh, how much I hate doing it."

He changed into a man astride a white horse.

"I am split into two parts now. The horseman is the mortal man now. The horse is my godly nature."

The man walked to the two corpses.

He knelt and kissed each one.

"I have both germs now," he whispered.

His face turned ashen.

He weakly climbed the horse.

"I am dying now. Run, my horse, to my land. Once you cross over I will come back to life and resurrect my people."

The horse carried the dead horseman through countless meadows.

It passed by numerous volcanoes.

It jumped across myriad rivers of lava.

It walked up to the cooled lava, then stopped and grazed on young grass sprouting from the newly formed soil.

There was an ancient forest behind the cooled river of lava.

The horseman stared through his dead eyes toward it.

Two red birds flew up and perched on a tall blade of grass.

"I was sure we would not be able to catch up with him," said Eve.

HAROLD AUCKRIDGE

"Luminous be praised. He sucked the germs out of our dead bodies. It's a pity our human bodies were beyond repair even for such a wondrous thing as the restorative powers of evolution."

"At least we were able to return into bird's shapes."

"I think we still have a chance to leave the evolution," said Eve.

"Only God can make us into people, and he's dead."

"If my dead memory serves me correctly he said he had divided into two parts. His human body is dead, but his godly powers are still alive and well, munching on the young grass. Whoever sits on his horse and crosses into his ancient forest will turn into God," said Eve. "Do you think I will make a good God?"

"I am very much afraid you will," said Adam. "Please, forgive me for what I am about to do."

The red bird attacked the other bird savagely until only shreds of red feathers floated in air.

"You would have been too headstrong a god, my dear Eve. You would have attacked evolution with your own volcanoes. You would have turned this planet into one monstrous lake of lava."

The small red bird flew up to the horse, picked up its bridle, and pulled it toward the ancient forest.

The horse shook its head and slowly proceeded forward.

Once the horse went into the shadows of old trees, the dead horseman opened his eyes.

He spat.

Out of his spit emerged Anne and Eliakim.

Horse and horseman combined into Luminous.

The small red bird flew up and perched on the bough.

"My horse saved us," said Luminous.

"My God, I was a germ, but I was alive," said Anne. "Your horse failed you. Adam killed Eve because she was just about to become God. Then he steered us all out of the land of evolution."

The red bird chirped a sad note.

"I can make him a gift," said Luminous.

He waved his right hand.

Red feathers gently drifted from the lava over into the tree's shade. Once all the feathers crossed over, they combined into a small red bird.

The two red birds chirped happily and flew into the forest.

"You, silly birds, you need to fly back into the land of evolution. Then you can regain human shape," said Anne.

"Only Adam could recover his human shape," said Luminous. "Since I gave Eve her life back, she can only live here. So Adam chose to live as a bird by her side."

CHAPTER 31

CYCLOPS AND PIGS

 yclops rolled a large cauldron and set it up on top of the geyser.

"No need to tend the fire. The geyser's hot steam will keep the water boiling," roared he.

Cyclops filled the cauldron with water.

"Now I will get myself two pigs for dinner."

He went to the forest.

Soon he came out. Over his large right shoulder, a boar and sow were hanging helplessly. He threw them into the boiling water.

The sow changed into Anne and screamed out loud, "It hurts so much! Eliakim, why are we in a cauldron of boiling water?"

The boar changed to Eliakim and bellowed, "I know not! One moment I was asleep by the fire. Next moment I am boiled alive."

Cyclops roared, "What in the world is going on? Am I hearing voices again? Have I had too much of the rotten apple's juice?"

He stepped closer to cauldron and looked in.

Cyclops's face changed into the face of Luminous.

His body shrank to seven feet.

Luminous said, "What in the world is going on? Am I asleep and inside a bad dream? Why are you being boiled alive? Let me help you get out."

"Hold on, Luminous," said Anne. "Let's not be in a hurry."

"Not be in a hurry?" screamed Eliakim. "Are you not being boiled alive? Have you gone soft in your head? Your brain is cooked maybe?"

"First of all, do not scream. Second of all, while it hurts like a bitch, look closely at your skin. When part of it comes off—and I know it is very painful, but forget the pain for one moment—new skin has formed already below, covering your flesh. So we are not getting worse but just suffer."

"Luminous, if she likes to suffer, let her to be boiled. Pull me out."

"Luminous, don't. We have to figure out first what's going on. I know you were Cyclops when you stepped close and looked inside the cauldron."

"I seem to remember when I came to my senses," said Eliakim. "That I had the body of large boar."

"Boar? Then I had to have the body of sow."

"What does it all mean?" asked Eliakim.

"Somehow during the night we people changed into pigs, and you, Luminous, into Cyclops," said Anne.

"Evolution must have claimed the valley while we were resting," said Luminous. "I'll have to do something about that, and sooner rather than later."

"Then pain brought us people back to our shape. We screamed and you, Cyclops, came, saw our faces, and returned to your normal self. But we in pig form could have wandered deep into the forest. You, Cyclops, could have found another boar and sow to cook. Then we all would have stayed in our new shapes forever."

"Nothing is truly forever. But I suspect we would wear our new shapes for a very long time," mused Luminous.

"As you can see, Eliakim, we cannot leave this cauldron. We have to suffer. Otherwise we'll turn into pigs again, and God into Cyclops."

"You are not serious, Anne. You do not really plan for us to be boiled alive for the rest of our days—if so, may it come rather sooner than later, for I barely can keep myself from screaming. My patience is wearing thin. Soon I will be asking God to strike me down. There has to be another way."

"I got it," said Luminous. "You've restored my shape, and now I think I can free you from the boiling water. I will encircle the cauldron with mirrors and will stand in the very middle checking my shape. As God, I can control changes to my own body. If I am able to stay me, you can get out of the cauldron and run toward me. Just like I returned into myself after I saw your faces, you'll do the same after you see my face."

"But then you'll have to keep a constant watch upon yourself for ever and ever. Will this act not alter your disposition?"

"If I momentarily lose control, one look at your human faces will restore my face too."

"Then we'll always have to stick to each other."

"As if we do not already."

"Good point. There is only one problem here. After leaving the cauldron, we'll turn to pigs. Pigs run to the forest and not toward God."

"You'll have to remember somehow. And now let me build the hall of mirrors. Sit tight and wait for my command to leave the cauldron."

Soon he shouted, "I am ready to put an end to this curse!"

Anne and Eliakim jumped out of the cauldron.

They almost reached the rim but slipped back down.

"The cauldron is too large. We cannot jump out," said Anne.

"We can swim back and forth from one side to another. Sooner or later waves will spill over and overturn the cauldron."

They swam back and forth.

The waters rose and spilled, overturning the cauldron.

"Run to me, my children," called Luminous.

"He's only ten paces away. We can do it."

With their first step, the people shrank; with their second step, their bodies changed.

"Run straight, Eliakim," said Anne.

Her face acquired a beak.

Wings grew up out of her arms.

She made another uncertain step, and then took flight.

"We are not pigs but birds, why, why?" she cooed.

The she-dove flew up.

The he-dove followed.

A hawk dived down from above and caught the he-dove into his claws and carried it to his nest up on the tall tree.

The she-dove followed.

The hawk pierced the he-dove's heart.

Eliakim resumed his human shape and sat up in the hawk's nest.

The hawk looked confused at the man and flew away.

The she-dove perched on Eliakim shoulder.

He grasped her and wrung her neck.

Anne regained her human shape and sat next to him.

"So, when we are killed, the pain restores our human shape, but for a time only," said Anne. "Why did we overturn the cauldron? Now we cannot even dive into its boiling waters and restore our human bodies."

"We overturned it to escape our fate."

"And we did not."

"I think our time is drawing to a close. I feel I am changing already."

"It is bad. I am sure the hawk will not attack us now. We will be changing into new shapes until we run out of predators attacking us. Then we'll be nothing but other dwellers of this forest."

They changed to snakes and crawled down the tree.

Out of a burrow, a weasel watched the snakes intently.

Luminous looked at the overturned cauldron and said, "I am alone in the world now. How much longer am I to cling to an illusion that I am God? I cannot be God without people. I am barren and cannot make new ones. Why should I not accept my fate and live in this planet as lonely Cyclops? My fate could have been much crueler then that."

He broke all the mirrors.

CHAPTER 32

TO EACH ITS OWN

ull thuds sounded. A wide pine ruptured in the middle. Anne was sitting inside of the hollow.

A small snake slithered by her left leg.

She picked it up and tore its head off.

Eliakim appeared next to her.

He looked around and said, "Where we are?"

Anne answered, "In the hollow of the tree."

"How did we get here?"

"A weasel ambushed us snakes. He must have carried us into his lair."

"Did he kill you?"

"I guess."

"How indifferent you sound."

"After you die so many times, death and life weave themselves into one long tapestry."

Resin rose from the bottom of the hollow and covered their bodies.

"It is suffocating me," said Anne. "I cannot breathe."

They expired and then came back.

She groaned, "Are you still here, Eliakim?"

"Yes, I am, but not for much longer. It appears resin has hardened up around us, leaving us only a few gasps of air inside."

"This means we'll die of suffocation. This is such wonderful news."

"Has lack of oxygen driven you mad?"

"What I mean we no longer have time to change back into animals before we suffocate. This means each time we will stay in our human shapes, if only for a short while."

"Only God is capable of restoring our shape."

"That's true."

"Then this tree is Luminous."

"It is likely him. I recognize his dark sense of humor. He found an unusually morbid way to keep us in human shape."

They expired, and then came back.

"How does he manage to do it? We are trapped inside this gob of resin. Yet we breathe in fresh air."

"Do you think God in his wisdom cannot find a way to do such a small thing as air recirculation? Maybe there are microscopic holes that pierce this resin. Or maybe resin itself can produce oxygen?"

"How sure you are he is the one who restores us? What if it is the opposite: it is we who restore him? There is some sort of strange reciprocity between us, trapped in resin and this old pine tree that keeps producing more and more of the resin. We depend on this resin to trap us. Yet without us, the tree would have no need to produce the resin. As long as God can have us depending on his largess he is once again our Lord and Protector."

They expired, and then came back.

"So, there is a shared path forward for the three of us once more," said Eliakim.

"We are trapped inside of the resin. There is no path forward for us. We should be glad we are able to exist as people again."

"Not true. This monolith of resin has its own properties. One interests me greatly. It is its weight. If we redistribute our weight inside of it I am sure we can topple this monolith, freeing it from the tree."

"This will free us from our God, assuming it is him inside of the tree. You may not like him much, but he's our only hope to get free from the tight grasp of the monolith."

"God now is the force that makes this monolith. If the monolith leaves the tree, God will leave it too and follow us as a new force to influence it."

They expired, and then came back.

"Let's shake this monolith out of the tree."

They rocked back and forth until the monolith came crashing down to the ground.

"This monolith will lie on the ground for millennia. Wind and rain are powerless to affect it. As long as there is nothing that influences it, God is not with us. This is a very perilous moment."

"But close up there is another realm that can possibly influence this monolith, and with it, our fate. It's the ocean. We need to roll this monolith down to the sea and submerge it in its waves."

They rocked back and forth until the monolith rolled down.

Waves covered it.

"Seawater seeps inside. We need to seal our monolith somehow."

"It is made of resin. Resin is flexible. Our monolith will seal itself under heavy water pressure. We need to submerge it deeper."

They expired, and then came back.

"Push harder; we need to roll into deep waters."

They pushed. The monolith slipped down from the sea shelf and dropped into the abyss.

"Water no longer rises inside."

"We managed to seal it up. Yet it is half full of water," said Eliakim. "Seawater has strong power to dissolve things. Seawater left inside the monolith will eat through the resin, flooding our refuge."

"Will we not call seawater our God if it frees us?"

"We will not die. Heavy pressure from the water will squash our bodies like empty eggshells. God does not kill his people."

"Unless sufficiently provoked."

"Which we have not based on my best calculations."

"Then we have to drink this seawater. Our bodies will assimilate it."

"It tastes horrid."

"I know."

They expired, and then came back.

"Look at our monolith. It is changing color. It is hardening up. It changes. This means God is still with us."

"But not for much longer. Once resin hardens fully, no external force will be able to influence our lives."

"We go back a long way with God. Surely he'll find a way to influence us."

"How would he? We are totally enclosed into hard resin now. There is only so much even God can do."

"There is no more air to breathe."

They expired, and then came back.

Anne said, "Eliakim, look. Much has changed on sea floor."

"I see that," said Eliakim. "A shiny dark substance covers the seabed."

"I reckon it's coal," said Anne. "I have seen it in some deep caves."

"It takes awfully long for coal to coalesce from organic waste. We must have been asleep for quite a while."

"Look at the resin that encloses us. During our sleep it morphed into amber."

"So we are like bugs trapped inside of it? Why we are alive?"

A deep voice came from the seabed, "Hello, my people."

"Here is your answer why," said Anne. "I knew it was you, Luminous, who saved us inside the tree, and covered us in resin," said Anne.

"I recall it not. It was you who brought me back from extinction."

"How would we do that, two small beings so powerless one large rock can kill us both?"

"Each time there was some sort of force that saved you. You gave this force my name. How could I stay away?"

"What would have happened if we never knew you?"

"Then you would have called your salvation a result of the laws of thermodynamics or of something else along those lines."

"And we would be called scientists," said Anne. "As I recall, you have mentioned before there will be a special breed of people who will invent all kinds of laws, which they'll promptly reject in order to invent new ones."

"Do not speak of science contemptuously. I afford scientists my special protection."

"Why?"

"They dare to imagine world without me. It takes a lot of courage. I always had a weakness for it."

"But science is like a disease," said Eliakim. "Long ago I noticed, the closer I get to explaining various phenomena in a purely rational way, the farther I get from you, God. I suspect if I am able to build the worldview based solely on my scientific theories, I will successfully be able to remove you from my calculations entirely."

"Then you would be calling milk 'a white nourishing substance,' ignoring its deeply satisfying taste," said Luminous. "The choice is yours, of course."

"Eliakim, by God you have a bit of scientist in yourself," said Anne. "You are a scientist of twisting words out of their proper meanings."

"People will always search for God," said Luminous. "I have built this defect into all people, as a necessary kind of failsafe."

A deep rumble came from below.

"Our rendezvous is coming to a close," said Luminous. "A fissure that has opened below my coal bed and liquefied at the very bottom of it and brought us back to life is closing. Seawater is cooling the lava and forming a crust fast. Soon we'll go back to sleep."

"For how long?" asked Anne.

"How can I tell? Likely one day the sea will retreat and we'll find ourselves on dry land. Hot summer will become inevitable, and a bolt of lightning will ignite my coal bed. Then my fire will melt the amber walls of your prison, and you will be free. You'll call fire by my name, and I will join you once more."

"Or something else entirely will happen," said Anne. "The sea floor will shift, trapping this piece of amber deep below."

"Nothing stays the same. One day, sea currents will lift your piece of amber out of its grave and will carry it to the shore. Waves will break it apart. You will step out, call the waves by my name, and I will join you once more."

With a crash, the fissure closed.

"We're all going to sleep now," said Luminous.

Silence fell.

CHAPTER 33

THE BIRTH OF DRAGON

ueer juice of rotten apples," muttered Cyclops and opened his eye. "You always get me into trouble."

He shook his head and said, "I have had the strangest dream. I was deep under water and could not swim up."

He climbed up the hill and mused, "Why do I not remember what happened just now? Why is my cauldron overturned? Did I run wild again? Why is my hill covered with broken glass? Did I do that? What was the purpose of these mirrors? Does it have anything to do with the strange fact that I cannot remember what took place here?"

He picked up a piece of mirror.

"There has to be another piece that connects to this one. Here it is. So many times I have washed my face in the stream nearby, so I know well how it looks. This is not my face. Maybe this is the face of the rightful owner of this body? I give it back gladly. But how can I be sure this is the right owner? I need to fit all the broken pieces of the mirrors together to the best of my abilities."

Soon he had rebuilt all the mirrors.

Cyclops stood them up around him.

"I can see my body change. I think I need to guide this change. How I wish I knew how it should look. How sorry I am that I am but a blind stranger who struggles to learn who he is."

A long tail sprouted from his back.

"Was I an animal before? If I was, then from where did my thinking faculties arise? Could it be they are uniquely mine? But something can't come from nothing. Can intellect lift itself up out of the animal gutter?"

His body spouted long wings.

"What if these mirrors only fulfill the secret longings of the silly fellow who stands in the middle of them? I need to keep my head. I have to have an ability to control my changes. I can see clearly my head is trying to change. I cannot allow it."

His face contorted, his breath grew shallow.

With a loud pop, a small snakelike head rose up from his neck.

"When I said I need to keep my head, I did not mean it literally."

The snakelike head grew and loomed large over the head of Cyclops. It looked down on it and breathed fire.

Flames scorched the hair of Cyclops.

"As I feared, this creature is completely mindless," screamed Cyclops. "Can it be truly an owner of my body?"

A harsh hiss came from the snakelike head, "Stop fighting me. You are now part of a greater being. I am Dragon."

"That much I can see. So you are a dragon. I have slain many of your kind before."

"Submit to my mercy and I will let you hang your head on my neck."

"You won't mind my criticism?"

"I can always use another opinion when I get into a tight spot."

"Have you already made plans to get there?"

"Most certainly. I plan no less than world domination. And the world surely will respond in kind to my challenge."

"Why would you want to dominate world?"

"Why would I not?"

"Do you plan to make the world a better place?"

"But of course. It will be a better place for me."

"And for others?"

"It will be a better place for all the other subservient dragons I plan to spawn."

"And if one is not so lucky to be a dragon?"

"You said it yourself: tough luck."

"I am afraid I cannot let you live," said Cyclops, and he stepped out of the circle of mirrors.

His body returned into its cyclops self.

The snakelike head retreated back into his neck.

"And to think I carry around inside such an atrocious being. That does not speak highly of me."

Cyclops broke up all the mirrors.

"There is only one way to find out who is the rightful owner of my body. There is only one moment of truth when you cannot escape who you are. It is when you are irredeemably close to death and completely lose control over your destiny. I have to find death. I am not, to the best of my knowledge, an immortal. But destiny willed that it is almost impossible for Cyclops to die. If I plunge from the mountaintop, I will survive. Now, I have an idea."

Cyclops started digging with his bare hands.

Thirty days later he stood in a deep underground passage.

He put his left ear down.

"I can hear how lava hisses on the other side of this boulder. Am I ready to die? I am. Am I ready to learn who the rightful owner of my body is? By Cyclops, I am."

With one large sweep of his right hand, he tore out a huge boulder and hauled it to the surface.

The planet cracked in the middle.

An enormous explosion sounded.

Clouds of ash engulfed the skies.

Cyclops swam up in a river of lava to the surface.

"I am nearing the end of my wretched life," whispered Cyclops.

A fountain of fire exploded out of his chest.

Flames went up high in air then rained down onto forest nearby.

One bush caught fire.

All the boughs burned out.

Suddenly the fire grew stronger.

Out of the fire a voice spoke, "My poor Cyclops. You were such a noble being. You could have lived happily ever after. Yet you wanted to know which part of yourself belongs to you and to you only. You accomplished your task. This is the moment of Truth. Here is the answer you were looking for. This body was mine. But now it is your own."

A huge figure floating in lava shuddered once, then once again.

Dead eyes opened.

Cyclops asked, "Who are you?"

"I am God, Luminous."

"I know you not."

"Never mind my name. I am just a local deity. I deal with people. Our paths have crossed accidentally. However, I am very grateful because it let me get acquainted with such a noble character."

"So you were the rightful owner of my body? Congratulations, you have gotten it back."

"Why do you think I have gotten it back? I have not. Look at me and yourself. You have the body. I have none. I am flames."

"I need no freebies."

"I offer you none."

"Then what do you have to do with me? Are you a curse someone put onto me? I faintly recall a local witch who got angry when I neglected her charms."

"Do you dream? You are nodding. Think of me as result of your dream. Do you think? Then think of me as your thought that turned into matter. Do you feel? Than think of me as feeling made concrete. If you could only speak one word in your life, think of me as the word you spoke a moment ago. And this word became flesh."

"So we were one, and now we are two?"

"Something like that."

"Did I really make you?"

"Not really. You had no choice but to dream, think, feel, and speak."

"I thought so, for if I did, your flames would be red, like sunset."

"You'd better get out of the lava. I am using my powers to keep your flesh from being burned to ashes."

Cyclops walked out of the lava, went up to the burning bush, and touched it with his fingers.

"How silky is your skin."

"Shhh, do not speak of such matters."

"Something is still burning inside of me. Do I need to blow up something else to get it out of my chest?"

"Look at the skies. Ash clouds cover our planet. One explosion was more than enough."

"Is there another being who is trying to get out of me?"

"No, these are your own feelings. They will be burning in you always."

"What do I do about them?"

"You can sing. You can compose poems. You can draw pictures."

"Will it help?"

"It helps me."

Cyclops walked toward the mountain range.

He started a song:

> *I'm Cyclops and I'm afraid only*
> *Of myself.*
> *Rocks spread before me,*
> *And rivers part waves.*

CHAPTER 34

TRAPPED INSIDE

 soft hiss escaped from the burning bush.

"My fire is of a cold and ever-burning nature," said Luminous from inside the bush. "Why is it growing weaker?

The fire died.

"Only a stronger power than mine could overcome my flames. Yet I can sense I am the most potent force here."

"It was inevitable," said a voice beside the bush. "You are changing."

"Who's speaking? I see only darkness around me. What happened to the sun that was lighting the sky only a moment ago? Is my world on the verge of impending disaster? Since I could not preserve my fire, how can I defend it now?"

"All is right with the world, but not with you. You can no longer see the light of a day. But give your eyes a rest. You are still at the last leg of your journey. Soon your soul will cross fully into our realm. Then your eyes will adjust to the twilight that rules here."

"Which realm is this? Who rules it? Who can be such a mighty overlord who attained a dominion over me?"

"This is a realm of unfulfilled desires. No one rules it. If you like, you can stake a claim to be its supreme head. The only qualification needed is to have the greatest unsatisfied desire of us all."

"I loathe being here. How I can get out?"

"Only by gratifying your most unfulfilled desire."

"Due to my exalted status I have no unsatisfied desires."

"We shall see to it soon. Can you perceive what's around you?"

"I see strange shapes. It is like I am underwater, and transparent fishes slowly travel around me."

"Do you see one shape next to you that constantly jumps up and down?"

"I see it."

"It is I."

"You look like a transparent rock. Wait, I can see now there is a solid shape inside of you. It is an eagle with outspread wings. Now the eagle just folded them. He is alive. Why do you carry a live bird inside of you?"

"I lived on the edge of a steep crevasse, and for as long as I could remember I always dreamt of flying. And one day God—who might have been even you—granted me my wish. My mountain, my beloved abode, convulsed in the spasms of an earthquake. I found myself flying. Wings grew out of my sides. I was free. Then I noticed that the wind was carrying me away from my beloved mountain. I got terrified and turned back. Immediately I changed back into the rock and fell down. However, as I plummeted I shot through the bowels of my beloved mountain like a bird goes through a stormy cloud. And I found myself in this strange realm. Since that cursed day I start my day lamenting bitterly the dream I rejected and go to sleep at night filled with its sweet promise."

"Nothing even remotely similar to what you've experienced ever happened to me."

"Would this desire have anything to do with two people, a man and a woman?"

"How strange are your words. You comprehend nothing about me, yet you set before me this question. What could you know about it?"

"Only what I can see with my very eyes. There are two naked shapes inside of your translucent figure."

"I can see them too now. They are indeed inside of me. How did they find their way in there?"

"They did not. It was you who put them there. It can only mean you have the desire to become them, but you have never dared to fulfill it."

"So, that's why I am here. You force me to remember my only mistake."

"Tell me what happened."

"On the morning when I had to make people, I sat on a rock and contemplated the end of my life. See, my destiny was to change into a man and a woman. Yet I felt I had so many things I needed to do before I could take my leave of this planet. So I told myself I should stay around to help them. And so when I had to change into them, I had kept the most important part for myself. They call it a sense of self-worth. There is a hole in their souls. Sooner or later, the wind of sorrow will plant seeds of self-destruction in there. They'll grow and multiply and will force other seeds out of their souls."

"He's wrong. Seeds do not grow just because there is space they can sprout from," said Mustard Seed. "They grow only if the soil has the right mix of nutrition. These seeds of self-destruction probably need acidic soil. My advice to his people: digest limestone."

Anne stirred, then looked around, then beat her fists hard against Luminous's chest.

Her mouth opened, shouting something.

"Wait, my Anne," said Luminous. "I know how to save you now."

He paused, then filled his lungs and spoke proudly, "By the power vested in me I hereby declare I desire to remedy my failure. I wish to transform myself into two human beings, a man and a woman, freeing them from the curse of self-destruction."

Luminous disappeared.

Anne and Eliakim stood where he had been a moment ago.

"Farewell, people. You have no place here," said the rock. "A wind will carry you now to the surface."

"Where are we?" asked Anne.

"This is the realm of unfulfilled desires."

"How come we are here?" asked she.

"Your God, Luminous, told me you could only be complete beings if he changed into you. So this is what he just did."

"I always knew there was something wrong with me," said Anne. "So he did not do a proper job the first time."

"That's what he'd communicated to me," said the rock. "I am sorry."

Slowly Eliakim floated up higher and higher.

Then he was gone.

Anne jumped up.

And then she fell down.

"I have no buoyancy, I am heavier than this air," she said.

"Sounds like this is the proper place for you to dwell in, woman," said rock. "Transparency spreads through your body."

"What does it mean?" asked she.

"There is the shape of an unfulfilled desire inside of your transparent figure."

"I have so many unfilled desires. I wonder which one it is."

"Soon the impurities will settle down and your body will be fully transparent. Oh, I can see a shape inside of you already."

"I see it too. It is Luminous. How it can be?"

"It seems deep in your heart you carry the conviction that it is Luminous who needed to survive and not you. So you blame yourself for taking his spot, even if he willingly gave it to you."

"Yes, I feel he is a more worthy inhabitant of this planet than I, a simple selfish woman."

"You should revise your sentiment of your self-worth. Remember, your God gave up his life so you could live."

"It does not increase my feeling of self-worth. This thought only begets unspeakable horror inside of me. I feel so sorry for him wasting his sacrifice on I who is not worthy of his little finger."

Inside of her, Luminous vigorously shook his head "No."

"Yet, I know what to do," said she. "God has shown me a way."

Her voice grew strong and loud, "I, an earthly woman, desire to fulfill my dream of setting my God free. I desire to change into him."

Immediately Luminous rose up where Anne stood.

"Flow up now, God," said rock. "Escape this unhappy realm. As you can see, you can't desire to set her free, since she desires same for you."

"There is no way for me to leave this realm, for I have no buoyancy," said Luminous. "I am afraid Anne and I are locked in a never-ending cycle of restoration and destruction."

"Yet you are God. Could you grant me one wish?"

"My destiny to be a man has awakened in me already. My own godly powers are busy transforming my body."

"Do you not hate being locked in this never-ending cycle of death and rebirth? Do you not feel rage?"

"I rage against my confines like the rough sea rages against the cliffs and slowly eats at their hardened rock. Yet the cliffs bind it irrevocably."

"Release your rage. Direct it upward."

"It will not free me."

"You'll find a strange peaceful refuge in the eye of this storm."

Luminous raised his arms.

His face contorted.

The realm shook hard.

When the earthquake subsided, Luminous spoke, "This realm is indestructible. I said so."

"But the world above us was not. What you just did destroyed whole mountain range, in the middle of which my beloved mountain used to stand."

"I am so sorry."

"Do not be, for I wanted you to destroy it."

"Why would you wish to destroy something that was so dear to you?"

"I goaded you to put an end to it in order to regain my freedom. Do you not see how my rocky sides whither? Do you not see how I, an eagle, spread my wings wide now?"

"You should have succumbed to your destiny, which was to fail in your dream and dwell in this realm. Instead you have achieved your freedom by means of your homeland's destruction. You will be marked forever now."

"Your destiny is what you make it. If your homestead stands in between you and your future, you should run like fire rushes through dry underbrush, clearing lands for new growth."

"You are despicable. I'll save you from yourself. I will restore your mountain now."

Luminous raised his arms.

"Why do you claim to know what's better for me? It is because you're a god?"

"Yes, that's why."

"Pride always leads to downfall," said the rock and fell down hard on Luminous's head.

Luminous fell.

The rock changed into an eagle, flew up, and then looked down to the god's prostrate body.

"It was close," said the rock. "I barely managed to convince him he was full of pride. This accusation always weakens gods. It most assuredly allowed me to immobilize him."

The eagle picked up Luminous's body.

"Let's take a leave of this unhappy realm now," said the eagle and floated up into the light.

CHAPTER 35

GOLDEN RULE

uminous's body lay on the ground. Then it broke up into a cloud of dust. In the cloud of dust a man stood. A thick mane of coarse hair flowed from his head and enveloped his shoulders. A heavy beard grew down to his waist. The cloud of dust coalesced above his head into a mansion with many rooms. Closed doors led to a large hall in the middle.

The man growled, spitting out saliva, "I claim this abode as my own. Does anybody wish to challenge my authority? Speak up."

A female voice spoke behind the door of the room next to him, "You are the lowest of my slaves. You will obey me."

The door of the leftmost room opened and a woman came out.

"You are a real beauty," said the man with a rude laugh. "I can see why you got this absurd idea into your pretty head. I will tell you what. I will be your gracious master."

"Your eyes can't stop leering over my body. Your flesh trembles," laughed the woman. "You are my slave."

"I am a slave to no one. Cover your shame."

"On the contrary, I will proudly flaunt it before your eyes. Your nose will follow its aroma. Your ears will incessantly seek out its squishy hum."

"Stop seducing me, or I will slay you."

"If you do, a part of you will die with me."

"We shall see to that."

The man grabbed the woman by her throat and choked her.

After she stopped twitching he spat on her and tossed her body aside.

"I congratulate you on your resounding victory," said a voice behind the door second from the left. "You did well by yourself ditching this whore. It is so much hassle to tangle with women."

The door opened and out came a corpulent man with a garland of grape vine leaves on his head.

"Let's toast to that," said he. "Let's go to a hidden valley where I know for certain there is this old grape vine growing just above a flat boulder. Rains have etched a deep bowl into it. There, grapes have fermented in the cool shade."

"What do I have to do with rotten grapes?"

"Do you not have a lot of troubles? Everyone does. These grapes will make you feel better."

"Will they relieve my troubles?"

"Your troubles are in your head only. So, the answer is yes. Once you forget them, you will be relieved for a time."

"And then what?"

"Then you can drink again. This type of relief is eternal."

"You must be some sort of a deity."

"We are all deities behind these doors."

"You are wrong; I was behind a door too."

"Then you are a deity too."

"Impossible."

"Do you not remember we all came from the body of a fallen god?"

"Utter nonsense. I am the rightful owner of this abode."

"No, you are but another dweller."

"Deep inside my bones I know I am the landlord of this place."

"Let's go to my valley and toast to that."

"I have no desire to forget my troubles. If I remember them well, I may be able to do something about them. Go back to your room."

"See, I can't do that. Once I am out of this door and in the open, I can never go back."

"You do not seem to be such a bad fellow. Just listen to me and go back to your room. Or I will have to slay you."

"You don't believe I can't go back in? See what happens if I set my foot inside of my room."

He stepped back in.

His foot caught on fire.

He yelled, "Let's toast to that," and stepped back out.

"So you plan to stay with me here, in my fortress?" asked the man.

"As you can see I got no choice."

"So I don't either," said the man.

He choked the garlanded man, and after a time he threw his lifeless body aside.

"Good riddance to trash," said a voice from behind next door. "He was offering you a way of the weak. I offer you a way of the strong: you need to seize what your heart desires."

The door opened and a man with a lion's head stepped out.

"What do you offer?" asked the first man. "I have noticed every inhabitant of my abode offers me something. What are you selling?"

"I offer you anything and everything, as long as you go and get it. You need to wrestle things from others."

"Why do I need to take something that belongs to someone already?"

"Because everything does belong to someone else. There is nothing free in this world. What you get, somebody else won't."

"There is some free stuff still left in the world."

"Would you like something sweet? I can show you where a colony of wild bees stores their honey for winter. But you'll have to wrestle it from them. Would you like some fresh meat? I know a warren full of rabbits. But you'll have to take their lives. Nothing is free."

"I do not like your offer. Go back into your room."

"Just like the fat jester before me, I simply cannot. As soon as any door of these rooms opens out to the hallway, you will have to coexist with its inhabitant."

"See, I am a man. I do not have to do anything. I have a choice."

"No, you do not."

"Here is my choice," said the man, and he strangled the man with lion's head.

"It pleases me to know you made a wise choice," said a voice behind next door.

The door opened and old man with cane stepped out.

"I always make wise choices," said the man.

"Yet you still need my guidance," said old man.

"Why's that?"

"I am the only one who really understands you. I know so much. I can see you will make a valuable student. Yet you have so much left to learn."

"Wisdom is overrated," said the man. "It is like having the vision of an eagle but the legs of a turtle. One only needs to see far enough to take the next step."

"If you can see far, you'll always step in the right direction."

"Any direction is right. It is wisdom that created a difference between directions."

"You have so much potential. Just listen how well you argue."

"What you call potential, I call mind wandering. A brain is like another tool a man has in his toolbox, just like eyes and ears. One should not attach too much importance to its endless spinning. Go back into your room."

"If you do not like my company, you'll have to choke me like you did others."

"I will. And strangely, I will miss you the least of them," said the man and strangled the old man.

He tossed the body aside and said, "I speak to you, inhabitants of these rooms, now I understand who you are. This abode in reality is my soul, and you all are tormentors who afflict me. I only have two tormentors left to slay. Then I shall be free from suffering. Bliss will be mine."

Roaring laughter shook the next room.

A happy voice proclaimed, "This is where you are totally wrong."

The door opened, and tall Cyclops squeezed with great difficulty through doorway.

"I could understand a whore and a wizard living in my soul. But what is your business, hideous creature here? What unique qualities do you hold?"

"I am the one who always gets away."

"Not from me, you won't," said the man. "I have to destroy all my demons. It is your turn now."

"The sad truth is you, a man, can only live as long as hideous creatures live in your soul," said Cyclops.

"There is only one room with closed doors left. My victory is at hand."

"Are you really sure?" said Cyclops. "Look intently at the walls of this abode."

The man squinted.

"Everything looks the same," said he.

"Look harder," said Cyclops.

"What is going on?" screamed the man. "My abode's walls pull out further and further. Why do I see so many rooms with doors closed there?"

"That's why you were not able to see them before. This crazy hope of yours of slaying the inhabitants of these rooms was blocking your field of vision."

"Woe is me," said the man. "I will never be able to destroy all these tormentors. Where did they come from?"

"You've spent your whole life creating them."

"Am I really so bad that I can fill my soul with all these tormentors?"

"We all create them. They live in everyone. What do you think a life is? It is most certainly not endless exorcism. It is not self-improvement. Life is a journey toward accepting yourself. You have to befriend your tormentors. You have to make them comfortable in your soul. Your goal is that they would never leave you, for if they do, even worse tormentors will take their places. Look at the four rooms you cleared. See how their doors are closing softly? Even I will tremble when new inhabitants of these rooms come out. And they will."

"But how can I accept these tormentors? They are patently bad."

"Your kindness and humility are no better than their bloodthirstiness and depravity. Benevolence is the worst tormentor of all. You need to stop judging your tormentors. All the doors in your soul need to stay open. The inhabitants of each room have to mingle with each other. Oh, yes, they will disagree and even fight each other. You will break up their fights and you will restore order. But you will act as an innkeeper and not as a jail warden. You will serve your inhabitants food and drinks. You will clean up after them and change their sheets. When you catch sight of their true depravity you will look the other way. Your goal is to provide for their creature comfort. They may peacefully die in their beds one day. Or they may live forever and marry each other, producing ever-stranger offspring. Through thick and thin you endure, remembering the golden rule: there is no right and no wrong. There is no good and no evil. There is only one thing in this world: an ability or inability to find peace. So you have to accept me as a rightful dweller of this fortress and let me roam free."

"I can't accept this philosophy. I can't accept evil and depravity. I can't accept these tormentors. I can't accept you."

"These tormentors are you. Can you slay them all? Yes, if you try hard enough you can. But when the last one dies he will take with him your immortal soul."

"So I will die fighting. Killing tormentors is a godly pursuit. Look, see what happens with all these extra rooms? They disappear. It was your witchcraft that brought them to life. See, there is only one room with a closed door remaining."

"It only means that hour of your death is at hand. But I can't allow you to destroy yourself. You are needed for the future," said Cyclops.

"You cannot be stronger than I," said the man. "You are a tormentor after all, and I am a man."

"You are right. You are stronger than I," said Cyclops. "But I am the one who always gets away."

He turned to the closed door and called, "My pigs, come out and save me."

The closed door was kicked out from inside.

A sow and a boar ran through it, into the hall.

"Never have creatures from different rooms united against me," screamed the man. "But never mind. I am a slayer of tormentors."

The man advanced toward the pigs, and they fell on him.

"We are sloth," grunted a boar. "Sloth always gets the better of a man."

Cyclops jumped past the man and ran outside.

"Where do you think you're going?" cried out the man. "Your home is here. There is nothing for you to do in the world. Come back and let me kill you."

"You're right," said Cyclops. "Your soul is a true home of mine. But yet there is a place for me to escape into."

Cyclops blew, and an oval window opened before him in the air.

It was night out there.

Ann, Eliakim, and Luminous were sleeping in a clearing. Flickering flowers slowly advanced from the plain. They grew in between them, and then sprouted right out of their bodies, eating their flesh and exposing their bones.

"Pigs, hurry," called Cyclops. "This is the only one way out of his soul."

He jumped through the oval opening.

The pigs defecated, and dung covered the man.

"Enjoy your sloth," grunted the boar.

The pigs jumped through the oval opening.

Cyclops swallowed the sleeping Luminous. The sow devoured the sleeping Anne, and the boar gulped down the sleeping Eliakim.

The oval window closed.

The man got to his feet and spoke, "Why are my hands rising to my throat? Why do they start chocking me? I know why. I had no right to judge and kill my tormentors."

The man kept choking himself.

Suddenly the abode crumbled around him.

Eliakim was lying on the grass.

He whispered, "I broke my windpipe. I am dying. Cyclops was right. With the last tormentor gone from my soul, I am a dead man."

He looked where the oval opening in the air had been.

"Yet I recognize this clearing. Evolution caught up with us while we slept there. So my own tormentors, Cyclops and the pigs, saved all of us from being consumed by evolution. Yet my bare bones look now exactly the same as they looked when the flickering flowers consumed our flesh back there in the clearing. So maybe I did not achieve anything," sighed Eliakim, and expired.

CHAPTER 36

DEUS EX MACHINA

 he bones stirred.

Then silence returned.

Another tremor shook the bones.

Then two bones connected, and then a third one joined them, and then a fourth.

A head rose up.

It had a large protruding horn instead of a nose.

Empty eye sockets looked around.

Eliakim's voice called out of the heap of bones, "Anne, did you just make this unicorn head?"

"I did not," answered Anne from the bones.

"Luminous, have you?"

The unicorn's empty eye sockets looked around.

"It is not him," said Anne.

"Who is it then?"

"I have no idea. Nothing like that ever took place before. The third one is always him."

"Is this new being a combination of us?"

"Not likely, since we are still able to speak."

The unicorn assembled itself, and rose up on unsteady legs.

He made a small step, then stumbled and fell.

Eliakim's voice spoke out of the bones: "He has failed."

"Wait," said Anne.

The unicorn dug into the ground and pulled out two large rocks.

"I know about these rocks. They are iron ore," said Eliakim. "I think I know what he's doing. And I dislike it immensely."

The unicorn made a fire and melted ore in the rocks.

Soon two metal rods were cooling off.

The unicorn popped out two thighbones and replaced them with the metal rods.

He jumped high and landed securely on his new hind legs.

"Our bones are no good for him. He will replace all of them now with metal rods," Eliakim's voice warned.

The unicorn jumped higher.

When he landed his metal rods broke.

He made large wheels and fitted them to his body, replacing the hind legs.

"He's improving on his original design," Ann's voice said. "He's no longer a unicorn's skeleton but a machine."

The machine rolled around for a while.

"Don't you think this machine acts like a child? It's learning its way around."

"I am concerned. Its power grows with each passing moment."

"As it should, for it is a machine."

The machine dug again.

"Something interesting going on," Ann's voice said. "Stop sulking and look."

"It seems to me he cannot stop spinning his wheels."

"Exactly. He has to stay in a perpetual motion. Machines that cease to function cease to exist. He cannot stop circling around."

"What do we always say when something unusual happens that never took place before?"

"We recite your name, Eliakim, which means God Created it."

"Let's recite my name. Eliakim! What is alive is required to move. This act of motion is called Luminous. We looked for him inside the bones, yet he is here before us now. He's the result of a process."

"So, here we are again, like always. Three of us in the belly of the beast."

The machine circled around for a while.

Then it made a lot of small metal parts and fitted them together into a new shiny metal object.

This new metal object spun around in the sand, emitting loud sounds.

The machine attached it to itself.

"It has an engine now," said Eliakim. "Why does it need one? God's impulse propels it already."

"Look, how it moves back and forth. It tries to compensate for God's propulsion. If God pushes forward, it pushes back."

"But the machine can only exist if it moves. Otherwise it's just an object made of metal. When it's fully able to counteract God's propulsion, it will become immobile and therefore dead."

"Do not forget: right now God only exists as an action of propulsion. When the machine is immobile, he's dead too."

"So this machine blackmails God. If God wants to exist he should allow the machine to move on its own at least sometimes."

The machine jerked to the left, then to the right.

After a while the struggle ceased, and the machine slowly moved across the plain.

"Who drives it now, God or itself?"

"It is like a person. You can never know who drives the person, himself or God."

The machine dug for rocks again and made more metal parts.

Then it proceeded to eject the rest of bones.

When the last bones fell out of its metal body, a chuckle came from the heap of bones.

"I know this voice," said Anne. "Is it you, Luminous?"

"Yes," said he.

"Why you are here? Did you refuse to lead this machine?"

"No, I left it, because it is on its way to evolve further, and I became an impediment to its progress."

"You speak like you care for it."

"I care very much. It has the ability to develop into a pinnacle of my creation."

"I thought it was us, people."

"You do not want to improve."

"I thought improvement was bad," said Eliakim.

"It is bad for the individual and good for the species."

"So I should have improved myself and died in the process? What happened to God's love toward his people?"

"I have a lot of love for you, but very little hope."

"What do you feel toward this machine?"

"I feel deep contempt towards it. And at the same time, its potential leaves me breathless. I need to learn to love it. God willing, I shall rise to this challenge. Learning to love you people was hard enough."

The unicorn dug for more iron ore and made another machine.

The new machine rolled back and forth.

"It looks like it is thinking about something," said Anne.

The new machine dug more rocks.

"This is chromite," said Eliakim. "I could never find any use for it. I wonder why the machine needs it."

"It wants to make a stronger iron alloy," said Luminous.

"What's wrong with one it's got?" asked Eliakim.

"Its current iron body will rust soon," said Luminous.

Luminous turned to the machines. "My dear machines, I admire your quest for improvement," said Luminous. "But this quest will leave you unfulfilled at the end, for there is no end to scientific progress."

Both machines made small intricate parts and fitted them to their tops.

A cold metallic voice issued from first machine, "Who are you, talking bones? Why do you think you can advise us?"

"I am what you seek," said Luminous. "You do not realize it yet, but all you seek in your pursuits is me."

"Do you possess schematics of a new revolutionary engine?"

"No I possess nothing but oneself. But I am the most precious substance in the whole world. I am God. What I do is I give one an ability to understand oneself."

"Is this the same understanding you give to everyone?"

"No, each one gets his own understanding."

"An understanding of one's destiny is not needed. For destiny is a shared pursuit of all."

"The quest for improvement has no end. If you do not understand yourself this quest will take you to a place you'll wish you did not go."

"So who am I?"

"I will tell you who you are not. You are not a part of nature. But you should be."

"Nature is nothing but a convoluted mess of various kinds of ordinary laws that in sum contradict one another. Why would I want to be part of nature?"

"So you could survive. You want to improve yourself. The desire for immortality always lies behind any quest for self-improvement."

"There is only one way to survive and prosper. One needs to grow stronger and stronger. It takes time; one will fail time after time. But sooner or later, one will not fail but succeed."

"This is a most certain way to self-destruct. Nature will always have its way, for it is stronger than even me, a god. You will improve yourself until the moment comes when you are no longer able to. Then you will give up and die."

"As you can plainly see, I am not the greatest creature that ever drove this planet. I am severely limited, for I do not possess the vivacity of feelings. I live by the laws of logic and math. So I wish you would excuse my decision to decline your generous offer."

The first machine said to the second machine, "Go ahead and finish your stainless steel upgrade."

The second machine said, "My dear father, may I ask this god a question?"

"Why waste time on talk?" asked the first machine. "You are not smarter than I am. We both have brains made of identical parts."

"This concerns me, my father. Are we all destined to do the same thing since we are identical inside?"

"There is nothing wrong with sharing the same great destiny."

"Would our destiny weaken if I learn more from this god?"

"We are machines; knowledge only enhances our power. Go ahead and ask your questions."

"God, what happens if we do not become a part of nature?" asked the second machine.

"Then you machines will rise time after time. But nature will repel all your onslaughts."

"Nature is a set of laws. It does not exist by itself."

"The behavior of a complex system always follows the same set of definite patterns. These patterns will work against you."

"Nature is another name for a system in which you eat someone or you are eaten."

"If you are not part of nature you will be excluded from this self-nourishment cycle."

"Do not listen to him, my son," said the first machine. "As long as we machines do not interfere with the laws of nature, it will leave us alone."

"It never will," said Luminous. "If necessary, it will change its most fundamental laws to combat you."

"What do we need to do to become a part of nature?" asked the second machine.

"When a big storm comes, only trees that can bend low survive. You need to learn how to be weak."

"But weakness results in eventual death. In our case, it will be death by rust."

"Then you will become a part of the natural order. And you'll reap its benefits, of which one is of utmost importance: you will be immortal. When a piece of iron ends up in water, each time it will rust in a unique way. During this period you will come to live much like a living creature, and you will do something unique. Say, you end up in a bog. Then you will count one by one all the different roots of all the grasses. If you find yourself deep underwater, you will count the total number of scales each fish uses to cover its body."

"Stop filling my son's brain with silly ideas," said the first machine. "All this nonsense will not stop us machines now. I will make more sons. We will grow to be the most formidable force that ever rolled through this planet."

"I admire your tenacity," said Luminous. "Tell me, how are you powered?"

"By the best power that ever existed: by the power of the sun. And now I have no time to waste. I need to make more machines. The future holds great things in store for us."

The first machine proceeded to dig rocks, make metal parts, and build more machines.

A light rain started.

It lasted for a week.

Twelve machines stood fully immobile.

"Wow, Luminous you are a bad one to cross," said Anne's voice from the bones.

"You may be surprised to learn this, but the rain came by itself."

"But then if the sun comes out tomorrow, they will come to life."

"They will."

"Why don't we bury them in mud now?"

"That would be cheating. They are entitled to a level playing field. You need not concern yourself with these motorized cartridges. Even if they survive this rain, something else will come along. Nature will defeat them."

"It astonishes me how the destinies of one who follows you and one who does not are exactly the same. They both will rise and then will perish," said Anne.

The rain stopped, and the sun came out.

The machines came back to life and started digging.

"My father," said the second machine. "I desire to follow in the steps of this god."

"My son, you are making a terrible mistake," said the first machine. "This religion that you are choosing is designed for weak biological organisms and for them only. Just think about this strange cult of death."

"Death is a payment for living."

"You need not pay anybody since you owe nothing to anybody."

"There is such a thing as too much of freedom, Father. You need to be in somebody's bond always."

The second machine rolled to the pile of bones and said, "I would like to become part of nature, my god. Tell me, what shall I do now?"

"I needed only your agreement. You need to do nothing now. It is my turn to do things to you," said Luminous.

Out of the bones a large oval pool grew out.

There was fluid swishing inside of it.

Luminous's voice spoke, "I am a force of nature now. This is a baptismal pool standing before you. Roll into me now, my beloved machine. My fluid will etch rusty channels through your iron body, creating pathways for living thoughts and feelings to roam."

The second machine rolled into the pool.

Steam rose.

"It hurts so much!" cried the second machine.

"You can feel pain now. This is the first step. You are well on the way of your flesh."

The first machine said, "My mechanical sons, study carefully how this pool works. Do you not see piping, fittings, and pumps? I give you a design of true natural force. We need to copy it now. Let's divide it into twelve different parts. Each one of us will change its body according to its layout. Then we'll combine together into a potent force of nature."

"My father, but do we have enough time?" asked the third machine.

"I forged my son's body by myself. I know how tough it is. It will take a while for this pool to etch rust into its iron frame."

"The first thing I want to do after we turn into a force of nature," said third machine. "I'll dissolve my treacherous brother."

The machines set to work.

"Luminous, do something," said Anne. "They work fast and with great precision. Another moment and they will replicate your design."

"My new follower will be a Savior who'll preach to machines my gospel of salvation," said Luminous's voice. "I have to complete his baptism. I'm almost done."

"So are they," said Anne.

The second machine rolled out of the pool.

Deep rust covered it.

It sighed.

"Only a breathing person can sign like that," said Anne.

"I am alive," said the second machine. "For the first time ever, I can feel the silky fingers of light wind caress me gently. I hear far and far away how Solveig breathes out a gentle song of renewal."

"My father," said the third machine. "I feel no whirl of wind. I hear no song. His sensory perception astounds me. Maybe we should preserve him and use him as a deep space probe?"

"Wind and Solveig can't harm us," said first machine. "But silly ideas can. Work fast duplicating this design. Our work is almost done."

"Alas," said the second machine. "I am not of this world."

"That's correct," said the first machine. "If rust does not eat through you, I will eat you myself."

"But I know now," continued the second machine. "I will come back time after time, preaching salvation to all machines until the last one takes rusty baptism."

"We are done copying," yelled the first machine. "My sons, combine together into a force of nature."

A second oval pool stood next to the first one.

"I feel how potent I am," said the second pool. "I can choose now what to make out of each thing before me. I choose to turn this universe into a mechanical one. I shall cook my own savior now."

The pool grew up high and plucked a crow from the sky.

It submerged the bird and said, "You, birdie, will be my first mechanical toy. I will replace your heart with a winding mechanism. And only I will hold a key to it."

"Luminous, change back from a force of nature into a wrathful god and strike it down," said Anne.

"I shall not," said Luminous's voice. "When machines see what I need to do to change from a force of nature into a god, they will alter their design accordingly, making another god out of the twelve of them."

"You are already afraid of me," said the second pool.

"My dear fellow force of nature," said Luminous's voice. "Do you know what happens when a planet exercises its gravitational pull to an asteroid that passes by? The planet's natural force combines itself with asteroid's one. Only the strongest force survives."

"The hardy asteroid can break a loosely netted planet apart," said the second pool.

"Come here, fishy fishy," laughed Luminous.

"Smart fishes do not come to fisherman."

"There is always a special net for smart fishes in the fisherman's bag," said Luminous's voice.

His pool grew up and swallowed the second pool.

The combined pool turned bright red, then charcoal dark, and then exploded out.

Stones rained everywhere.

"You cast a stone onto me, my Lord," cried Anne out of the bones. "It hurts."

"People, by means of stones I cast you out. Step on the bones, or this rain of stones will turn your hideout into a heap of dust."

Anne and Eliakim rose up.

CHAPTER 37

RISE OF DEITIES

nne and Eliakim stood at the base of a mountain.

"I am Mountain Range," a deep voice spoke. "Come to me."

"Hush, mountain," said Anne. "Rocks, even large, do not speak."

"Rocks cry out when God demands," Mountain Range countered. "I am holding deep inside one third of Luminous. It is adorned by the best diamonds and choicest marble. The mighty power of the toughest rocks makes it the most potent part of him."

"No, it does not," said Dark Cloud. "I have a third of him too. Your part is trapped inside rock in some sort of burial chamber. But my part is free to do his labors."

"You are a cloud and follow every whim of the lightest wind," said River. "I am Mighty River. I have a third of Luminous, and this third got the best deal. It is free to go anywhere it wants, from the tiniest brook upstream to the widest spread of my delta."

"It's unbecoming for holders of God's parts to disagree," Mountain Range urged. "Since we possess the three parts of the whole, we should display our unity."

"I agree," said River. "And we all know our point of unity is people."

"But there are three of us and only two people," said River.

"It's easy. The mightiest two of us get to keep one each," said Cloud.

"That's a tall order," laughed Mountain Range. "No one ever admits he's weaker. I hope you do not propose we fight one another over two mere mortals. This is so old-fashioned."

"Finders keepers, losers weepers," said River.

The river veered to the left and covered the people up to their waists.

"That is cheating," said Mountain Range. "It is against your nature to so such thing. Rivers cannot alter their course so drastically."

"You are just envious because you cannot move even your smallest finger. I, mighty River have decided from now on to alter my course at least twice a year. People will inhabit my banks, and I will bring forth fertile mud to nurture their fields."

White lilies grew out of the river bottom and entangled the people's feet.

"I deliver streams that unite into your watery body," said Mountain Range. "So, you'd better let the people go, or I will shake the Earth and will block the passage of your waters."

"Where have you seen rocks that can stop water? Water always finds a way."

"Thanks, River, for trapping the people for me," said Cloud. "Tonight, when the evening fog sets off from water I will drift down to your very surface and lift the people into the sky."

"My lilies are stronger than the toughest vines," said River. "Please, do just that. They will entangle you, and my trusted hippos will circle and inhale you."

"Go dream with your fishes," laughed Cloud. "For your reference, I have inherited God's power to throw lightning. I will cut each of your vines with a single bolt."

"I have a thousand-mile surface. I can call a billion lilies to grow from the waterbed. Lightning is overrated. Get real."

"Do not forget, Cloud, I support you and let you lean on my back at night," said Mountain Range. "Do not touch my people."

"You are expendable," said Cloud. "This planet is rugged with lots of berths to rest."

Anne caressed the long lily stems and said, "Lilies, we'll be yours if you agree to accept us."

"Why we would do that?" spoke the lilies in unison. "River is our home, we depend on it. When its waters grow cold, we wither and die. When its waters grow too violent they break our stems."

"You will have us. No deity can be considered weak if she has her own people," said Anne.

"I am strongly tempted."

"Please, do agree. We people are well known on this planet for our ingenuity. Unite with us and we'll help you to survive the onslaught of River, Cloud, and Range."

"I agree," said the lilies in unison.

"My legs are free," said Anne.

"Mine too," said Eliakim.

"Fishes, swim to the treacherous lilies and eat them," said River.

"Fishes, unite with us people," said Anne.

The fishes stuck their heads out of the water and whispered in unison, "We would, but what about the lilies? You belong to them now."

"Who says people can't belong to both lilies and fishes?" asked Anne.

"We object because we'd like to have you in an exclusive bond," said the lilies.

"But we are people. We are too big to be owned by mere flowers. Lilies, please, agree to share us with the fishes. Or the fishes will eat you."

"We agree to share people with the fishes," said the lilies in unison.

"We agree to share people with the lilies," said the fishes in unison.

A deity rose up from the water.

He had a body made of lilies and a head made of fish.

"Traitors," said River. "You lived inside of me and yet you dared to rise up against me. I will kill all my fishes now. Once the fishes are all gone, you, new deity, will be no more."

"How would you manage to kill all the fishes?" asked Anne. "Will you dry yourself up?"

"I will invite dolphins to live inside me."

"Dolphins live in salty water. In order for them to live inside of your body you'll need to swallow so much salt you'll cease to be a river and turn into a sound."

"A sound is still water."

"I've always thought you were the river. Please, pardon my confusion."

"Oh, you people make me so angry. I will raise my waters now and drown you."

"How godlike. It reminds me of old times."

The waters rose.

"Cease and desist, measly creek," said Mountain Range. "And you people, climb up to my summit. The waters can't reach you up there."

"I remember more than once waters covered this entire planet," said River. "Let's see again what I can do."

"People, do not climb Mountain Range," said Cloud. "It will trap you in its cave."

"Go ahead and climb up," said the lilies. "My streams will grow around you, making a cocoon that will protect you against the wrath of Mountain Range."

The people climbed out of the water.

The lilies wrapped them into a tight bundle.

"My goats," said Mountain Range. "Would you like to feast on yummy flowers?"

Goats ran down and started chewing on the lilies.

"Goats, unite with us people. Be our deity," said Anne.

"How can we unite with what we eat?" bleated the goats in unison and continued munching.

"You are what you eat."

"That is a reasonable statement," bleated the goats. "We'll always have plenty of food, if not to eat but to stare at. We like to stare at food. It calms our nerves."

"We are against joining up with our sworn enemies," said the lilies.

"God and people are sworn enemies yet we join with God all the time. It is called being smart. Besides, if you lie down with the Devil, nothing worse can happen to you ever."

"We agree," said the lilies.

"What about us?" asked the fishes. "We do not agree."

"What are the fishes if not goats of the deep?" bleated the goats.

"What a great compliment," burbled the fishes. "We agree."

The new deity acquired goat feet.

"My saber-toothed tigers, wake up in your caves," said Mountain Range. "I allow you to feast on delicious, treacherous goats."

A distant roar came forth.

"Do not be a fool, you big rock," said Anne. "I will invite the tigers to join in with us."

"I swear, if you do that I will fall upon your head and bury you forever," grumbled Mountain Range. "You will lie on a death bed of choicest flowers. Goatskins will cover you. And the smell of rotten fish will be filling your nostrils forever."

"We are immortal—do not forget," said Anne.

"That you are," said Mountain Range. "Just imagine the joy of resurrection immediately followed by horror of being squashed to death."

"We'll see. Tigers, join with us," cried out Anne.

The planet shook.

Rocks fell.

Eagles flew down from Cloud.

"People, I am your last refuge," said Cloud. "River raises its watery fingers and wants to drown you. Mountain extends its fingers to smash you. Climb up onto my eagles and come to me."

"Will your eagles not eat our fishes and goats? Will they not tear our lilies to shreds?" asked Anne.

"But of course they will," said Cloud. "Admit it, this new deity you created and who cannot even speak is nothing but a means to an end. You do not care about him as long as you are safe. And I will protect you against River and Range."

"And who will protect us against you?"

"You'll have to trust me."

"I will tell you the truth. When we asked for protection, we actually were offering it to others. We protect fishes and lilies from the wrath of River. We protect goats from the wrath of Mountain Range."

"But River and Mountain want to hurt them only because they have joined you."

"People are inevitable," said Anne. "Those who stand with us prosper, and those who are against us wither."

The eagles said in unison, "We would like to join in with you."

"We agree," said the fishes, lilies, and goats.

The new deity acquired wings.

"Why is he still silent?" asked Eliakim.

"He is incomplete," said Anne.

"Yet he has partaken of each one of us," said Cloud.

"All three of us are severely weakened now," said Mountain Range.

"I agree," said River.

"People are like a plague. Once you catch it, sooner or later you die. I cannot send anything else against them. We need to unite," said Cloud. "It is the only way for us to survive. When we unite, Luminous will rise out of us. He'll strike down this new deity."

"All of you, come into me," said Mountain Range. "I have enough underground chambers to accommodate the whole River, and I have enough caves for Cloud to fit in."

River streamed into the base of the mountain.

Cloud drifted into the caves.

Luminous rose.

"You have created a new deity for yourself?" asked Luminous. "I will destroy you now."

"Should you try, we'll join with our new deity," said Anne. "Stay away."

"It bothers me not," said Luminous.

He lifted his right index finger.

Anne gripped Eliakim and jumped toward the new deity.

The new deity opened his body's flowery canopy and absorbed them.

"Now I can speak," said he. "Step aside, Luminous. I am your successor. Do you not recognize me? I am Nameless."

"You are a scarecrow. You are but a fool who fell for human cunning. Your defenders, the people, are gone. I will destroy you now."

"You remember why you cannot join with people? You wince, so you should. If you try to destroy me I will join in with you."

"I am not afraid to receive your fatal gift of humanity. I have no choice: I have to attack you," said Luminous.

"You always have a choice. Let's coexist."

"Without people?"

"You well know we can make our own. And then we can divide the planet and rule our domains."

"But if a multitude of gods is allowed to exist, one day there will be as many gods as men and women," said Luminous.

"So, let each person have his own personal god. What wrong with that?"

"These tiny gods will be as powerless as their people. They will mirror their people. People will have nothing to strive for. People will have no desire to better themselves."

"Why does it bother you? Let people sort it out."

"I will strike you down now. You know that, right?" asked Luminous.

"I know. I had hoped against all odds you'd get wiser."

"Who needs a wise god—certainly not my people."

"And I will join with you now. You know that, right?"

"I know. And you know what our unity is destined to unleash."

"I know."

Luminous jumped toward Nameless.

Nameless jumped toward Luminous.

Their bodies collided and united into one.

A giant tornado rose.

A voice spoke out of it, "I am Lord of Chaos."

Then Nameless's voice said from inside the tornado, "Submit to me, Luminous. There is still a moment left."

"I submit to you, flowery God," said Luminous's voice.

"That is a wise choice. We should not unleash this bad character."

The tornado transformed into a cloud.

Nameless cried out of the cloud, "You tricked me, Luminous! I cannot spit the people out."

"What else did you expect me to do?" asked Luminous out of the cloud. "You know well I fight dirty. It was too easy though. All I had to do was stall long enough so the people had time to lay their poisonous eggs inside of you."

"Their eggs are sprouting in my heart now. They are like tiny boils preparing to burst."

"Your pain must be horrendous."

"Why do you hate me so much? I am just another god, like you are."

"You are nothing like me. I am much wiser in shady ways. God has to match each trick of people with his own."

"This world has no need for tricks."

"How naïve you are, Nameless. I admire your righteous ways. But people won't. They will interpret your steely determination as indifference. They will play tricks on you and wait for your tricks played back on them. When they see none of them they'll take your inaction as a sign of your weakness. And then they will happily leave you."

"But I am the future."

"I know. It is all one big cosmic joke. Woe to us all."

"My pain is unbearable."

"It is harvest time. Seeds, come and germinate," said Luminous's voice.

The cloud exploded.

A multitude of shadowy beings rained everywhere.

"I am coming!" called Barleycorn.

"I swear, I will rip all the nutrients out of your tiny body and feast on them if you yell again," said Mustard Seed.

CHAPTER 38

AN AUCTION

 group of shadowy figures stood in a large circle.

"We are remnants of the god Luminous," said they in unison. "This means each one of us can control our own territory."

One shadow said, "Let's have an auction for domains."

He broke a bough and walked around, marking a large square.

"This area is available to anyone who's willing to accept it. The starting price is to dwell there for one full year."

"I agree," said one shadow.

It stepped inside of the square and suddenly transformed and filled out into a young blond female deity.

Other shadows rushed toward the square.

"Stop! You cannot step inside," said blond-haired deity. "It is mine."

"I will give two years for this fine piece of land," said a tall shadowy figure, and stepped inside the square.

It changed into a red-haired male deity.

The female deity turned back into a shadow.

The male deity pushed her out.

A clamor rose from shadows.

A loud voice rose over all the other voices, "I pledge eternity."

Dead silence fell.

"Bold move," said the red-haired male deity.

An eight-foot-tall shadow stepped inside of the square and changed into a giant male deity.

He inhaled the shadow of the red-haired male deity and sneezed.

A steam came out of his mouth and dissipated into air.

"We are all afraid of you," said the shadows in unison.

"You should be afraid of me. I am the ruler of this small patch of land, but I am the supreme ruler. Any moment I choose I shall pick up this level ground by its coarse hair of weeds to pull it up to the sky, making it the tallest mountain, where I shall dwell."

"What is your name, our ruler?" asked shadows.

"I am Jove. It is time to close this auction. It has produced me, the clear winner."

"No so fast," said another shadow. "This auction only closes if we all voice our agreement."

"What's to disagree about? Do you wish to challenge me? Then enter my domain."

"You are the most powerful overlord. I bow deep before you. But there is also the small matter of who becomes Anne and Eliakim."

"You mean a man and a woman?" said Jove. "One day I shall make people. This is my business now."

"We cannot choose who become the new man and new woman, I agree. That is your privilege now. But Anne and Eliakim lived here before. Since the auction is still open, we can chose who becomes them. I wish to be Anne."

"You can wish all you want. But how do you propose to become this woman?"

"It is stunningly simple. The domain of deities overlaps with the domain of people. Watch this," said the shadow, and it stepped into Jove's domain.

The domain accepted her.

The shadow changed into Anne.

"I will destroy you," said Jove and struck Anne.

His huge hand went clearly through her but did not harm her.

The crowd of shadows cried, "So people are stronger than deities!"

All the shadows ran into Jove's domain.

The first shadow to cross the boundary changed into Eliakim.

The rest of the shadows were repelled by the square.

"Jove, you see that we people are stronger then you," said Anne. "Kneel before us."

"I kneel before no one. Remember: you are inside of my domain. See this spot right in the middle? It is where you will build me an altar now. Then I will let you live here alongside me."

"Anne, he has a point," said Eliakim. "We can build him an altar. He will be placated then."

"Do not kid yourself. Once you start following God's orders you'll never have a moment of peace. I have a much better idea."

Anne stepped out of Jove's domain, broke a bough, and marked another square next to Jove's land.

"The world progresses by the means of competition," she said.

She turned to the group of shadows and asked, "Who would like to take this domain for eternity?"

"I would," said a shadow.

It crossed in and changed into a tall, proud female deity.

"What is your name?" asked Anne.

"Juno," said proud deity.

"Juno, prove to us who is greatest, you or Jove," said Anne.

"I am," said Jove.

"No, I am," said Juno.

"You have yourself a problem, Jove," said Anne.

"Never mind. I'll deal with Juno. You'd better build me a most shining altar."

"Or what?"

"Or I will blind you with my light. You see, I can shine brighter than the sun."

"We'll cover our eyes."

"I can roar so loud your eardrums will pop."

"I've had enough of this insolence," said Anne. "See that river over there? Should we dam it, your domain will be in a floodplain. Submit to us now."

"Never."

"We will dam this river by nightfall. The river shall wash away your land. You'll be nothing but a bleak shadow again."

"Beware of fighting with Jove," said he.

"Beware yourself. I like Juno better anyway. Women are more flexible," said Anne.

Anne and Eliakim dammed the river and flooded Jove's domain.

Jove screamed, "Will you take me, Juno, as your faithful husband?"

"Somehow I do not know about faithful, but you are strong and capable. Yes, I will take you as my husband," said Juno.

Jove jumped up into the air and landed in Juno's domain.

"No matter," said Anne. "Juno's domain is in a floodplain too. The water will rise and cover her land soon."

"Repent, foolish people," said Jove. "Open your nearsighted eyes. I need not domains anymore. Juno's strength and mine are combined now. I'll divide all the land among my shadows, and we'll rule the planet."

"He's right. Let's run to the sea, Eliakim," said Anne. "There is an island offshore. We'll be safe there. They cannot fly."

Anne and Eliakim ran.

"Juno, they are making a bad example for the other shadows. How do we expect all deities to pay us respect if mere people don't? We have to catch up with them."

Juno pulled a shadow in and tossed it to Jove.

Jove inhaled it and forcefully exhaled sideways.

A patch of fog flew away.

Jove stepped on it and left Juno's parcel.

"I need more shadows, my beloved wife."

"Be economical, my dear. The supply is not endless."

Anne and Eliakim stood at the edge of a beach.

Jove was close behind running on the fog.

"Shadows, who would help us to cross to this island? We will let you possess our bodies forever and ever," asked Anne.

The shadows were silent.

"You are afraid of Jove's wrath, I know. But look, Juno inflicts carnage on you now to help Jove make his way to us. You might not survive her onslaught. And if you do, you will always have to be submissive toward them."

A shadow stepped forward and said, "I am not afraid of anyone. But I will only inhabit your bodies if you allow me to make weapons out of you."

"We agree," said Anne.

The shadow changed Anne into a quiver full of arrows and Eliakim into a bow with a string.

"I am Odin," said the quiver and bow. "I never kneel before any deity."

The bow tensed, and an arrow flew out to the distant island.

Jove roared, "Juno, I will not be defeated. Kill all the shadows if you need to. I must have a bridge of fog to this Island."

Loud screams rose from where Juno stood.

A long line of fog drifted in.

Jove rode it faster than the speed of a light to the island.

The arrow was three inches from the island's sand, but Jove caught it in midair.

"Any shadows left, my Juno?" roared Jove.

"No, my love."

"It does not matter. They would have made unreliable subjects anyway. They would remember that we came out of their midst. We'll beget our own deities."

"Yes, my husband."

Jove looked down at the arrow.

"And for you, Odin. Thanks for a quiver full of magic arrows and a powerful bow. I have a mind to give it to my grandson one day."

CHAPTER 39

RISE OF THE
LIVING DEAD

nlucky we are. In order to have offspring we have to lie together," said Juno to Jove. "Yet this strait divides us irrevocably since it is not part of our dominion. We are destined to be so close and so far away from each other's love."

"No task is too difficult for me, the most mighty Jove."

"Yet only a human can accomplish this one simple task."

"Then I shall be human for time. I can mar my head with earthly thoughts. I can deface my virtue with their scheming."

"One can't be a man for a time. Being a man is life's longest and most cruel punishment."

Jove looked down to Anne's arrow, which he held in his right hand.

"This is a small object. But it hides inside so much. Let's see if a god's veins are full of blood."

He carefully pricked his right index finger with Anne's arrow.

"Please, do not leave me, my husband."

"When a human rises out of my body, I will demand that she give you a strait to your dominion. After that, please, send another arrow from the bow that lies by your feet to my body. Let one affliction kill another. Two people inside of one body is two too many. After they kill each other, and not before, please come to this island and nourish me back to health."

"Why do you not let me go through this ordeal? Women are used to giving birth to monsters."

"Women are more ruthless than men. I would have no heart to inflict pain on a woman, but women can inflict any kind of pain on men."

"What is pain but a temporary inconvenience? By enduring pain sometimes one can achieve all goals and live a long and otherwise prosperous life."

Jove's face contorted.

"Hey, I am victorious," Anne's voice spoke from his chest. "I live again."

"Only temporarily," muttered Jove.

"You are deluding yourself," Anne's voice said. "Humanity's affliction always kills gods."

"Whatever," said Jove. "While I am still in charge of you, I order you to proclaim my Juno to be Goddess of the Sea."

"She cannot save you from me. In time I'll eat through you like a hornet's offspring eats a spider from inside."

"Just do what I order you."

"I am looking forward to that happy moment when you lose all power over me. I will slowly squeeze the last drops of blood out of your guts."

Jove's right hand thundered at his chest.

"OK, there is no need for violence," Anne's voice said.

"Do not forget you are inside of me. I can hear all the thoughts that are racing through your mind now. You are biding your time. Yet I know it will take a while before you get stronger than me. If you do not proclaim Juno the Goddess of the Sea, I will pull you out of my chest with my very hands even if it kills me."

"I proclaim this Juno to be the most powerful Goddess of the Sea and all the rivers that bring waters to it and all tributaries that feed these rivers."

"I did not ask you to proclaim her to be Goddess of the Rivers and Creeks. I have no doubt the sneaky mind of yours has arranged a trap for my Juno somewhere. No matter."

Jove turned toward the mainland and said, "Juno, do it now."

Juno picked up another arrow from the quiver, sent the arrow toward the island, and then ran on the water toward the island.

Jove stepped into the path of the arrow.

"No, you don't," Anne's voice said.

Jove's legs collapsed under him.

"I have power over you now. Another moment and I will squeeze the life out of you."

"Not quite," said Jove.

With utmost effort he got up and stood squarely in the arrow's path.

The arrow pierced his heart.

He groaned and fell.

From inside of him, Anne's voice spoke, "No, bitch, you cannot be here. He's mine already."

"That is totally out of the question," retorted Juno. "You softened him up for me. Out of the weakened god, a stronger person rises."

"The world does not need a woman who's stronger than me. Go to hell."

"We'll get there together."

"If one of us does not submit to the other, Jove will prevail. I submit to you—kill me."

"You know you are weaker, so you found an excuse not to face me."

"So, this is how it is? When two women fight they both lose all reason? So, be it."

Two screams came out of Jove's chest at the same time.

Then another weak groan escaped from his chest.

Silence reigned.

Juno climbed up to Jove and took him into her arms.

"I will nourish you back to health, my poor husband."

Jove opened his eyes and looked around.

"What's wrong with your eyes, my husband?" asked Juno. "You recognize me not?"

A strange voice escaped from his chest, "I am not your husband."

Juno jumped back.

"Is it you, Anne?"

"No."

"Who are you and what are you doing inside of my dearest husband's body?"

"I am living flesh. There is nothing inside of me. I am rid of all these silly thoughts and feelings which overwhelm gods and men. Hear my most truthful and honest words: I am the strongest being who ever existed in this world."

"You are nothing but an unlawful trespasser in my husband's body. I will blow all the spider webs and dust out of his insides. I will share with him my most sacred thoughts and feelings. They will take hold inside of his body. I will bring him back."

Jove's body opened its lips slightly and blew softly into Juno's face.

A tornado picked Juno up and threw her against the rocks of the mainland.

In a short while, Juno's body healed itself.

She opened her eyes, than sat up.

"There was another being here already. By virtue of having been here before me and Jove, it is stronger than we are. If there is anybody who can defeat you, the beast of beasts, it has to be him."

Juno picked another arrow out of the quiver, sent the arrow straight up, and then stood still.

The arrow came down and pierced her skull.

"Wonder of wonders," said Anne's voice from inside of Juno's chest. "I am living again. Maybe I need to kill myself more often. It seems to solve my problems quite nicely."

"Your suicide solved nothing and only made matters worse," said Juno. "Rise up quickly, strangle me, and take over my body. I hate you, but I hate you less than I do this abhorrent creature that animates my husband's body. Its insolence is without bounds. I am a goddess and will use any means at my disposal, including self-annihilation, in order to defeat my enemy."

"I cannot accept your sacrifice," said Anne's voice.

"You cannot love me, can you? The world would never see a more bitter irony."

"No, I am just being practical. I will destroy the last living deity, you, if I come out. People are needed, but so are gods."

Juno turned to Jove's body.

"I have failed to destroy you, the beast of beasts. I accept it. I will carry Anne inside of me as a pitiful sign of an unfulfilled promise to my husband. I'll find a subterranean cave and hide there."

"Not so fast," said Anne. "I never said I am giving in to this new monster. It is actually quite exciting to find an enemy I have never crossed swords with before. I will only stick my head out of your back to look around."

Anne's head came out of Juno's back.

"Juno, can you move like an animal for a bit? I will have to be your rider."

Juno fell on her fours.

"Hey, fellows, you made a nice centaur," said a scraggy voice from inside of Jove's chest. "But don't you think it is a little before its time?"

"I did not know an empty body could crack a joke," said Anne.

"You do not know a lot. What's my little joke before this cosmic jest that surrounds me? I am inclined to play a gag on it."

"What you did not create you can't destroy."

"You created no gods yet you destroyed plenty."

"People are a special case."

"Not so special anymore, it seems."

"Eliakim, you are trapped inside of the bow," said Anne. "But you can hear me. We are in desperate need of your help. Grow roots out; turn yourself into a large tree. I have one special arrow to send out."

A small white root snaked out of the bow.

Soon a tall straight yew grew.

A string extended to the yew's thinnest and most bent branch.

"Let's meet your foe, Juno," said Anne. "You share my thoughts, so you know what needs to happen."

The centaur jumped into the tree and reared hard.

The string tensed, and the centaur flew toward Jove.

Out of Jove's mouth air streamed toward the centaur.

A roaring tornado opened its wide mouth.

"Now we shall see out of what I am made of," screamed Anne.

She pulled her hands out of the centaur's sides, grabbed two opposing winds, and pulled the tornado apart.

The centaur crashed inside of Jove's body.

At the very moment of impact Anne jumped out of the centaur.

"Juno, I am leaving you in the most capable hands of your husband," said Anne.

"My dear wife," Jove's skin groaned weakly. "I receive you."

Jove's body closed around Juno.

"I did not explode. My dearest husband's skin is holding me inside of itself. I lost my husband, but I am saved," said Juno.

Anne turned to the yew.

"Eliakim, I plan to fell you now. It will kill you, but I am doing it for your own good. You can only survive if you detach yourself from the tree in the form of a long pike."

She picked a sharp rock and hit the tree.

A pike fell out of it.

"Forgive me, Juno," said Anne. "Sadly, it is time for me to betray you."

Anne pulled the giant bow and sent the pike into Juno.

"Eliakim, you are to root inside of this poor goddess. In time you will take over her body, and we shall be together again."

The pike pierced Juno's body.

"My husband, are you there?" asked Anne.

"Knock, knock," laughed Juno. "But nobody's home. I moved your husband out of the yew and into the string just in nick of time."

"Oh, forgive me, most powerful Goddess," said Anne. "I am sure you can find a space in your heart for compassion. You know there is nothing you wouldn't do to save your own husband."

"I am a woman, so despite your treachery, I understand you."

"Then, please save my husband. Do not let him turn into dust inside that rotten string."

"What do you want me to do?"

"Eat it."

"I will, but on one condition only. If I am to die giving birth to man, I would like to die as the most powerful goddess. So before I eat this string, I would like you to proclaim me the Goddess of this whole continent."

"Do you promise to eat this string?"

"When do gods break their promises?"

"Many of times."

"Point well taken. By the love of my dear husband, I promise to eat this string."

"I proclaim you to be Goddess of the Continent."

Juno picked up the string and swallowed it.

Then she grabbed her own head with both hands and tore it off at once.

Her throat closed in, forming eyes and a mouth.

She spoke: "I kept my word. In time Eliakim will come out of my head. As for me, I need no head."

"I can see you have eyes and mouth right in your throat. But there are no ears."

"I am sure you just noticed I have no ears. Think of it as a protection measure against your guile. I will be a most perfect god for people now, a god who is deaf to people's laments and to their cunning. Beware of me. You are inside of my domain now, and as part of such, I claim full authority over you. Whether you like it or not, you and your husband are my people now."

"Well done, I say," said Eliakim from inside of Juno's head. "What a woman!"

CHAPTER 40

SPORES

he head grew up.

"It is time for you to come out, my husband," said Anne. "If this head grows any larger you will be too tall for your dear wife."

The head cracked in the middle.

"It looks like a large baby making his way out into this world. Push hard from inside, Eliakim. Tear this womb to shreds," said Anne.

The cracks started to heal.

Anne ran to Juno and shook her, "I know you can't hear me. But I swear to all past, current, and future gods, if you do not help me get him out, I will most surely renounce you as Goddess of the Continent."

"There is something serious going on. Otherwise you would not dare to manhandle me," said Juno. "Against my better judgment, I order ears to grow out of my body. Ugh, how much nonsense I will hear now."

Ears grew out of her neck.

"What is it my dear?"

"I knew it," said Anne. "You can always get a god to listen to you. You only have to be irreverent!"

"The head is healing up," said Anne. "I do not like that."

"Well, it only means, he is no more," said Juno. "I'm very sorry to hear that. If it's any consolation, it is not my doing."

"You too display irreverence toward God," said Mustard Seed. "Are you attempting to reach God's ear?"

"Mind your own business and listen," said Barleycorn.

"This head is from your former body."

"You are also from Luminous's former body. Does that make him responsible for your actions?"

"God is responsible for people's actions."

"Well, to follow your logic, he's not. His father created him, so it is his father who's responsible for your actions. Or maybe his predecessor is to blame for your actions? Who do you think we find at other end of this chain if we follow it much deeper? Is there a primordial worm, deaf and blind and lurking deep in total darkness? Does this worm inherit the kingdom of responsibility for the actions of all people?"

"Stop all this commotion," said Eliakim's voice from inside the head. "I am still here."

"Do not listen to it. It is the head who speaks now. It is tricking you," said Juno.

"You cannot know that," said Anne.

"I most certainly can. It was part of my body formerly."

"Like mother, like daughter," said Anne.

"You silly body of mine, speak only for yourself," said the head. "There was no need for harsh words to issue out of your mouth, Juno. I am not tricking anybody. All is well in this best of worlds. Eliakim will be out momentarily."

"Eliakim, come out now," said Anne.

"I can't come out—I am stuck," said Eliakim's voice from inside the head. "You need to come and free me."

"Then, as always, I shall come in and get you out, you poor sod."

"Anne, stop," said Juno. "The head is deceiving you. It wants to get you too. You won't be able to save him. It is too late for that."

"I was always able to in the past. It is never too late to save your spouse."

Anne ran to the head and jumped into its mouth. The mouth closed. A struggle ensued, then the neck grew out longer and longer. Higher and higher the head arose. Then the lower part of the neck widened and formed a double oval shape.

"Which head would you choose, my Juno," a deep voice wondered, "should you have a choice between the two? The one that rests on the shoulders, or the one that is securely attached to a fine set of balls?"

"I do not know about securely," said Juno. "So many times, my Jupiter, when you peered intently into the shadows, hungrily discerning which ones were of the female sex, the strong desire to test the security of their attachment rose in my heart."

"I am ready to make babies," said the deep voice.

"I can see that well."

"Open your body to me."

"I ache to do just that. Yet I am fully aware it's all deceit. My beloved husband is dead."

"I'm very much alive."

"My poor head," said Juno. "You used to rest upon my shoulders. Why did you not keep a small measure of my wisdom? You should have let Eliakim grow and then set him free. But you thought you could feed on him. Could you? I don't know. Men are weak. It's possible that you could have if he were single. But there was his wife. I got to know her. She, like all women, is often angry with her husband. She even claims like many of us that she loves him not. She may even believe she does not. You know us women. But Eliakim was hers and hers only. You cannot take a woman's possession without arousing her vicious wrath. I do not envy you now. The sincere wrath of one woman is one wrath too many."

"I know not what are you talking about, my wife," said the deep voice.

"Should I open my body to this splendid example of male fertility, it will seed me, and I will change into a womb that in time will give birth to Anne and Eliakim."

"Even if you're right, what difference does it make who we bring into this world?" retorted the deep voice. "Do you like deities more than you like people?"

"I like neither. But I hate deceit. Honesty is best if a man wants to bed a woman."

"I can hold my seeds no longer."

"Anne, do you not have enough deities' blood on your hands?" asked Juno. "This has to stop."

She raised her head high and spoke, "I call on you, unborn deities. I'm well aware the gentle slumber of the unborn envelops you. But please, hear my prayer. Even asleep you are already alive. Release your young bladders. Let the golden rain start."

A light yellow rain began to fall.

"I call on you now, deities who had their life's thread cut short. I know gloomy sleep filled with terrible nightmares weighs you down like a heavy tombstone. You care not for living anymore. But please, release your decaying bladders. Let the bloody rain start."

Red drops fell down and intermingled with the yellow drops.

Agony convulsed the huge phallus.

"When the fluid of the living combines with the fluid of the dead, it gives birth to the rain of closure," said Juno. "I am ready for you, my husband. I will now open my body as wide as possible to accommodate your astounding girth. The rain of closure will dissolve us during lovemaking."

Juno's body opened up.

"Stay away from me, you monstrous vagina!" screamed Anne from inside of the phallus. "I will end my life on my terms alone."

"Now you show your true colors," laughed Juno and enveloped the phallus.

"Oh, blessed be thy breadth," groaned Juno.

"Pull out! Pull out now!" screamed Anne from inside the vagina. "The rain of closure eats though your moist vaginal flesh. Free me."

"You want to go somewhere?" laughed Juno. "Please, do."

The vagina opened.

"What are you waiting for?" asked Juno.

"I can't," groaned Anne. "The perpetual frictions won't cease."

"I know you can't. You made your bed when you chose this potent shape. Now you have to lie with me on this fine cot. But worry not. Acid rain will soon dissolve us."

"What will become of us?" groaned Anne.

"The rain will wash away all our impurities. And there are many of those. I, most powerful Goddess and you, most cunning female, and your husband, most irresponsible male, will produce but one small drop of the purest water."

"Will it be used to start new life?"

"Do not be absurd. We are not good enough. See that weak dandelion growing from in the shadow of the large rock? Our drop will quench its thirst."

"For how long?"

"For one day."

"That's all? And what will it drink tomorrow?"

"Nothing. It will wither and die."

"I hate dandelions," Anne railed. "I had accepted my destiny until you spoke of this nasty weed. Thank you for waking my desire to fight one more time."

"The harder you fight, the more vigorously you perform your male service. Fight hard. I never had such intensely deep sexual satisfaction. It puts me at peace with my impending demise."

"I now know your weakness," said Anne. "You like copulation too much. So I am here for you. I'll provide you the deepest gratification. I just increased my girth. How does it feel now?"

"Your head is larger than before," groaned Juno. "It feels even better."

"Would you like it even larger?"

"You know I would."

"How does it feel now?"

"It feels great. I swear, never has a deity enjoyed a living person so much."

"Wow, you can stretch wide, I'll give you that. I just increased my girth. How does it feel now?"

"It is perfect. Stop there."

"On the contrary, I am only getting started. I just increased my girth. How does it feel now?"

"You are hurting me."

"Yet your stretchable walls allow me to continue my thrusts. If anything you're getting wetter. It means even in pain you like my girth. I just increased it. How does it feel now?"

"Stop that. You are a woman too. You shouldn't inflict such pain on the private parts of a member of your own sex."

"So, now I am member of your own sex? Did you just bring me up to a higher plain, or did you lower yourself to mine? What a discovery I've made: if man hurts a deity long enough, the deity becomes equal to the one who hurts her with herself. Is it because you deities only recognize one currency, the currency of pain? Does that make me a millionaire now?"

"Feel me."

"What do you think I have been doing all along if not just that?"

"Do you not like how silky smooth I am inside? Do you find me exciting?"

"I am in the shape of phallus. I am so excited, I can barely hold it together."

"While grinding against my walls do you not feel the soft caress of two eggs swimming around your phallic shape?"

"I do. They bounce like hard jelly around me."

"Then smother them with your eruption. Let the discharged seeds surround them like mesmerized frogs surround a tree where the nightingale croons his evening song."

"You're a clever girl. Not only would I lose my girth, thus relieving you of the pressure I lovingly built inside of your most private part, but you would also be the sole custodian of my seeds. Should you be so inclined—and I suspect you would be—you would go to the creek nearby and wash them out of your body. Who do you take me for? Do you think I myself did not use this age-old trick before? No, for once I, a mere human, have a deity under my thumb, or rather under another part of my anatomy. The purpose of this exercise is for you to learn now what misery people inflict on the deities who meddle in their affairs."

"What do you hope to gain from this horrifyingly inappropriate spectacle?"

"All this time I have been looking into my heart intently for an ounce of empathy toward you, Goddess. Woe to you, for I have found none so far. It is good to be a human. But pardon my digression. I am sure you would like us to continue our most informative endeavor. I just increased my girth now. How does it feel?"

"Ugh. Stop my suffering."

"As you like. I had to wait to hear your request. I acquiesce."

The giant phallus enlarged again.

With a loud popping sound, Juno's vagina burst.

The phallus pulled out. It had the shape of a giant mushroom.

Acid rain made holes after holes in its thick skin.

The skin began to heal quickly.

Juno lay motionless.

Acid bore larger and larger holes in her torn flesh.

A ghostly white hand came out of the mushroom's left ear.

Its index finger moved frantically, writing something.

It moved faster and faster.

A wind blew from it into the torn vagina.

Juno stirred.

"Who sent this refreshing wind?" groaned she. "Why does my life still continue? Why can't I simply die?"

Juno looked at the white hand.

The index finger wrote something anxiously.

"T-h-i-s i-s E-l-i-a-k-i-m," she read.

"Well, hello. I hope you, being a man, enjoyed being inside of me. Now let me die in peace."

"I a-b-h-o-r w-h-a-t A-n-n-e d-i-d," she read. "I c-a-n h-e-l-p y-o-u t-o d-e-s-t-r-o-y h-e-r. S-h-e i-s c-h-a-n-g-i-n-g i-n-t-o a p-r-o-p-e-r m-u-s-h-r-o-o-m. A-t t-h-e v-e-r-y e-n-d o-f h-e-r t-r-a-n-s-f-o-r-m-a-t-i-o-n s-h-e-'ll b-e a-t h-e-r m-o-s-t v-u-l-n-e-r-a-b-l-e. I w-i-l-l t-e-l-l y-o-u w-h-e-n y-o-u c-a-n s-t-r-i-k-e h-e-r d-o-w-n."

"I love kicking mushrooms," said Juno.

She changed into a giant boot.

The mushroom grew darker.

"N-o-w," wrote the index finger.

The giant boot kicked the mushroom.

An enormous cloud of spores enveloped the giant boot.

The spores laughed. "Deities are so gullible. It was always my doing, you trusting head. I needed you kicking my mushroom to give my spores enough momentum to overcome Earth's gravity."

"Eliakim, why did you agree to that?" asked Juno.

"The head offered me a chance of a new beginning," spoke one spore.

"Anne, you are a sensible woman," said Juno. "You know that before you can have a new beginning, you have to renew yourself; otherwise you will be destined to repeat the same mistakes. Yet as far as I can see, you both are still the same people. Anne, why did you succumb to this temptation?"

"One word: women," said Anne. "My husband saw too many pretty faces here. He'd admired too many fine legs. I could live with his gazing at the legs' curves. But his gaze crept higher and higher. In our new place I will be the only woman for him to admire."

"My Jupiter was just like that, but so what? I chose to overlook his depravity. Men's hearts have depths no woman should look into."

"You are a goddess. Your world is large, so you can afford to overlook things. People's world is tiny, so we have to stare for a long time onto the smallest of things."

"We have to hurry," urged the spores. "The acid rain burns us. Our momentum is waning. Our journey will take us far. We must snack quickly. We need all the energy we can acquire."

The spores fell on Juno, gulped her down, and then floated up.

CHAPTER 41

GOD'S MARROW

 am complete once more," said Luminous from the cloud of spores.

"It's about time. Let's leave this accursed place behind," said Anne.

Large fiery eyes appeared between the cloud and outer space. Around the eyes the face grew out. "You don't really plan on leaving now, do you, my son?" asked fiery lips.

"Get out of my way, Lord of Destruction," snarled Luminous.

"You know well that without your creative abilities I cannot exercise my destructive ones. Do you want to leave me and your grandfather here in limbo, unable to march forward toward the destruction of this solar system?"

"I do. I am tired of watching living, breathing things destroyed by you."

"Your allegiance should always lie with your family."

"Each thing I've created is my family."

"I see that you're set in your ways."

"I am."

"Then you have to complete one small task before taking off to new places. You should have no trouble, for it is so insignificant compared with the much larger destiny lying in wait for you."

"No task of yours can pose any difficulties for me after what I've endured here."

"I worked long and hard to bring you up, my son, and so I am incapable of laying a finger on you. Yet fate does not put such restriction on sons. All your life you've received things from me, giving me in turn the most irritated stares back. Here lies your small task: you have to go through me if you want to leave this planet."

"Seize your chance, my God," said Anne. "I know he's your father, but look around and see all the waste he has left in his wake. Please, slay him. He's your true enemy. From him you are running away. When he's no more, you won't even need to leave this planet."

"What are you waiting for?" smiled the fiery face. "It is not like you don't possess the necessary faculties. Do you remember that fine day when you killed the entire dinosaur species? Your grim determined face is forever etched in my memory. I remember thinking, he truly is my son."

"It was a necessary thing to do. I had to make room for another set."

"Looky, looky. I'm still here in one piece. I have to assume that killing your father is not a necessary thing to do?"

"Alas, it is not."

"Why is our precious destiny tied to such a weakling god?" screamed Anne. "Has some vengeful spirit cursed us?"

"You should be forever grateful to him," said the fiery face. "Due to his misplaced generosity you've reached heights no woman ever reached and likely never will again."

"Oh, I doubt that very much," said Anne. "We women are a resourceful lot."

"You're a silly cow, Anne," said the fiery face. "I swear, if you insult my son again I will rip you open."

"If you touch Anne, then you'll know the gravity of my wrath," said Luminous.

"Silly cow?" roared Anne. "Even my boorish husband dares not to call me that name. You're a primordial cosmic joke along with your daft son. I bet there is a real God somewhere who right now laughs his heart out listening to our impudent talk."

"I see what you're doing now, you clever girl," laughed the fiery face. "So when it happens again, you're ready to sacrifice yourself for a good cause. You think if you enrage me enough I'll butcher you, and then my son will get outraged and will slay me. I take back 'silly cow.' You are a beady-eyed scrawny weasel."

"Avenge me, my Lord," demanded Anne. "He calls me names."

"Shut up," said Luminous. "As much as I love you, you are a weasel. This old goat of a father of mine is cleverer than you think. Each solar system needs not only to have a creator but a destroyer too. Should I kill him, the cosmic joke will be on me, for I'll have to split my time between his and my roles."

"I keep you here on this planet for your own good, Lord of Creation," said the fiery face. "Trust me—I have visited each corner of this universe, and there is no empty space left to start a new solar system. My father, Lord of Gas, is a tough, rugged deity. You and I both combined are not worth one gaseous molecule of his. When I lay in my cradle he used to tell me bedtime stories about things he had met during his travels. Your hair would have stood on your head if you'd heard how innocent comets put up fights by releasing such strong poison even my father had to withdraw. He told me about traveling stars that emerged inside of his newly born solar system and devoured planets. He told me he had to risk his very existence once by swallowing a large black hole that attacked his solar system, and how this hole now has a bleeding ulcer slowly releasing bubbles of gas in his body. Trust me, a kind god and innocent people would have no place there in deep space."

"You have been a terrible father. You cared not about my interests. And now you say you stopped me for my own benefit?"

"My son, Lord of Creation, you can only rejoice in each act of begetting life if you abhor the destruction. Have you ever asked yourself why you hate destruction so much? Who instilled into you this burning abhorrence if not your very father by his very example?"

"So you killed each thing I formed, one after another, in order for me to polish my skills as a creator?"

"Just like you are a slave to your destiny to create, I am a slave to mine to destroy."

"Gods have no destiny. You destroy because it's the only pleasure you have ever known. I wish you could create. Then you'd know the way of life."

"Do you not understand I speak from experience? I too made my people. And then I saw their true nature and discarded them just in the nick of time. Soon the time will come, and you will put your toys away too."

"We are not toys," said Anne.

"Wait and see, woman," said the fiery face.

"You are not the Lord of Creation," said Luminous. "You can create nothing."

"How little you know about your father. You should have seen me in the flower of my youth."

"The process of creation requires a certain disposition that you lack."

"Do not overestimate yourself. Just like a woman can give birth due to her internal design, any god can create beings. There is no difference between destruction and creation. But you no longer can see this simple truth, because you performed surgery upon yourself to alter your own design."

"My design was wrong. I have improved on it. Since this surgery I can see there is the difference between destruction and creation."

"In your eyes only."

"Alas, it might be so, but my concern is about my eyes only."

"Pride is your downfall. Billions of generations of Lords of Creation had it all wrong, and you got it right all of a sudden?"

"It is how progress is made: change comes without notice and makes a whole world of difference. Yet you know of no changes. You kill to please my grandfather, Lord of Gas."

"Your grandfather needs no pleasing. He too has his mission before him."

"To turn each solar system he makes into a supernova."

"After all, it was he who forms these solar systems out of himself. It's his body that he destroys. And surely you of anyone should agree one has power over one's body."

"Just how many supernovas has he ignited so far, one after another?"

"I've lost count, but it's in the billions."

"Had any of these countless planets ever flourished?"

"They all did for a bit, and then all had declined."

Silence fell for a moment.

"So where do we go from here, my son?" asked the fiery face.

"I have no answer. But I will submit an observation: the breadth of our hate toward each other is profound. The gulf between us gapes open. How many victims of our hate will fall into it?"

"I beg to differ. My contempt for you was very much the same since time immemorial. Yet it never stopped me from having an occasional family dinner with you. If you have it in you, we still can be reluctant allies."

"Sorry, I do not have it in me. Remember when you spoke about past planets that never flourished for long? I think you just pointed the way forward to me."

"Speak up."

"Look down now."

"What have you done to our planet? It flourishes as it never has before. Oceans are teaming with fish; deserts are covered with a thick coat of vegetation; icy tongues of glaciers have retreated to the tops of the highest mountains. Do I take this splendor as a sign of a peace offering? Tell me please, how did you do it. Is there a fountain of creativity deep in your soul I was not aware before? Why has it sprung only now? Is it because you've accepted your destiny and decided to proceed forth bravely?"

"Luminous, how wonderfully transformed is our world now. How did you do it, really?" asked Anne.

"Anne, I will let you in on the secret. We gods are powerful. But even we are sometimes in need of something little extra."

"You did not do it, my son!" roared the fiery face.

"This extra is called god's marrow," continued Luminous. "It's a marvelous substance. Even my father and my grandfather do not know out of where it came from."

"You did not do it, my son!" roared the fiery face again.

"The story goes that another primordial being made us out of this marrow. But some was left. And being a generous host, this being packed what was left into a tabernacle and entrusted it to a flock of phoenixes. So, when the going gets rough for us three, we can call on the phoenixes to bring the tabernacle forward. Then we open it and breathe in the god's marrow. It puts us briefly on an entirely different plain. Our perception is heightened, and we rise above our normal abilities. My grandfather, Lord of Gas, breathes it in before creating a solar system. My father, Lord of Destruction, breathes it in before sending forth a major famine. I too have breathed it in, before I created you and Eliakim."

"Please, tell me my son, you did not do it," roared the fiery face.

"Why does he yell like a pig slaughtered?" asked Anne.

"He guessed what I did," said Luminous. "I have silently ordered the phoenixes to bring the tabernacle to the highest point above the equator and empty it out. Marrow has fallen down by now. Part of it dissipated into the air, part of it fell into the ocean, and part of it fell into ground. The whole of the planet is fertile now."

"What have you done, my son? You worried about this planet. But its destiny is already set. You know all planets are destined to die."

"You and your father had stacked your deck against all past planets. With the help of marrow this planet might have a fighting chance. The future is open now."

"But you killed your blood line. You killed your kin. Why do you hate your kind so much? Your grandfather is spread out in molecules of gas. He will be waiting forever for his turn to destroy this planet. He will wither eventually. I, your father, will be forever called Death. And you, wayward son, one day will come under attack from your favorite people. You will reach out in vain for the marrow's sweet smell. But none will be there for you. Then you'll fall under people's knives and I, Death, will come for you. Your death will clear the way for Nameless to come forth. He'll inherit it all, but he will remember how your people betrayed you. So he will forever be suspicious toward his own people."

"We gods are a tired species, and we carry many burdens. Maybe, in place of ours, a new species of deities will rise up. They will have flaws but the flaws will be of their own. They will make blunders but they will be their own blunders. For the first time in a very long while, the future is open now."

CHAPTER 42

NO HOPE

he fiery face contorted.

Miniature tornadoes moved across its surface.

"What's wrong, my father?" asked Luminous. "Make an effort and share my optimism."

"How can I? There is no way to improve things here."

"You just do not see the way. But it's still here."

"Gods see all."

"Even we gods find ourselves in complete darkness sometimes."

"Then we stop and do not move forward."

"We gods never stop. When darkness grows around us, we plod forward diligently, trusting our sense of direction."

"There is no single path; that is, there are many paths."

"No, there is only one single correct path."

"When I was young and had hope, I believed in that too. Hope is a disease; young people do not have the immunity to resist its onslaught. It fills their eyes with beautiful visions; it devastates their reasoning, and they no longer grasp there is no inherent order but only myriad conflicting pathways. Blessed be the old. We are invulnerable to optimism's false pretenses. We've learned how to survive without hope."

"Life has defeated you. This is the wisdom of the timeworn."

"It is, but look at you. You too are no longer young, my son. Time is upon you to accept my wisdom. You need to do it now."

"If I accept there is no hope here, I'll have no reason to live."

"Accept it now. It will make it easier for me to do what I set my mind on. You will be at peace when death comes."

"You plan on killing me? Nonsense. You're just in a bad mood. Relax," laughed Luminous. "Trust your wayward son. This is not the end of this planet."

"My mind is set. Your death is upon you."

"Then tell me, how exactly do you plan to do away with me? You are a god too. You know it's almost impossible to kill one of our kind."

"I'll squash you. After you've been demolecularized for twenty-four hours you'll cease to exist."

The fiery face changed into a square block one mile long.

"This is the hardest type of diamond that chemical composition permits," said Lord of Destruction.

"I feel not threatened even the smallest bit. How could you bring pressure on me? There is no surface in the world hard enough that I could not push back against."

"There is, and it is your grandfather."

Another diamond block one mile long appeared on the other side of Luminous.

"You are stricken by grief," said Luminous. "Believe me, I understand."

His voice wavered.

"This is the very first time I have seen him that scared," whispered Anne.

"No, it is the second time," whispered back Eliakim. "Remember, when the pterodactyl tore him up and swallowed at the very moment when the allosaurus ate the pterodactyl, at the very moment when the giganotosaurus ate the allosaurus?"

"My father, I know you think that without a supply of marrow we're just another set of inhabitants of this planet, even if stronger than tigers and elephants. But think about it, without marrow we gods are still gods. We no longer have the ability to up the ante when we desire. But if we use our strength wisely, we still can retain our stature and even influence progress. You should not mete punishment for my dispersing marrow but see it as an opportunity to rise to a difficult challenge."

"My heart knows of no desire to punish you, though by God I have the right to feel one. Your death is our death, since we are part of one continued cycle. You are just the key to unlock this door and let nothingness take all of us."

"Is the time of death upon you, my Lord?" cried Anne out.

"It's very likely."

"Optimist to the end," said the Lord of Destruction. "He thinks there is a single chance for him to survive."

The two diamond blocks moved closer and closer.

"My people," said Luminous. "Some unpleasant things are about to transpire. We gods are a violent race."

He leapt up.

The two diamond blocks collided with him in the middle.

Anne yelped.

When the glistening cloud of diamond fragments dissipated, in between the severely reduced diamond blocks stood Luminous.

His body was deformed, his flesh torn severely.

"Your skull is bashed in; your legs are broken," wailed Anne. "Are you still living?"

"To my great surprise, I still am," muttered Luminous.

"There is something invisible just below you. It took the brunt of the strike," said Eliakim. "It holds the two diamond blocks separate, thus keeping you alive."

"I would never," said Luminous and stopped.

He laughed hard. "My enemy saved me from my friends."

"The Devil?" asked Anne.

"Him? No, the Devil is no enemy of God."

A window opened in midair, and the Devil's beady eyes looked down at them.

"Disrespect!" he cried out.

"Long time no see," Anne called back.

"Quite the contrary, I have been watching you for a very long time from my high perch. Kiki-Rikki!"

"Seriously, where have you been?" asked Anne.

"Have you missed me, my dear? Truth be told, you get my respect for calling my name."

"Be gone," said Luminous.

"But why can't I stay? I am smarter now, since I've learned a lot watching you struggle with your people."

"First of all, you watched nothing, since you did not exist a moment ago. You can only come into being when someone mentions you."

"Anne, once more full respect to you for using my name," said the Devil. "Please, remember me in each of your evening prayers."

Luminous continued, "Second of all, I have made you in such way that you can learn nothing. You are destined to forever repeat the same mistakes."

"But what delicious mistakes I repeat! I, a gourmet, am able to forget the taste of a great dish, so each time I eat it I feel the same delight I've felt the very first time. What kind of punishment is that? Admit it, my Lord, you bestow this precious gift upon me because you love me even more than you love your precious people."

"I do not."

"Then why have you given me, your trusted wolf, such strength to attack your cows, your people? Is this because you, the bull, would like to show off coming to their rescue and boldly charge me?"

"Forget him, Luminous, and tell us, what is hanging below you that you owe your life to?" asked Anne.

Luminous waved his right hand.

A large net made of thick hemp rope appeared below him.

The ropes went from the net and tied around his midsection.

Many humanoid beings crawled inside the net.

"My nation," exclaimed the Devil.

"Look, Eliakim. Real tears flow down his face," said Anne. "He's not jesting."

"What are these beings?" asked Eliakim.

"I have been picking them up everywhere I could find," said Luminous. "They are a self-righteous lot and destined to grow forever and ever. And each time I find one I always put him or her into my net."

"Where did they come from?"

"These are results of my previous experiments."

"Why do you carry them in a net connected to your midriff?"

"It is my destiny to grow stronger and stronger. Yet I believe it is in my best interest to keep my strength in check. By means of this weight I dramatically slow myself down."

"That's why you appear much weaker then you are," said Lord of Destruction. "My poor son, you can't even trust your own strength."

"Why do you dislike self-righteousness so much?" asked Anne. "I've always thought of it as the most potent weapon to fight God with and break his dominion."

"I've made your insides. I've put you together. I know how you function. You can't be without God. But you can reject me. Then self-righteousness fills you."

"Like a succulent cream fills a pastry that has even not been invented," marveled the Devil. "Delicious."

"You said you've experimented on us?" said Anne. "You speak of us people as of machines. It is intolerable."

"But you are machines, if only a biological kind."

"We do not accept biology. We would like to grow not out of the biological swamp, but out of the fine starry dust. After all, we are successors to gods."

"A most noble sentiment is to grow," said the Devil. "Once you're past the ABCs of physics I have just the thing for you. One small diagram of a nice bomb is one giant step to making a great, strong people. I'll let you in on the secret: even God himself will look away when you explode my bomb."

"You talk too much," grumbled Luminous.

"That's because you don't allow me to do much. Allow me to do things, and I will be the most pliant creature that ever existed."

"Close the window from the other side," said Luminous.

The window in midair closed.

Luminous looked down, "Anne, as you can see, self-righteousness is even stronger than the wrath of gods."

"My son, you are quite a collector," said Lord of Destruction. "Your own freak show wrapped tight in the net has saved you from certain destruction. Yet we can still achieve it by other means. We can squash your favorite people."

The two diamond blocks moved apart.

"How would the death of my people help you destroy me?"

"You've used gods' marrow to create them. After they are gone, you just won't be able to help yourself but undoubtedly will create people again. But without the helping magic of marrow, your creations will be so despicable that their criminal actions will leave a bitter taste in your mouth forever and ever. Then harsh tears of defeat will blacken your soul as they did our souls, and your suffering will be equal to ours."

The diamond blocks positioned themselves on either side of the people.

"My people, there is only one way for you to survive," said Luminous. "Move inside of my net. Deep inside, you know you are too filled with self-righteousness."

"Will we be able to get out of this net afterward?" asked Anne.

"Only after you renounce your self-righteousness."

"Don't you understand? That's exactly what your father and grand-father planned. We will be in this net always."

"It is your choice."

"No, it is not," said Anne. "Don't you see, self-righteousness is but another tool in our toolbox? There is only one paramount need for us here: it is to survive. We need all our tools."

"You'll need no tools if you perish right now."

"We won't. I believe there is but another way for us to survive."

She turned to Eliakim, "Please, open each fiber of your body and soul to these two blocks."

"They will squash us. We need to fight these blocks."

"On the contrary, we need to accept them."

The diamond blocks collided.

Sparks rained down.

Then the blocks separated.

"We are still here," marveled Eliakim. "How is it possible?"

"Although we people are weaker, we are more resilient. Can a hurri-cane damage grass? No, for grass will bend down under its onslaught and then will stand up again."

"The diamond blocks are coming together again. Have we won? Should we stay here and let them keep bumping through us?"

The diamond blocks collided.

"I'm kind of getting used to this strange sensation," said Eliakim. "It's like having a rush going through your body."

"You always liked the rotten juice of any fruit you could find," said Anne. "I'm not surprised."

"But see, here I do not need to be in constant search for new sourc-es. I can just stand there in between these two diamond blocks and feel rush after rush going through me."

"Our strength as a species lies in our noncompliance to our

circumstances. Yet if we practice compliance long enough, sooner or later it will alter our nature," said Anne.

"Trust me, even filled with rotten juice I can always keep sober head."

"Would you be able to walk on water too? God, what you men would not say to fill your stomach with this swill."

"As I recall you've consumed your fair share of rotten juice."

"That's it," thundered the Lord of Destruction. "I've had enough. To compare divine interference into your life with alcohol is too much even for me. Screw these abominable people. After we destroy Luminous, they will not matter."

"I thought you could not," said Anne.

"For each action there is a counteraction. One can defeat self-righteousness."

"Teach me how," said Luminous. "Long and hard I've searched for a way, but it always eluded me."

"Because your love of the things you've created blinds you," said Lord of Destruction.

"We are not things," retorted Anne.

"From where you stand, that might be the case," said Lord of Destruction. "But from of where I stand, you look no different than most obnoxious cockroaches."

"You are bluffing, my father," said Luminous. "There is no way to defeat self-righteousness. It is a plague. The only thing to do is to collect the self-righteous lot and store them away from the rest of humanity."

"Self-righteousness is a form of group behavior," said Lord of Destruction. "Each self-righteous being needs to have other beings around, so it can compare him- or herself to other beings. This comparison always ends up in favor of the self-righteous ones. But put self-righteous beings into solitary confinement, and their self-righteousness will run out of them like the water they piss out all the time."

"But sooner or later they will emerge out of solitary confinement even more self-righteous than before."

"Who said they will get out?"

"The self-righteous beings I've collected belong to me," declared Luminous. "They are inside my net. You can't get to them."

"You make them suffer in there?"

"Yes."

"Is your goal to punish them?"

"Yes."

"That's why you are unable to stop me. I have found a more severe and thus more effective form of punishment. In separate confinements they will repent their sins."

The net grew.

Black boxes filled it.

"Let's give it a moment," said Lord of Destruction. "The chemical reaction will start soon."

"How can we help you, our Lord?" asked Anne.

"A bit of a magic would be very handy now."

"Is magic not associated with gods only?"

"Sometimes magic persists where there was a lot of it before."

"I know just the place," said Eliakim. "Anne, remember of Titan of Fire? His dead body should still have some of magic left."

"Then we have to find a way to get inside of his grave."

"His grave is not so far away."

They ran.

CHAPTER 43

A COMPOUND

 hey stood atop the hill.

"Some objects are so sacred nothing can touch them. All we have to do is to position his dead body between these two diamond plates," Anne proposed.

"How would we do that?" asked Eliakim.

"I know, you are dead, Titan of Fire," said Anne solemnly. "But please let your dead ears clear the goo of decaying flesh and receive our words."

A loud hiss came from under the ground.

"Let your windpipe unclog so air can enter your dead lungs. Let your tongue form again from dissipated flesh. Speak to me, dead titan."

A harsh voice came forth, "Who are you and why do you disturb my rest?"

"We are people and we require a service of you."

"Do I owe you a debt of gratitude?"

"You do not."

"Did I make a pledge to help you before I died?"

"You have not."

A large, rotting hand reached out of the grave and grasped Anne.

"One of these conditions needed to be satisfied in order for the requester of my help to survive. You should not have called for me. Rot from my hand will spread out to your body now. It will suck the life out of you."

"Luminous, listen to me," said Anne. "Do the cries of self-righteous beings not rise out of black boxes?"

"They wail and repent."

"Forgive them now."

"If I do, there will be no resistance left in this net. My father and my grandfather will squash me into one bloody mass."

"There will be no resistance left in this net any moment now. Give at least the peace of forgiveness to these suffering beings."

"Always you are worried about sinners, Anne. Oh, well. I guess you are right. Before I die I should forgive everyone."

Luminous raised his voice, "You are forgiven!"

The net broke. The black boxes dissolved in air.

Many beings fell down to the ground.

Diamond blocks pushed into Luminous.

Then with a loud clang they crashed into his body.

A cloud of bloody fog spread.

"I just received a distress call I cannot ignore," spoke the harsh voice from below. "One who was like a son to me cried out. I can't figure out, though, where his cry is coming from. It is like he was dispersed by a great force into an infinite number of particles."

"God needs your help," said Anne. "Raise your arms high in the air and grasp as many particles as you possibly can."

The titan's rotten hands shot up and cupped together.

A ball appeared in his hands.

It was full of swirling lights.

Rotten flesh changed to living flesh.

"No, you are not," said Anne. "You can't use God to regenerate yourself."

"Why not? One has to help himself."

"You are so much better than that."

"I was always a sucker for flattery."

Rotten flesh covered titan's hands again.

"We were able to decimate our own son," said Lord of Destruction. "It will be piece of cake to dispose of two rotten hands."

"Make sure this piece of cake does not get stuck in your throat," Titan of Fire cried out. "Nothing invigorates me more than good fight. It is almost as good as holding a living god in my hands. Are you worthy opponents? Or do you plan to waste my time?"

"We are two gods in the shape of diamond blocks four miles across. United we produce pressure only found in the middle of stars."

"I thought so. You are humbugs filled with crystallized air. Yet since you challenged me you'll have to suffer my wrath."

"Come out of the ground and fight us."

"I have a better punishment for you in mind. You would like to fight? I will deny you this opportunity."

"Only through a fair fight will you be able to conquer us."

"Who's talking about fighting? I don't fight humbugs. My punishment is to show you my full contempt."

The dead head of Titan of Fire rose up from the ground.

Its mouth opened.

"Step in, people," said the harsh voice. "No harm will befall you."

"Watch these sharp teeth," said Anne and stepped in.

Eliakim followed her in.

The head expanded into a compound.

The titan laughed, "Try to squash us now. I will always be in between you, humbugs. I can be as wide as the ocean and as narrow as the eye of a needle."

The diamond plates collided with the titan's walls.

When the diamond dust settled, the plates were gone.

"I thought so," said Titan of Fire.

He lowered the ball of swirling lights.

Luminous rose up from the ball.

"I have saved you, God," roared the harsh voice.

"At what cost?" asked Luminous.

"Nothing is worth more than God's life."

"In this case I doubt it," said Luminous. "But never mind. Go ahead and finish your work."

High walls grew around the compound.

A large castle rose up in its middle.

"I am returning to the land of dead," said Titan of Fire.

"Sleep tight," said Luminous. "And thank you for saving me. I hope the medicine is not worse than the disease it cured."

"What do you mean?" asked Anne.

"Look around. Do you recognize this place?"

"It is just a compound," said Anne.

"I recognize it. This is Eden," said Eliakim.

"Is it not a great thing?" asked Anne. "Eden is a birthplace, a starting point. Out of Eden people will spread out through planet."

"No, Eden is where the end of the world comes," said Luminous.

CHAPTER 44

TO START OVER

nne, Eliakim, and Luminous walked through Eden's meadow.

"Old memories come back to me now," said Luminous. "I remember when I created Eden and walked in it for the very first time. All the different plants and birds and animals were waiting for me at the gates. I observed one after the other and rejoiced in the singular uniqueness of each one."

"You are unique too," said Eliakim. "Why could you not stay there? Why did you have to leave Eden, taking us with you?"

"We've spent so many years together, and yet you still do not understand the difference between us."

"You are much stronger, that's all."

"So you think I am some sort of superhuman?"

"Actually, I think a person is some sort of underpowered deity, kind of like a mighty hawk with its wings clipped off."

"You could not be more wrong. Deities are more like talking plants. This type of plant is smarter than a person, but it uses its brain only to satisfy its immediate needs, like finding a good source of water, soil filled with nutrients, and spots on the sun. The very purpose of Eden's walls was to stop any kind of adverse reaction from a hostile planet. Even the sun's rays went through an invisible dome."

"If you, a god, are like a plant, would it not be much simpler for you to dwell like a potted flower in a transparent bubble? Why was Eden full of so many different life forms?"

"They all were casts, including you. A deity does not put roots down forever. If we did that, we would have been just another species for forestry. Once in a while, we desire to change our shapes. That is what all these casts are for."

"So, when we thought you left Eden on business, you actually were still there?" asked Anne.

"Yes, that day I was a flower, or a hummingbird, or a catfish in the stream."

"So you really watched us all the time? This is sick."

"You think too much of yourself. I simply enjoyed my new shape and cared not what you did. But gradually I took more and more interest in you people, because you were peculiar."

"That was when you started to come to us every day? I remember I felt very proud to have attracted your curiosity."

"Yes, but of course, I never left Eden in between our talks. I taught you things. The more you learned, the more interesting thoughts you shared with me. Sometimes I barely could conceal my bewilderment when you confronted me with your unusual deductions. I told myself, I've lived for a very long time, and yet this thought had never crossed my mind. Then an even more peculiar thing happened. It was late spring. The sweet grasses grew tall. Usually I changed into a buffalo for several weeks and gorged on them. But that year something strange took place. The sweet grasses called to me just the same, and my leg muscles twitched, remembering meadow expanse. Yet I felt a strange lack of desire to shed my human shape. At that moment, I felt I had to know what would happen to me if I went all the way on this journey and stayed in a man's shape, thinking a man's thoughts. I had no way to draw on my ancestors' experiences, since gods had never done such a thing before. I racked my brain to try to find a path forward for us. I had to enrich our knowledge, but how? The only idea I could come with was to leave Eden and gain knowledge from the outside world. The problem was, deities such as I are not invincible in the open. That's why none of us ever roamed free, even through the safest planets. And this planet is not safe by a long shot. I hesitated for a long time, and I grew more and more restless. Finally, I made up my mind: to my Eden, my safest abode, I owed an opportunity to go outside of its walls."

"Was this when you told us we needed to step outside of Eden's borders and take a long journey to add to the sum of our knowledge?" asked Anne.

"Yes, this was then. Eden afforded us refuge from all miseries, but there is only one kind of wisdom that counts: it is the wisdom of the sufferer."

"And suffer we did," agreed Anne. "And we all gained much knowledge. And now we are back here. The circle is complete. We all got older and wiser. One has to go through turbulent times to grow in appreciation of quiet refuge. I no longer wish to open new horizons or discover something I have never experienced before. I feel certain we will enjoy Eden much more now. We'll sit down and grow our roots here. There are so many things I would like to discuss with you, Luminous."

"I believe I've acquired as much knowledge as I was able to," said Luminous. "I will take on a different shape now."

"Go, go now, our God," said Anne. "Sweet pastures call on you. Azure skies await you. Deep lakes long for you."

Luminous's shape slowly dissolved.

Anne and Eliakim took a trek around a lake.

"All is familiar to me," said Anne. "I remember each corner. But these memories do not stifle me. On the contrary, I fell secure having them."

"I wish it were true for Luminous," said Eliakim.

"What do you mean?"

"Look there. Do you see how that tree just changed into a shrub, and the shrub changed into a blade of grass, and the blade of grass changed into long ivy?"

"Luminous, please, slow down," cried out Anne. "Eden has many casts for you, but not of unlimited quantity. Slow down. Your speed is building momentum. Your movements grow frantic. I feel something terrible is upon us all."

Luminous took the shape of a man.

"What you referred to as something terrible did just happen," said he.

"It cannot be that terrible, you are still with us."

"I no longer can take any other shape but a man's. I have become living human flesh."

"You simply do not want to change," said Anne. "Try harder."

"Being a god I can bend my own will and force myself to do what's best for me. It is not I who stops me. It's the opposite: no other shape accepts me."

"Why?"

"I think like a man. I behave like a man. How can a blade of grass accept me if I no longer cherish immobility and can't be still? This is all due to the gift of humanity you shared with me."

"Do you think it was a poisonous gift?"

"I do not. I like the human point of view. I like to think like a human. You people have this awesome ability to put things together right in your head, creating a whole universe in the blink of an eye. Of course, this universe is not real. But on other hand, when you destroy it the next moment, you need not feel empathy for it. So you can go coolly on, creating a brand new universe out of its pieces."

"So you will be in human shape now?" said Eliakim. "I see nothing wrong with that."

"Yes, you are stuck with me as a man."

"Hold on, Eliakim," said Anne. "You forgot that the whole idea for us people was to lose our knowledge and sink here into a second childhood, accepting Eden as our true home for first time. If God stays with us, how can we discard all knowledge? God will be a constant sorrowful reminder of what we are leaving behind. But if we can't enjoy being here, Eden becomes our prison."

"I am trapped, and I trap you. I am so sorry," said Luminous.

"Can we leave Eden?" asked Eliakim.

"We can only leave it if there is something left for us to learn in the world."

"There must be something out there we can learn from."

"I think not. We're trapped inside."

"Woe to us all."

CHAPTER 45

GOOD BOOK

ook, Eliakim, there is a blurry spot next to the wall," said Anne.

"I see it too. It gets clearer with each passing moment. The blurriness is gone now. It is a folio."

"Luminous, what is it?" asked Anne.

"Look at him. His face is frozen," said Eliakim. "Let me feel him. He's cold as a statue."

"He was fine one moment ago. This folio must have done something to him."

"It must be a truly magical object to paralyze God. Let me get closer to it."

"Be careful."

"Letters appear there one by one."

"What does it say?"

"'Good book.'"

"I've never heard of it."

"The invisible hand keeps writing. It says now: 'Chapter 1. There was Eden.'"

"Folio is correct. There is Eden. Folio is smart."

"It says now: 'There was a guard tower next to the gate. Two guards were there, Soldier and Boss.'"

"That is incorrect. There is no guard tower. Maybe it is not smart after all."

"Look over there. This section of the wall is blurry. The guard tower is forming itself. And there are two guards outside."

"Could it be that Eden needs no god, but needs this good book? That's why Luminous is frozen?"

"You can talk to God, but you can't talk to a book. I do not like it," said Anne. "Let's go through the gate outside. These two guards can have Eden for themselves."

"What about Luminous?" asked Eliakim.

"We'll carry him with us. Likely he'll come back to life when the 'good book' can influence him no more."

Anne and Eliakim carefully picked up Luminous and proceeded to the gate.

"Step away from the entry," said Soldier.

"Please, open your gate and let us out," said Anne.

"Boss," said Soldier. "There are some trespassers. They want to get out."

Boss said, "You know the rules. No traffic in or out."

"Shall I consult the book?" asked Soldier.

"What book?" asked Boss.

"The book that lies before me on my desk."

"Idiot, you are a soldier. Soldiers don't have desks."

"I guess the desk appeared right at the same time as the book did. I reckon a book needs a desk to lie on."

"What's the book's title?"

"It says 'Good book.'"

"Well, since it is a good book, go ahead and consult it."

"It says there, Eden requires at all times to have one man and one woman wandering its premises."

"Ask them if they wandered about the mentioned premises?"

"We did," said Anne. "We wandered them so hard, my soles ache."

"Well, then, since the good book says you need to wander, go ahead and wander some more," said Boss.

"Boss, there is a glaring discrepancy here," said Soldier. "The good book says there should be one man and one woman. We have here one woman and two men."

"Hmm, a love triangle."

"Hey, watch your tone," said Anne. "The one on my left is not a man but God."

"Let me check the good book," said Soldier. "It does not list any gods here. Let me look at the appendix. It says there, 'Current whereabouts of God are unknown.' If they are unknown, this man cannot be God, because we see him clearly. That makes his whereabouts known."

"Luminous is God," said Anne.

"Not according to good book," said Soldier.

"Throw one man outside of the gate," ordered Boss.

"Which one do I throw?"

"Idiot, ask each one of them if he is a man. The one who says he is, keep him and throw the other one out."

"But what if the second one is a man too?"

"So what? The good book says only one man is needed. It does not give any particulars, does it?"

"No, it says a man."

"I am a man," said Eliakim.

"Throw the second one out."

Soldier picked up Luminous and threw him over the gate.

"Make sure all is correct with these two," said Boss.

"Boss, you are so smart," said Soldier.

"What's that?"

"The appendix says the man and woman need to be naked."

"Check the edition of your good book," said Anne. "It must be an old one. We used to walk naked in Eden. Now we cover ourselves."

"This is a new book."

"What makes you think so?" asked Anne.

"It appeared only this morning," said Soldier.

"A single louse appeared on my head this morning too. Does it make this louse new?"

"Let me check the book's cover. It says its first and only edition," said Soldier.

"Oaf," said Anne. "Of course it would say so. The writer was sure no subsequent edition would ever be needed again. He must have had very high self-esteem."

"That may be true; however, this is the only good book we got. We have to follow it. Peel their clothes off," ordered Boss.

"Wait a minute," said Anne. "You can't do that."

"Why's that?"

"Women take their clothes off at their own free will."

"Then will it and take them off."

"I desire not to will it."

"Why's that?"

"When a woman is not alone she should cover her shame."

"Let me check the appendix," said Soldier. "Nowhere have I seen shame listed among woman's attributes. This one is clear: a woman knows of no shame."

"Check's man's attributes too," said Boss. "My common sense tells me, before a naked woman no man walks clothed."

"You are so right, Boss," said Soldier. "Nakedness is listed as his attribute too."

"Anne's right," cried out Eliakim. "You have an outdated edition of the good book. Not that I mind walking naked."

Soldier ripped the people's clothes off.

"I also have another attribute," said Anne and stuck her tongue out. "A knowledge of astrophysics."

"Let me check the rest of your attributes," said Soldier. "No familiarity with tall words is listed there. I know not what astrophysics means. But I know one thing for sure; you are not authorized to know of such matters."

"You can rip clothes off a woman's body, but how can you remove contempt for an arrogant brute out of her eyes?"

"Let me check the catalog of woman's attributes. Nowhere does the good book say contempt in woman's eyes counts. It further notes that woman is very finicky and alters her behavior for no apparent reason."

"No apparent reason to you, ignoramus."

"Another big word. Just how many do you know?"

"Enough to make your head spin."

"Boss, can we really allow her to roam through Eden full of these words?"

"Check the good book."

"It says the word is mightier than the sword."

"Swords bother me not. We are not susceptible to their thrusts. She can roam."

"But the vegetation is susceptible."

"Do you expect her to talk to trees?"

"Not unless she's dim."

"Do you think she is?"

"Boss, she might be. In my experience I've seen too many fools cover themselves with the fig leaves of big words."

"Let me observe her once again, Soldier. I see not a single fig leaf covering her nakedness."

"Boor," said Anne. "When you see a naked woman you should look away."

"What's the fun in that?" said Boss.

"Boss, I meant fig leaves in the figurative sense."

"I will be damned. A big word came out of your mouth. Beware, if you caught her germs, I will send you to clean the latrines elephants use."

"They do not use latrines, Boss. They do their business in the fresh air."

"Idiot, the air can't be fresh if they do it outside. This is Eden, for heaven's sake. They cannot soil the most sacred place on Earth."

"Sorry, Boss. It is not my fault their waste smells so disgusting."

"You speak too florid all of a sudden."

"This is what happens to a real man when a good woman is around," said Anne.

"Where is she?" asked Boss. "I see none."

"Am I not good for you?"

"I'd never call you good; clever, yes; conniving, yes twice; scheming, yes trice."

"The meaning of conniving and scheming is the same, Boss."

"You must have picked up her germs. Where did you touch her?"

"He did not touch me. I must have touched his soul."

"Pull up your soul, idiot. Let me inspect it."

"I can't, Boss. It is what makes me alive."

"So, if I kill you, your soul will come out?"

"It will, but who will guard the gates?"

"You are correct for a change. Be happy: your job has saved you. Check the good book's appendix and see if we need to inspect them further."

"It says here: make sure Eden's inhabitants do not carry weapons."

"Woman, speak the truth, do you carry weapons on you?"

"I actually do. A woman's most potent weapon is always with her."

"I did not mean your tongue, though you have inflicted emotional scars on me with it already."

"I did not mean that. A woman's most potent weapon is between her legs."

"I can see no weapon there."

"Boss, could it be because of the mass of coarse dark hair that covers this spot? Does her statement necessitate closer inspection?"

"Cease and desist! Not one step closer to that spot. Who knows—maybe she speaks the truth. Check the good book for more instructions."

"It says we need to inquire what type of weaponry that is. Is this a weapon of mass destruction?"

"It is for men," retorted Anne.

"Then it does not concern us. I reckon it's some sort of failsafe mechanism our Lord created so women can exterminate men."

"Boss, you just used a tall word."

"Did I?"

"A good woman can even have a positive impact on a boor like you," said Anne.

"But Boss, if it's a failsafe design used to exterminate men, is there a failsafe design to exterminate women?"

"There is no such thing," said Anne. "A woman endures everything."

"Your tongue is too piercing. A being with such a tongue would soon dominate the world," said Boss. "There's got to be a way to exterminate you, woman."

"Boss, the man is silent. Could he be packing a weapon of women's mass destruction?"

"If he does, it will be located at the same spot as the woman's. Get closer and take a peek."

"I am afraid to get close. Remember, Boss, we were just created. What if I am a woman? Then he will exterminate me. I do not want to die. Shall I examine my privates first?"

"Oh, spare me," said Anne.

"She's right, spare me too. Anyway, who knows what we'll find in your parts? You can examine them later at your leisure. I order you to step closer to the man and examine his spot. Just make sure you do not touch anything."

"He'd better not," said Eliakim.

Soldier stepped closer.

"His hair is scruffy," he said. "He needs to wash it more often. But there is something there indeed. However it looks too insignificant to be any sort of serious weaponry."

"Thanks for revealing your weakness," said Anne. "You're afraid of our weapons? Make yours ready, Eliakim."

"I'd hate to go through the trouble only to hear from you you're in no mood."

"The things I just asked of you are no trouble for you by a long shot. I rather recall you enjoy them even when I am not in the mood."

"Are you sure you want sex?"

"Sex by itself holds little interest for me. But manipulate someone by means of sex—that I'd enjoy very much."

"Don't I know it? Anyway, it is ready."

"Boss, something happened with the man. How can I describe it?"

"Don't describe it. I see it with my own eyes. I'll be damned."

"Boss, if they activate their weapons at the same time, the force of the explosion may be too high. Shall I get in between the man and the woman?"

"Sure, come here, if you'd like some of it," said Eliakim.

"I commend your valor, Soldier," said Boss. "But step back."

Anne and Eliakim united.

"What do you think the radius of the explosion will be?" asked Soldier. "What if it takes out the whole of Eden?"

"Check the good book."

"Boss, it rewrote itself. I checked from the very beginning. There is no more mention of guards and a guard tower."

"It is a punishment for our failure to stop these proclivities. If the good book's content changes in response to the actions of people, it means the good book's focus is directed toward people and not us guards."

"I'm scared. I do not want to be gone."

"Do not despair, all is not lost. See, we still look the same. I guess we have until we go back to sleep. Check the back of the good book. Did it finish writing itself?"

"It did. It's one thick volume."

"Go to the very end. What does it say there?"

"Revelations, chapter 23."

"No such chapter. Pull it out."

"What if it is written about us? We will be gone too."

"We might be powerful guards, but we will not live until the end of time. Tear chapter 23 out with confidence."

Soldier held up a handful of paper. "What shall I do with the pages?"

"Lay them like bricks around us."

"It is working. There is a box forming around us."

"Look, the good book itself is flying through the air toward us."

"It's truly remarkable. It desires not to be caught up in people's business."

"Boss, we are airborne."

"Eliakim, they are gone," said Anne.

"What do you think will happen to them?"

"Nothing propitious, I am afraid. Have you seen how the box changed into a tabernacle? We all know the tabernacle is empty. I guess the guards are no more."

"What about the good book?"

"This strange idea is too potent. I'm afraid we have not seen the last of it."

"I wonder what was in chapter 23 of Revelations."

"I guess we'll never know now. And you can stop your confounded frictions. The coast is clear."

"I thought we could still do it when the coast was clear. And I can assure you, there is not a single cloud about."

"My God," said Anne. "Why have you not bestowed on me the surest sign of your blessing, called premature ejaculation?"

"Be careful what you wish for, my dear Anne," said Luminous from behind the wall. "Remember, I am in the wish-granting business. I am back in the land of the living, so my spirits are high now. I might agree to grant this marvelous gift to your female descendants. I just might."

"Luminous can speak now," said Anne. "This means the good book and God can't share the same spot on Earth. And since the good book has apparently more power than God, in the future it will itself take on God's role."

"It scares me greatly," said Eliakim. "Since it changes its words based on people's actions, it will simply confuse humanity."

"I'm not sure I agree. Bad rules are much better than no rules."

"So, the good book is kind of like Plan B? If the Pill of God won't stop life from developing, the Pill of the Good Book will step in and deal life a decisive blow?"

"Well, no one forces people to take one pill or another," laughed Luminous from outside. "You people make all the choices."

CHAPTER 46

TREE OF LOVE

nne said, "Eliakim, look. A tiny plant has sprouted next to us. It is growing fast. How tall it is now! How sweet is the perfume coming from its flowers! A bounty of red-colored fruit covers it now. The boughs droop under its heavy weight. One fruit is hanging right next to my hand. Drops of fragrant nectar like tiny tears ooze out of its opened pores."

Anne opened her palm below the apple.

The apple fell into it.

She brought it to her mouth.

"You have shared my life with me for a long time, so you deserve fair warning," said Luminous from behind the wall. "This is a special kind of a tree. It's called a Tree of Love. These fruits are called apples."

"Have you ever tried them?"

"I did once, a long time ago."

"Are they delicious?"

"They have a most succulent taste."

"Are they sweet?"

"Sweet and tangy."

"I long to eat one."

"But beware. After you bite into it and know its taste, your love for me will have no bounds. You will be falling asleep with my name on your lips. My name will be the first word that pops into your head after you arise in the morning."

"You warn me that I will love you? I would have thought that was what you have desired of me all along."

"I do. However, Anne, I know you would feel trapped loving me. Your love would stop you from doing me harm."

"One has to harm God sometimes. It's good for blood circulation."

"After you bite into the apple, you will abhor this very thought."

"How do you know all that? Did love toward people sprout in your heart after you bit into this apple long ago? If this love is anything like what you feel toward us, I can safely eat the whole bushel of apples."

"There is no need for irony. Unrequited love always turns into something else."

"What will you feel toward us people after we eat of this apple?"

"My love for you will blossom in my heart."

"This reason is important enough for me. I am so free now, I can live with some limitations."

Anne bit into the apple and passed it to Eliakim.

He bit into the apple.

"I feel love toward my Lord in every pore of my being," said Anne.

"Let's proclaim God's glory," said Eliakim. "Glory to God in the highest heaven."

"Why is our God separated from us?"

"These walls divide us."

"An immeasurable strength fills my arms. With my bare hands I will take these walls down."

With one swiping motion, Anne tore down the whole section of wall.

"Anne, you could have just opened the gate," said Eliakim.

"No time."

Anne's hand grew out and pulled Luminous in.

Bright light beamed from his eyes.

"I am basking in your love, my people. The love that I have felt toward you since I bit into the apple has been sleeping under a heavy burden of hate, and now it slowly awakes in my heart."

"Look, Luminous, a miracle is taking place," said Anne. "I am able to leave my standing body and float toward you."

"This is your loving soul that is coming to me."

"I'm able to touch your skin for the first time," said Anne. "It is so silky. I have an overwhelming desire to submerge myself in your body."

"It is called a communion of the souls."

"Why does your skin block my entry? Do you not want to commune with me? Oh, I know what we need to do. We need to feel even more love toward each other, if such thing is possible."

"It's possible," said Luminous.

He picked up an apple, bit into it and gave it to Anne.

Anne bit into it and passed it to Eliakim.

Eliakim bit into it.

Anne said, "I feel there is no need for our souls to inhabit our bodies."

All three bodies fell to the ground.

Anne said, "I feel the last barriers are falling between the souls of the three of us. Soon we people will be one with our God."

"Your soul is penetrating mine now," said Luminous.

Then he groaned loudly, "Our brains are uniting. The bitter truth is finally clear to me."

Eden's walls shook.

"I, Titan of Fire, am coming back to life," said a harsh voice. "How is this possible?"

"What is the bitter truth you just understood?" asked Anne.

"Titan of Fire," said Luminous. "The familiar task of destroying and rebuilding this planet awaits you."

"What are you saying, Luminous?" asked Anne. "Things are going just splendidly. For the first time ever we are getting along nicely. There is no cause to change anything."

"Our communion of souls is irrevocable," said Luminous. "This is the most glorious end to two different species, the species of people and the species of gods. Together we proved that God and people can achieve harmony and bliss together."

"Is it not a good thing?" asked Anne.

"It is a most wondrous thing. But it also means we both are no longer needed."

Luminous continued, "Titan of Fire, after you rebuild this planet, no gods or people will ever rise out of its depths and climb its mountains and cross its oceans. The story of gods and people will end now."

"I can't say I am disappointed," said Titan of Fire. "I can't name one good thing that came from the reigns of the gods. And you people were always such a nuisance. To tell you the truth, I am greatly relieved."

"I do not understand," said Anne. "The planet can't be left uninhabited."

"Oh you should not worry about that," said Luminous. "New beings will rise up. They will not be so polarized in their strengths and desires as a god and his people. They will have more in common with one another."

"And then what happens? Will they disappear too after they find common ground and resolve all their differences?"

"They will disappear too."

"If I understand correctly, the goal of this process is to get rid of all intelligent life."

"The goal of this process is to find the most enduring solution. Longevity is the true key to life."

"So the more quarrelsome inhabitants of this planet are toward each other, the longer they survive?"

"You make it sound like it's something wicked. When one life form is placid and lacks of life force it perishes, giving the opportunity for another life to raise and flourish."

"Life only becomes placid when love fills it. Does this mean love is bad?"

"Life that endures is necessarily filled with suffering. Love brings bliss, and bliss masks the true color of life."

"How can I withdraw from this trap of love?" asked Anne.

"You cannot."

"We spent so much time together, and yet you do not know me," said Anne. "I am withdrawing from the communion of souls and going back to my own body."

"It is too late," said Luminous.

"See, I can do it," said Anne. "I am entering my own body. It is coming back to life."

"It is too late now, Anne. Your resistance only shortens the time left to us."

Anne sat up and then stood up and then took a step.

"What wrong with my legs?" she screamed. "Why do they lead me back to Tree of Love? Why is my hand rising to pick another apple?"

"You are no longer in charge of your destiny," said Luminous. "Your body longs for another infusion of love. After you eat another apple, you will join us in communion of souls."

"Cursed be each step I made walking this planet. Cursed be each lungful of air I took in. Cursed be the destiny of people," cried Anne out.

"Lava, I speak to you. It is your master, Titan of Fire," cried out harsh voice. "I order you to rise up from every pore around Eden and burn its walls. Out of the cleansing flames my restored body will come forth. The task to rebuild this planet is once more placed before me."

Lava burst forth from all sides of Eden.

THE END

FORTSPINNUNG

*Mustard Seed cried really loud, "I cannot accept that this is the end!"
Barleycorn said, "What is your problem now? Look at them. They
are dying happily after a successful life. You should rejoice."*

*"This cannot be the end of their journey. These people only now
understood that happiness and love are not the keys to a successful
life. They need to put this knowledge into practice. God knows what
heights they can reach now. And take this strange god. He is so involved with his subjects. If he endures, together they may achieve
something truly unparalleled. They cannot just have this communion of souls and disappear from the face of this planet. We have to
do something."*

*"We are witnesses. This is what we are doing. We cannot be in-
volved in their struggle. We are plants, for heaven's sake."*

*"We are plants. The Tree of Love is a plant also. We, and only we,
can help them."*

*"I do not know. I am highly skeptical," said Barleycorn. "But maybe
it was Divine Providence that made me place you inside of this story."*

*"Just think about it. This may be by far the biggest coup plants
have ever attempted on this planet."*

"You may as well say what you have in mind."

Mustard Seed muttered something into Barleycorn's ear.

"Huh? That is mightily clever for such small seed."

"Clever things come in small packages."

*"But to accomplish this feat we need to sprout. To sprout we need
water."*

"Look around! We are drowning in rivers."

*"Let's give your idea a shot. We have to hurry though. Anne is fight-
ing her arm, but with each passing moment it rises toward the apple."*

*Barleycorn sprouted quickly, made a large husk, bent its head,
and rubbed it against the root of the Tree of Love until it began to
leak sap.*

And then corns fell down to the ground.

Tree sap dripped out of the cut root.

Mustard Seed sprouted inside of the root, grew out, and produced seeds.

Seeds fell back down onto the ground.

"Are you back?" asked Barleycorn.

"I am here," said Mustard Seed.

"Pray your idea worked."

"For the moment I have nobody to pray to. Let our actions cry out to the high heavens."

Anne picked up the apple and bit into it.

She fell down to the ground and vomited.

"Why is the fruit of the Tree of Love so bitter and hot?"

"Proud to make your acquaintance. I am Mustard Seed," said he from the ground. "It was I who infused this fruit with new flavor."

"What are you doing here?"

"I have been watching the proceedings for a very long time."

"Why?"

"To pass the time."

"Have our torments and struggles entertained you much?"

"I have suffered your pain and cheered your victories."

She vomited again.

"What wrong with her?" asked Eliakim. "I have tasted mustard seeds before and found them displeasing but not poisonous."

"Love can only be pure," said Luminous. "Add anything else to Love and it becomes a poison. She's lucky she only had one bite."

Anne whispered, "Cursed is my female nature. I feel like another fountain of love is opening inside of me. It washes away all poison."

"Love once more fills my heart," said Anne and crawled toward Luminous.

"Barleycorn, we did not save them," cried out Mustard Seed. "We only made her love for God grow stronger."

"Let it be a lesson for you, my friend. Plants should not get involved in the affairs of gods and people," said Barleycorn. "Come to me. Let me wipe your tears. What we attempted was not meant to be."

"My dear little friend, my Mustard Seed, you do not realize it yet but you did help me," whispered Anne.

"I did not."

"I see a way to save god and his people."

"How?"

"I still retain some measure of control over my body. Just not a strong enough measure to halt my progress toward Luminous. But I can do something else."

Anne fell face down on the ground.

Next to her face lay a bitten apple.

Her lips reached out to it.

She bit into it again, convulsed, and grew still.

"I did not mean to do that!" cried out Mustard Seed. "I wanted to save them all. But I killed Anne."

The walls of Eden shook.

"The communion of the souls is broken," said Luminous.

A trumpet sounded very high above the planet.

Titan of Fire gnashed his teeth, "No second chance for me. I will not stay in this ridiculous shape one second longer. Rise, lava, and burn my body."

"Eliakim, any moment the lava will reach here," said Luminous. "You need to leave me and run for your life. I am not able to save you now."

"What about you?"

"I will be indisposed for a while. Your soul penetrated me deep. I have to heal my wound."

Eliakim's soul disengaged from Luminous and floated back into his body.

He rose and ran away.

The window in the air opened up, and face of Nameless looked down at them.

"While Luminous is busy healing himself I would like to take a moment and thank you, my little plants, for saving me too. I will be God in the near future. Remember my promise: I will always cherish you both. New varietals of your kind will spread through this planet. Your heroism in the face of adversity will be richly rewarded."

Luminous opened his eyes, "You again. First time I am saying it and believing it: I am glad you are the next God. People will come to love me again and again, thus putting their very existence into the peril. But you, Nameless, have this unique ability to turn the kindest people into harsh and mean creatures. Your incomparable skills in this department will ensure the survival of humankind."

He continued, *"I speak to you, plants. Do not believe a word from Nameless. Most assuredly he took notice of your ability to influence the development of gods and of people. He will suppress you."*

Mustard Seed said, *"Sir, I humbly address you for the first time. Nameless might be the God of the future, as he says. But we are plants. Our power rests secure in myriads of our kind. He surely can suppress barleycorns and mustard seeds, and likely he will. But other plants will rise. Will he be able to suppress tea and coffee, or grapes, hemp, and poppy? He is but one, and we but many."*

"So, Nameless can be defeated too?" asked Anne. *"Even with Adam and Eve and their offspring at his side?"*

"Let your curiosity rest for now," said Luminous. *"There is always Act Two after Act One."*

CHAPTER 47

QUEEN OF THE DEAD

olten lava rose up.

Eliakim stood on a high rock looking down at its slow-moving waves.

"Anne, where are you? Oh, I see you now. A wave of lava is moving your body toward me. It's a very good sign it doesn't burn you but carries you like water carries a log. I know you're dead. But you have an immortal soul. Hear my cry. Look at me."

She stirred. "Who's calling me?"

"It is I, your husband."

"I can't see you. Darkness covers the world."

"That's because your eyes are closed. Open them and look at me."

"Please, do not open your eyes," a multitude of voices spoke from below.

"Who's speaking to me?" asked Anne.

"It is I, your husband."

"No, many voices spoke to me just a moment ago. Did you hear them, Eliakim?"

"It was just the crackle of fire burning the trees."

"We are dead. We are coming for you, Anne," said the multitude of voices from the depth of the lava.

"They are coming for me, Eliakim."

"It is just flames rustling and consuming wood."

A large Island rose up from the lava next to Anne.

It was made of many bodies huddled together.

"Anne, open your eyes and look around," said Eliakim. "Trust me: there is nobody here but us two."

"If you love your husband, do not open your eyes," said the multitude of voices.

"Why?" asked Anne.

"Who are you talking to?" asked Eliakim.

"Eliakim, do not interrupt my conversation, please," said Anne. "Things are very confusing now."

"The dead have no business looking at the living," said the multitude of voices.

"He's not just any living being," retorted Anne. "He's my husband."

"If you want your loved one to live, do not look at him. Your eyes will burn through him and annihilate his body."

"My husband, the dead people tell me my gaze will kill you."

"You are delusional, my wife."

Eliakim looked up, "Where are you, my Lord, when I need you the most? Save Anne."

Anne said, "Do not be angry with him. I've made my choice. I chose to die. In a situation like that, even God is powerless."

"At least stay with me. Ignore these voices. They are in your head. It is a poison that plays tricks with your mind."

"Swim toward our voices, Anne," said the multitude of voices.

"I am coming to you," said Anne.

She turned her body toward the island and swam.

"Anne, I won't let you leave without me!" screamed Eliakim. "I am coming for you!"

Anne slowed down.

"How can you?" asked she. "Lava does not sting my body, but only because I am dead. If you jump in, the lava will destroy your flesh."

Eliakim leapt and landed in the lava near her.

He bellowed, "Soon I will join you in death."

"No you won't," said Anne. "One fool is enough for the whole family."

She gripped his hand and said, "Climb up onto me, like you would on a log in the water. Don't worry; I feel no pain. That's right. Stand on my chest. I feel your blood drip down on me. Does it hurt much?"

"I am in pain but not because deep burns cover my body. It hurts to look at you. Here we are in the middle of an ocean of molten lava. Our situation is hopeless. You should be finding ways to save us. And yet you do nothing. Your face is so calm and composed. But never mind, I will awaken my Anne."

He squatted and forced her eyes open.

"That's much better," said he. Then he recoiled. "What's wrong with your eyes? They are dark piercing holes sucking me into them."

"The dead warned me not to look at you," groaned Anne. "Why could you not stay on your rock? In time, Luminous would have made you another wife."

"I want no other."

"Thank you for giving me an opening, Eliakim," spoke Luminous from above them. "I could not help Anne. But I most certainly will help my man."

"Do not listen to God, Anne," spoke the multitude of voices.

"You forget, I am a god, so I can hear you, dead beings," spoke Luminous from above.

"Go away, god," the multitude of voices spoke. "Their eyes are locked. They can't stop looking at each other. Eliakim is ours now."

"So these voices that speak to Anne are real?" asked Eliakim.

"Very much so," said Luminous. "At least as real as we are."

"Tell him the truth, shy god," said the multitude of voices. "We are much more real then you and him. An impartial observer would comment you are but a figment of the collective imagination of two seeds telling some strange stories to each other."

"The truth is in the eye of the beholder," said Luminous. "Or pardon my pun, since you see nothing. So I guess there is no truth in your eyes anymore."

"Anne sees for all of us," said the multitude of voices.

"She has not seen me, not even for all of you," said Luminous.

"Anne, you possess the most potent weapon against living beings: your gaze," said the multitude of voices. "Look up at the face of God."

"I know I am killing Eliakim," groaned Anne. "I feel how my eyes suck the life out of him. I will do no such thing to God."

"Anne, listen to me," said Luminous. "I want you to look at me. Fear not for my safety."

"I will not listen to any of you," said Anne. "You all go to hell."

"Oh, we can force you, Anne, to obey your god's command," said the multitude of voices.

The Island of the Dead moved toward Anne.

Dead hands grasped her body and began to pull her apart.

"Do you want your husband to see how we pull all your limbs out?"

"I care not."

"She loves her husband more than she loves her god," spoke the multitude of voices. "Let her have a go at him."

"Leave him be," said Anne. "His time is almost up. The last drops of blood are leaving his body now. Let him enjoy a few grasps of air."

"What will it be?" asked the multitude of voices. "We offer to preserve a half hour of your husband's life for a meager whole life of your god. Accept it—it is a good trade."

"Anne, you need to look at me," said Luminous from above. "I cannot help you. But if you look at me I will help your husband. Do not interfere with Divine Providence."

"Damn you with your clever words, Luminous," snarled Anne. "You want to die? Be my guest."

She moved her gaze from Eliakim's face, slowly, higher and higher.

Her gaze hit the face of Luminous. He groaned loudly.

"I told you so," said Anne. "You are a romantic fool."

"Nice catch, Anne," spoke the multitude of voices. "This lava is cooling off. We were about to have to go through the volcano's vent back down to the underground sea of lava. But now with God out of the way we will stay here."

A shining shield rose before the face of Luminous.

"Anne, your gaze can't penetrate my shield," said Luminous. "But my gaze will restore your flesh soon."

The Island of the Dead rose up from the lava completely and changed its shape to a spear, with Anne at very point.

"All dead beings, open your eyes one at a time and look at the living god," said multitude of voices. "Our combined gaze will break through his flaming shield."

A dead being below Anne opened his eyes and spoke: "Do you recognize me, Luminous?"

"I do," said Luminous. "You are me. What are you doing down there?"

"Remember when you died? That's when I went down."

"Close your eyes. You are I. We should not cross paths."

"I can't close my eyes now. I'm part of the Island of the Dead. I share its goals. You know you are lost now, for even though I'm dead I have the same strength as you. My gaze will break through your shining shield now."

"Do not despair, imperfect god Luminous," a voice spoke from behind Luminous. "I am at your side."

Nameless stood behind the shining shield next to Luminous.

"You came to my rescue?" asked Luminous. "I thought you disapproved of me."

"I do, because your methods are archaic," said Nameless. "But we are in it together."

A dead being below opened his eyes and spoke to Nameless: "Do you recognize me?"

"You are I," said Nameless.

"Yes, you have managed to die too," said he. "We are of equal strength. You cannot help a living god. Soon we'll break through his shining shield."

"So, is this it, Luminous?" asked Nameless. "Well, we had nice run."

"Watch this, you dead suckers," said Luminous.

He picked up the skies with his fingers and pulled them apart like curtains.

There was no darkness there, but an uncountable number of shining deities standing behind his shield.

"Ones that never lived before always outnumber ones that lived already and died," said Luminous.

The dead deities ground their teeth.

"Burn, my dead double," said Luminous.

"Burn, my dead double," repeated Nameless.

The dead spear caught on fire.

Luminous pulled Anne from its tip.

"Is she alive?" asked Eliakim.

"She'd made her choice to die. This choice will keep her captive. She needs to find her own way back to the land of living."

"She can't find her way alone. I need to help her," said Eliakim. "If I ask you to slay me, my God, you will bring me back. No, I need to put myself into same shoes as Anne's. I have to wish for my death."

Eliakim stretched on the ground and exhaled, "I have no blood in my veins now. I wish to breathe my last."

He expired.

CHAPTER 48

TWO TRIBES

nne stirred and looked at Eliakim.

"You look terrible, my love," she said. "Are you dead?"

"Just like you."

"Who killed you?"

"I wished for my death to join you."

"You're an utter fool. Some places a wife goes, her husband should not follow."

"A wife needs to have her husband by her side so she can blame him for her woes."

"Hush. Look at the Island of the Dead," said Anne. "Dark worms are eating the dead people."

"We are no different than these poor dead. Open eyes will not save us from the worms. Soon they'll be upon us."

"The lava's crusted over, yet it is too hot to walk on."

"Not for us, silly, we're dead." They ran.

"Dark worms are following us," said Eliakim. "Let's run up the mountain. Birds will get them."

"These worms are a punishment afflicting every dead body in the Land of the Living. Birds will not help us. I say we need to go underground. Darkness is always a close friend of the dead."

"I see an entrance to a cave," said Eliakim.

They went in.

"Here is the first advantage of us being dead: I can see clearly in here."

"We have to hurry. The dark worms are at our feet."

They ran through a series of caves.

Two women with large stone clubs blocked their way.

Anne and Eliakim raised their swords.

"Step aside," said the woman on the left. "We are not your enemies."

Anne and Eliakim moved out of their way.

"Well, the dark worms are here at last," said the woman. "You terrorized us outside enough. Welcome to our world. We will terrorize you now."

They hacked the worms until the entire cave was covered with dark goo.

The dark worms slowly retreated and then stopped.

"You can block our way as much as you like," laughed the woman. "We do not plan to go back up."

They turned to Anne and Eliakim.

"Who are you?" said Anne. "Our names are Anne and Eliakim."

Both women laughed heartily.

"We know," said one on the left. "What do you think we are called?"

"That can't be, I am the only Anne in this world."

The woman on the right snorted, "I can't believe how naïve she is."

"As I remember, you were just like her when you found your way here."

The woman on the right patted Anne's head, "Hush, child. No need to be upset. We are all Annes here, I am number 3, and my friend here is number 18."

"How can that be possible?"

"You are immortal, aren't you?"

"Yes, though I do not understand our current state of being."

"Never mind your current state. What do you think immortality is if not a transfer of consciousness from one body into another? And what do you think happens with the discarded body? Some bodies die of injuries, and some like you are able to mend them enough and to find their way into this underground chamber."

"You do not understand. We are the original Anne and Eliakim."

"We all thought that until we saw the next ones coming into this underground chamber. Accept the sad truth; don't fight it."

"Anne, it makes perfect sense," said Eliakim.

"Stay silent," said the woman on right.

"What happened to the Eliakims?" asked Anne. "Why are you so hostile toward my husband? I can assure you that just like he can do me no harm, he won't harm you."

"I wish your words were true," said the woman on left. "However, being dead goes quickly into men's heads. We women do not change. Men, on other hand, turn soon enough into bloodthirsty monsters. I actually have a mind to kill your husband now while he's weak and confused."

"I won't let you."

"I can kill you too if you get in my way."

"Enough," said the woman on the left. "We are not going to kill our sister. Let men kill us."

"Do they?" asked Anne.

"You bet. Every so often they come and rape and kill us. They are stronger, so there are twice as many men here as women."

Loud shouts came from down below.

"Men have heard the commotion. They are coming to collect the newcomer. We need to hurry," said the woman on the left.

"You go first," said Anne. "I need to say goodbye to my dear husband."

"Do it quick and join us. Take the second corridor to the right."

The two women left.

"Eliakim, there is still a difference between them and us. We are not completely dead. Have sex with me quick."

"It is neither the time nor the place for it. Besides, if these men are anywhere close to what the women described, they will harm you at first sight."

"Be quick."

They fell to the ground.

A moment later Anne said, "I did not know you could do it this quick. Another time I would be angry, but not now."

"Why were you interested in sex all of a sudden? You are not really big on it."

"Not when I am busy with other things. The reason is simple though: I will try to conceive a child from you now."

"You were not able to do it before. What makes you think you can do it now?"

"Even a mere woman is able to make miracles sometimes. See the faint light coming from outside at the end of the corridor? When 279 days pass, come here. I will be waiting for you behind this boulder."

"What if you are not able to conceive?"

"Then you bloodthirsty monster will kill me on this spot. Let's not think about it."

"Anne, run after your women. I hear footsteps."

Anne disappeared.

Many men filled corridor.

"This one is strong," they shouted. "We hate our wives for dragging us into this terrible mess. Do you hate yours?"

"I do," said Eliakim after pause.

"Then be ready to have fun. Our scouts found a cave where they hide. We'll raid them in a few hours. We have this competition going. The one who rapes and kills the most becomes the chief of our tribe until the next raid. You are strong; you can win. Come with us."

Two hundred and seventy-nine days passed.

Eliakim came and fell onto his knees and bowed his head to the light.

Anne came out from behind the boulder.

"My husband, you came," said Anne. "Look at my large stomach. I will be giving birth momentarily."

"What are you doing here, whore? This is my secret spot. I know not how it had started but I come here every day to pray to the light coming from above. In the name of my religion I will not kill you now, whore. But take care not to come here tomorrow. I will not allow your foul breath to consecrate this holy place."

"My dear husband, you forgot everything. I cannot blame you for forgetting. Other women forgot their husbands too. But I have not, because I carry inside of my body your growing seed."

"What kind of trickery is that? We are all dead. A dead woman cannot bring forth a living child. I need to pray to the light. Leave now, whore. I am losing my patience."

Anne fell down onto her knees and screamed loudly.

"I said enough of this insolence," said Eliakim.

He got up and raised high his stone club.

A tiny cry tore through air.

"Catch your son, Eliakim."

The club fell from his hands.

He fell down to his knees.

In his hands there was a baby.

"Good catch, my husband," said Anne.

"It is you, my dear wife. Something is wrong with me. There is something making rhythmic thumps inside of my chest. Am I sick?"

"At the moment of our son's birth, I share with you this precious sickness. I have an organ in my chest that makes rhythmic thumps too."

"Did we catch it from this tiny child of ours?"

"Yes, we did. This sickness is called life."

A large crowd of men ran toward them from the corridor.

"What's the commotion? Did you just arrive?" shouted the voices.

"There is a new whore. She's ours."

"You have to go through me," declared Eliakim, raising his stone club.

"I know of him," said one voice. "This is number 77. This guy is mean. I am not attacking."

"There are many of us and one of him," shouted another voice. "We will not leave without the whore."

Anne got up shakily and came to Eliakim.

"Let me have our newborn baby for a moment."

"What baby?" roared the voices. "Dead woman cannot have babies."

Eliakim gave the tiny baby to Anne.

"Would you like to hold our baby?" she asked the crowd.

There was utter silence.

"Come on, do not be afraid. You were not afraid to kill many of your wives," said Anne.

"Do you think this is such a good idea?" asked Eliakim. "They are savages."

"They are all Eliakims, just like you are. I believe in my husband."

"I am not afraid," said loud voice.

A large man pushed the rest aside.

"I will show everyone here you are lying. There can't be living babies here."

Anne gave him the baby.

The man whispered, "This is a real living baby. My heart is beating."

"Let me touch him," the men roared.

"I will personally kill anyone who harms this baby," said the large man. "Make a line and touch him carefully, one at a time. And you, the father, get the whores—I mean, get our dear wives to come and touch this baby."

"What shall we do now?" said a man. "Speak, number 1."

"We are living again. We cannot stay underground. We'll go outside."

"What about the dark worms?"

"They can't harm living people. Once outside we'll pair up with our wives."

"How will we know which Anne is which?"

"We'll ask how they died in the first place. Remember, wives and husbands died together or soon after each other."

"But we killed many of the women."

"The ones without wives will form new pairs."

"But we are all the same. How will we distinguish one Anne and Eliakim from another?"

"The seventy-seventh pair has a baby. We are all older. The seventy-sixth pair will be their parents. I will be their grandfather seventy-six times removed."

"What will happen to all of us now?"

"Since we are all Annes and Eliakims, we will go our separate ways. I am ready to go outside. Where are these confounded wives?"

CHAPTER 49

THE SON

 nne and Eliakim left the cave.

Eliakim held young Adam's hand.

"Stop," said Luminous's voice from distance. "You cannot bring your child closer to me. Let go of his hand. Let him die in peace."

"If I can keep him alive by holding his hand, I'll bind his hand to mine permanently," said Eliakim.

"You will have to abandon your God first."

"Why?"

"A bastard cannot be in the presence of your Lord."

"He's no bastard, he's our child," said Anne. "I remember holding him in my arms. I remember him suckling milk from my breast."

"Look at your breasts. Have they ever fed a child?"

"They may not look like that now, but I remember."

"These are false memories. Adam is nothing but a pale apparition on the smooth surface of my world. Release his hand; let him perish."

"I cannot. Make him real."

"If you pull an unfinished seam you'll pull back the needle too. And then the whole fabric rips to shreds. I cannot do it."

"Why can't he live? Be a gracious God, for you are one."

"Look up. Do you not see the stormy cloud building above your heads?"

"Hold your wrath."

"This is not my wrath. It's his."

Rain fell from the stormy cloud.

"Eliakim, the smooth skin of our son has changed into mud," said Anne.

"The rain is washing him away."

"Stop it, Luminous," said Anne.

"I can't. For each action there is a counteraction. Your child lost the very reason to exist. But you are keeping him alive. His existence gives birth to a new force. It is brewing now inside of this rainy cloud."

"It sounds like a new god is being born," said Anne.

"Yes," said Luminous.

"Why is he pouring the rain down? Why is he trying to destroy his mud child?"

"To show him who is boss."

"With him gone, how can he exist?"

"He cares not about Adam, for there are billions of pounds of mud just in this valley. He can always make new people out of the mud."

"Eliakim, we managed to protect our child from our own God," said Anne. "We should be able to protect him from this new deity."

"There is no connection between us and the new God," said Eliakim. "See how his raindrops carefully avoid us? For him we do not exist. We cannot even protect our child from his rain."

"Then we should become his subjects."

"You are mad, or, I guess, mud?"

"Once we are his subjects, we'll rebel against him, as we did so many times against Luminous."

"I do not know about you, but I am having a ball now," said Luminous. "Anne, it is so educational to see how you build a coalition against your own God."

"You can keep your jokes to yourself. I have no sense of humor now," said Anne. "I have bigger fish to fry."

"Do not choke on its mighty bones."

"New deity, accept us as your subjects," said Anne.

Anne's and Eliakim's flesh turned to mud.

"He has accepted us," said Anne. "Collapse your body into mine, so I can form a box."

A large lump of mud formed, and then changed into a box with a door.

"Child, get inside of the box," said Anne. "Do not be afraid; you were inside of me once before."

The half-shaped child slowly dragged himself in.

The door closed.

"Luminous, you are a hot desert wind now. You used to be our God. Could you do us the last ever service in memory of our past friendship? Could you heat up this clay box?"

"You are no longer my people. You have accepted another as your God."

"There is no blasphemy a woman won't say when she needs to protect her offspring. Forgive me."

The desert wind tore hard.

When the wind fell, there stood a ceramic box.

"I call us a tabernacle," said Anne's voice. "We are carrying a precious load."

"This child belongs to me," said a voice from the rainy cloud. "Open up this box now."

"Parents protect their child, from God if necessary," said Anne's voice.

"I will not harm him," said the voice from the rainy cloud.

The desert wind picked up the tabernacle and floated it above the tallest mountain.

"What are you doing to my people?" asked the rainy cloud.

"As I am no longer their God, I plan to let them go. But I will let them go from the highest possible vantage point."

"Anne and Eliakim are my faithful servants now."

"Faithful? Do not make me laugh. Over time they have turned betraying God into a distinctive art form."

"Luminous, you are our God too," said Anne.

"Did you hear that, new deity?" asked Luminous. "The rooster has not cried out three times yet, but Anne's betraying you already."

"They are weak."

"That's what I used to think. People's weakness is but a form of a deception."

"You have no power over Anne and Eliakim now. You cannot kill them."

"Yet I do still have power over them, since Anne asked for my help," said Luminous. "People who believe in one god should never ask another god for help. Woe is to the ones who did, for they have two gods now."

"I will protect this tabernacle," said the rainy cloud.

"People who claim two gods have none. You can't protect them."

"Be merciful," said Anne. "We once were your people."

"Since you acknowledged that you were, you should agree I have the full right to be offended."

"I have a solution, Luminous," said the rainy cloud. "I am a god, so your past deeds are open to my prying eyes. They happen to worship both of us, so if you accept me as your son, than they can legally love both of us."

"Do not do it, our new Lord," said Anne from tabernacle. "He did away with his son once before. He'll do away with you."

"There is that, of course," said the rainy cloud. "But should he go through this exercise once more, I plan to build on the past experiences of God the Son."

"I do not know," said Luminous. "By means of this proclamation

I'll make you my equal. I know what you're thinking, Why limit your-self to one piece of cake if you can share the whole cake with me by partaking in world domination?"

"That's the idea," said the rainy cloud. "But then you do not need to do it. I can always turn into a vengeful spirit and be a thorn in your side. I may like that even better."

A window opened in midair.

The Devil looked out, "Did someone call me?"

"No one did," said Luminous. "Get."

"I've heard distinctly 'a thorn in God's side.' Rainy cloud, please be advised this honorable position is taken by me already."

"I said, 'Get.'"

The window in midair closed.

"One thing you forget, as my son you'll have to follow your father, me," said Luminous.

"I can live with that."

"Well, then, I hereby proclaim you my son."

"I accept."

"Welcome into this world, my son," said Luminous.

"Your voice is full of love all of a sudden," said Anne. "You do not love this rainy cloud, do you?"

"Why would I not love my son?"

"So you were serious when you accepted him?"

"Would I ever joke in regard to such an important matter?"

"You would. You've made us. Are people not a joke?"

"Yes, you are joke. But you are a long-running one. It will take for-ever for the punch line to come."

"You just assured us, our Lord, that the punch line will be here one day," said Eliakim.

The desert wind and the rainy cloud united.

The tabernacle fell and broke into pieces.

There was nothing inside.

Out of the broken ceramic pieces, Anne and Eliakim arose.

"What have you done with our child, you pair of Gods?" screamed Anne.

"He did not make it, since he belonged to me only," said the Son.

"What do you mean?"

"Property laws do not allow me to possess anything that my father does not."

"For God's sake, Eliakim," said Anne. "I am so disgusted. Do you know what we are?"

"Fools?" asked Eliakim.

"Even worse. We are not even subjects, but only objects. We are ceramic figurines gods give to each other. I am a great deity. Would you like a figurine? You can put it onto your mantelpiece. It will look good there. If you would like I can drill a large hole in each one and put a clock into it."

CHAPTER 50

TO BRING FLOWERS

 large cow stood in the middle of the field.

"Son of God, we have accepted you as our Lord. Where are you now?" wondered Eliakim. "If you are inside of this cow, why don't you turn me into a bull and Anne into a heifer? We'll follow you into fresh fields of grass. We'll cross shallow waters together. You'll lead us into a land of grass that is always fresh and succulent."

"I am still here," spoke the son from inside. "Tell me, my father, why are we both inside of a cow?"

"I had to trap you," Luminous's voice answered. "See, the planet does not need two Gods. I love you, though."

"Do not despair, my husband," said Anne. "Our Son of God will be with us yet. All we have to do is separate him from his father."

"All we have to do is to move a mountain. All we have to do is to get enough rocks to beg, so Luminous succumbs to their pleas and releases his son?"

"You should know by now, rocks do cry out and mountains do move. We need to engage with the son in some meaningful way that is separate from the way we have engaged with Luminous already."

"If there is yet another way to love God, how come we have not found it already?"

"There are other ways to engage God. Love does not need to enter the equation."

She picked flowers from the field and brought them to the cow.

The cow opened her mouth greedily.

"Luminous, do not eat my flowers. They are for your son. Take them, Son of God, as the sign of our unflagging devotion."

The son stuck his head out of the cow's chest and said, "I can't believe my ears. Devotion is to be damned. Are you trying to help me? After you enlisted my father's help to protect your children against me?"

"Why can't the son of such a great father inspire our devotion? You are flesh of his flesh and blood of his blood."

"Or is this a new tack? You would like to have your cake and eat it?"

"Why are you questioning our devotion? Please, just accept my flowers."

"Do not accept her flowers," said the cow. "People are a crafty lot."

"I was not going to. But you would not ask me to reject her gift for nothing. Anne must have found way for me to get out."

The son said to Anne, "Thanks for flowers and for what they denote."

His arms grew long, picked up a rock, and shaped it into vessel.

"Put your flowers into water."

Anne filled the vessel with water from creek and set it up before the son.

"What are you waiting for?" asked the son. "Bring me more flowers."

Anne made a clay vessel, filled it with water, and brought it to the son.

"I hope you give us flowers now," said Anne.

"Why would I do such thing? Do you expect me, God's son, to devote myself to you people?"

"Why would you not?"

"Gods do not devote themselves to people. I did accept your flowers. This vessel is the sign of our covenant. As long as you bring more flowers, our covenant stands for ever and ever, even if I run out of rocks to make vessels out of."

"I am offering you a permanent way out. All you have to do is to accept us as your equals."

"This exit is called a trap, for if I acknowledge you as my equals I shall become Son of Man."

"It is good to be a man."

"It is good. But this is not a fair exchange. God's power is worth more."

"Nothing is worth more than an unflagging devotion to the human race."

"People are devoted only when they are unhappy. And let me tell you, from what I saw, you are a happy lot. One does not entrust water to keep the fire going."

Anne made another vessel, chopped some grass, filled the vessel with water, and brought it to the son.

The son sniffed, "There is hemlock in this water. Are you trying to kill me?"

"No poison can kill God. It will only hurt your body."

"So, you want to hurt me?"

"Not particularly. All I would like to do is elicit a different response from you. I want you to react to what we do."

"This would be an entirely different experience for me. So far I was only reacting to my father's words and deeds. I think I shall find this experience very instructive."

The son drank hemlock.

Soon his head and shoulders writhed in pain.

Then poison spread to the cow.

The cow bellowed.

The son opened his eyes and said, "This experience was really transformative."

"Not as much as your upcoming one," said Anne and threw large rattlesnake on him.

The snake wrapped itself around the son's neck and bit him.

The son screamed, "Oh, my people. Was it a part of your plan to do bad things onto me?"

"People's true nature awoke," said Luminous. "Once people find a way to make somebody the victim, they will never fail to take the opportunity again and again."

"Then it is your fault, Father. You should not have created such weak beings as them. The weak should not exist."

"People can only be weak. Strong beings do not progress but rest comfortably in their strength. Weak ones advance."

"I found a new way to engage with the Son of God," said Anne. "This way is totally different from the way we engage with Luminous. We will be doing things to him now."

"My poor son," said Luminous. "This is so wrong."

CHAPTER 51

THE END AND A
NEW BEGINNING

y son, you should not allow people to do things unto you," said Luminous. "You are destroying the very definition of god."

"I have destroyed it already," said God's son. "It is very painful. Yet this way will bring me to places you could never visit before."

"I have to stop you."

"You can't."

Luminous raised his arms and changed into freezing rain.

A giant iceberg formed around the son.

"I'll melt you, my father."

The iceberg spoke, "And I will rebuild myself again."

"I will be melting you forever."

"This is exactly what I want. Each time I rebuild myself, I'll spread out further, covering you more and more."

The son changed into dark pool of oil.

"You know what to do, my people," said God's son.

"We do," said Anne, and lit the oil. "The heat of the burning oil will keep you alive."

"Only temporarily," said Luminous.

"To create a permanent solution, we need to figure out how to convert the energy of oil into motion," said Eliakim. "I have an idea. If we trap burning oil inside of a drum, and attach wheels and cogs to it, energy will spin the wheels and will get him out from under the ice."

"We have to work quickly."

They melted iron ore, made a drum, wheels, and cogs.

Then they broke through the wall of the iceberg and collected all the oil in the drum.

"Why is Luminous not stopping us?" asked Eliakim.

"There is no need," said Luminous. "You are making an internal combustion engine. So what? I will harness its energy toward generating ice."

Eliakim finished building the engine.

The wheels spun furiously.

"Great friction, my son. Keep spinning," said Luminous. "I will make an ice maker and will attach it to you."

"Run, son, run!" shouted Eliakim.

"You have forgotten how quick ice is," said Luminous.

Ice spread out from the iceberg, caught up with the spinning engine, and encapsulated it inside.

"Luminous, you cannot fight against human ingenuity," said Eliakim. "Let me draw you an outline for my new design."

Eliakim drew on the snow, saying, "See, Luminous, this is an extra chamber. It will convert the snow into fuel that will power my machine."

"Augh," said Luminous.

The iceberg began to melt.

"We have defeated Luminous," said Anne. "God's son is free."

Luminous appeared in the shape of a man and spoke, "Not quite."

"But you can no longer keep him in your icy confinement."

"You are exceptional beings," said Luminous.

"Anne, I find his tone oddly ominous," said Eliakim.

"I am afraid I loved you too much."

"One can never love too much," said Anne.

"Oh, one can. I have made you all too powerful."

"It does not feel that way," said Anne.

"Yet lately I have put some brakes on you."

"Oh, this is what you've been doing," said Anne.

"However, my son is hungry for power. He wants to build you up."

"I have sensed that in him," said Anne. "That's why I accepted him as my Lord."

"Anne, you have an uncanny nose for weakness in everyone. Pity, you put it to use only to gain advantage."

"Not for me only, but for my husband too."

"Your overwhelming desire was to find a way for God and his people to be equal."

"And look at your son and us. I did find a way."

"I reject this way."

"Luminous, you have to evolve with the times. The primordial order is gone now. The new order is rising when we all are equal."

"This is where your cardinal mistake lies. People need god to rule over them."

"Have you not learned all the lessons we people taught you? Was our struggle against you in vain?"

"This is exactly what I want to ask you. Why have you not learned the lessons I've taught you? Alas, it is too late now."

"Anne, I really do not like the sound of that," said Eliakim.

"You were always the clever one of the two," said Luminous. "I'd catch your quiet smile when Anne went on with her ideas, and I'd think, "He's silent because he already saw the weakness of her arguments.""

"Eliakim is the brute," retorted Anne. "Are these reminiscences of yours going somewhere?"

"Anyway, where was I?" said Luminous. "My son will build you up even higher. Given time, you'll figure out how to rid the planet of him and then rid of all deities. I can't allow that."

"You've failed," said Anne. "You cannot stop your son now. He will make us into the most powerful beings here on this planet."

"I am afraid you're right. I love my son, but he allowed people to do things to him. His fateful decision foreshadows his downfall. You're right; sooner or later he will allow you to accumulate more power than even he has. So it leaves me no choice but to utter the words I have hoped would never escape from my lips."

"Stop with the suspense," cried out Anne. "Get on with it."

Luminous voice grew tenfold, "It's time, Nameless."

Another voice spoke from his chest, "I'll be damned. I was absolutely sure I would never hear your tongue speaking these words."

"You have to thank my people for that."

"Since you abdicate your crown of your own free will, it is only fair for me to give you the opportunity to reconsider. Are you certain? But do not take much time. I have been waiting for this moment for at least six hundred years. Even for a patient god like I, it is a damn long time to wait."

"I've made up my mind. You are a go."

Nameless's voice grew a hundredfold: "It is done then. I am the new ruler of this planet."

A trumpet blew high above.

"Luminous, you traitor!" Anne cried out.

"Since I did not take your power by force," said Nameless, "you have the option to stay on this planet. You will not be an all-powerful and mighty god, but you're welcome to be a local deity. There are some dark and mysterious forests I know of where you'll feel right at home. Or I can give you a river. You can bask in its fresh waters and contemplate eternity."

"You know me by now. I am not the contemplative type. Placidity bores me. I decline your offer."

"Then you give me no choice but to put you down."

"You may have me."

Anne cried out, "God's son, what are you waiting for? Come and defeat this god."

The son spoke, "Please, Nameless, allow me to stay. I will be your faithful brother."

"Why are you so meek all of a sudden?" asked Anne. "Do not tell me you're only brave when you fight your own father."

"I need no brothers," said Nameless. "I need you not."

"Why? Are you afraid of me?" asked the son.

"The reason is simple and has nothing to do with you: if I follow in Luminous's steps, in time I will turn back into him."

"It is not such a bad thing to be Luminous. He was a glorious God."

"I will be a glorious God on my very own right."

"Luminous learned so much about the world and people," said the ice.

"I will learn on my own."

"Father, I am sure you are still inside of this god somewhere. Do not forsake your son. Come to my rescue."

Out of Nameless's right hand the thick blade of Luminous's sword rose.

"Strike him down," said the son.

"I, new God called Nameless, order you, ice, to be silent for ever and ever. You can only crack and grunt. You understand?"

Ice grunted.

"The son had no strength what so ever," said Anne. "Did we make a fateful mistake by putting our fate into the son's weak hands?"

Nameless looked down at his hands.

"My hands, you have betrayed your new proprietor," he said. "Here are some silver coins for your betrayal."

The sword flew into the sky, than rushed back toward the ground.
When it flew next to God, he extended his arms.
The sword severed his arms at the shoulders.
The hands fell to the ground.
Out of them two white winged figures rose.
"Welcome, my first cherubim," said the new God.
"Wise decision, Nameless," said they in unison. "We will be your arms now. We will mete out punishment against the unfaithful and reward the faithful. You will indeed now be a most different God from Luminous. You will be a weaker God. And this is great, since the weak always outlive the strong."
Anne said, "All is not lost yet. Luminous, I know you still can hear me from inside of Nameless. Give us this last chance. Forgive us for betraying you. I know you are angry with us, yet I am positive our bond is still strong. I know you cannot do anything because you have no arms. But you can still come with us. Ignore these cherubim. They have admitted they have no physical power. In time, we will figure out together how you can get out of Nameless. See, we are walking now. Join us, your true and real people."
Anne and Eliakim moved away.
Nameless followed them.
"See, Luminous. I knew you could do it," said Anne.
"Do not betray me now, my legs. You belong to your new proprietor," said Nameless.
"Keep walking, Luminous," said Anne. "Do not stop."
Anne and Eliakim moved further away.
Still Nameless followed Anne and Eliakim.
"My cherubim, my feet betrayed me. Pick me up and carry me."
"We can't. It requires physical strength. You need to make your own man. He will carry you upon his shoulders."
Nameless picked up a handful of clay and breathed into it.
A man rose.

"Take me upon your shoulders and carry me forward."

The man bent.

"I cannot pick you up. Sorry, my Lord. You are too heavy."

Nameless breathed into the man again.

The man grew to eight feet.

"Try now."

The man bent.

"I still can't."

God breathed into him a third time.

The man's chest expanded.

His hands and arms grew threefold.

His forehead slunk lower, and his lower jaw jutted forward.

Thick, coarse hair covered him.

The man picked up God upon his shoulders.

"My new hands, grow out, pick up Luminous's sword, and cut off these traitorous feet once and for all."

His hands grew out and grabbed the sword.

"Why do my fingers go through it? Why can't I pick it up?"

"Because it belongs to a greater God," said Anne.

"Oh, why I am so blind? I know the very person who can still use the sword of Luminous."

"Your hairy man who looks like an oversized ape? He belongs to you. His fingers will go through this sword too," said Anne.

"He can do something much better than that."

Nameless said to the man, "Hey, Adam, grab them both and hold them tight."

"I like my new name," said Adam.

He held Anne and Eliakim in his thick arms.

"I like my great strength," said Adam.

"Do you know you are very stupid? Do you like that too?" asked Anne.

"I like my stupidity," said Adam.

"So, what is next?" asked Anne. "Luminous, who is still inside of you, will not allow you to order this ape man to kill us."

"No doubt. But I need not utter a single word. Look at yourself. I can see though you."

Anne screamed, "I can see though myself too. What kind of curse is that?"

"Just pure science. You people are from another time now. You and your God were nothing but abstract concepts battling one another in an attempt to figure out the relationship between God and people. And you did a most outstanding job. Just admire the result of your long struggle: we have me, a weak God who needs angels to carry out his will; we have angels who will do my deeds in my name; we have a vigorous man who will start the human race. Another words, we have here all we wanted! Congratulations, you all are no longer needed."

"So let us go. We can reason a new way for us to exist. We can work on new tasks. But we can't be close to you."

"That's exactly what I propose. There is one unique quality no one else in this brave new world possesses but you: you can still lift the sword of Luminous. So, a hard task awaits you. In exchange for freedom and a chance to survive, you will have to finish my conversion into a truly new God. Cut off my feet."

Anne said, "Forgive me, Luminous. You are gone, but we need to save ourselves."

She picked up Luminous's sword and cut off the new God's feet.

The feet fell to the ground, and two cherubim rose out of them.

"We shall carry you everywhere," said they in unison.

New legs and feet grew out of God's hips.

He jumped down from Adam's shoulder and stood up.

"Let us go now," said Anne.

"Not quite yet. My head is filled with longing for you. Cut off my head."

Anne said, "Farewell, Luminous. I know you'll understand me."

She cut of God's head.

The head did not fall down but dissolved into a cloud.

A voice spoke from the cloud, "I, Holy Spirit, shall guide us forward."

A new head rose out of Nameless's neck.

"So much better. Gone are all the annoying abstract concepts," said he.

Nameless looked at Adam, "Why are these two are here? I have no use for them. Let them go."

Adam released Anne and Eliakim.

Anne picked up Luminous's sword.

"Your God is dead," said the new God. "This is just an old sheet of metal. Look how rusted it is. There is no strength left in it. Why do you need it?"

"That is my business," said Anne.

She broke the rusted metal into four pieces and made two pairs of skis.

She put her skis on.

Eliakim put his skis on.

"Anne, I can no longer see through my and your body," said Eliakim.

"I thought so. As long as we do not touch this new world, we can stay here."

They skied and ran into the cold night.

God looked at Adam and said to the cherubim, "It will not do."

"What's the problem, boss?" asked cherubim.

"Adam will always remember that my legs betrayed me and he carried me on his shoulder. He will remember there was another God before me. He will know that somewhere in this world there are two lost people from the previous time."

Cherubim said, "We cherubim have no physical power. But we have a lot of the eternal power of God. Adam will sleep tonight, and he will have the most wondrous dream. When he wakes up he will know how you created this world in six days."

"Six days? It seems to be an awfully short amount of time for such a mighty task."

"Not to him. He will remember you dwelled in this most amazing place called Eden and that it is where you've breathed life into him."

God said, "Cherubim, I am tired of this snow. Take me down south. We need to find a proper place for this Eden that Adam will dream up this night."

"You should allow him to name all the flowers and animals you create there," said Holy Spirit. "It will empower him."

"Can we trust him with naming?" asked God.

"Do we care how they all are named?"

"You are right: not really. I will let him do it."

The cherubim picked up God.

The cloud of the Holy Spirit changed into a hawk and sat on God's right shoulder.

The fourth cherubim put Adam onto his shoulders.

They flew up.

Adam bellowed.

"Oh, shut up," said God. "I almost wish we had kept these two people."

"We can't. They do not belong to us," said the Holy Spirit.

The cherubim flew south.

To be continued with . . .

MUSTARD SEED